. . .The Dream Continues

FULL-TIME

RVING

How to
Make
it
Happen

Gypsy Press

Sharlene "Charlie" Minshall

...The Dream Continues

FULL-TIME

RVING

How To Make It Happen

Sharlene "Charlie" Minshall

Edited by
Janet L. Wadlington

Gypsy
Press

Copyright (C) 1997 by Gypsy Press
101 Rainbow Drive, Suite 5024
Livingston, Texas 77351-9330

First edition 1997.

Printed in the United States of America

Library of Congress Catalog Card Number: 97-93848

ISBN: 0-9643970-2-1

About the Author

Sharlene "Charlie" Minshall began writing monthly columns, and free-lance articles, about her RV lifestyle in 1986. They range from the "how-to" to the "why-not." Sometimes, she delves into the nitty-gritty humor of real RV problems, like using the telephone, the intricacies of life with a computer, and loss of memory. She touches on the serious, the silly, and the sad side of life. A reader from Florida says her columns are more like "essays."

At present, she is publishing regular columns in Camp-Orama (SE), RV Traveler (Midwest), Texas RV (TX), RV Life (Northwest), Two-Lane Roads, plus Wagon Train Travelers Magazine in Canada, and contributes other freelance writing.

"Charlie" is the author of:

RVing Alaska! (and Canada),
Full-Time RVing, How to Make it Happen,
RVing North America, Silver, Single, and Solo,
In Pursuit of a Dream,
and
Freedom Unlimited,
The Fun and Facts of Fulltime RVing (co-authored)

The author gives seminars on the RV lifestyle. She tells positive, humorous, and very personal tales, of the joys and woes of life on the road as a silver, single, solo gypsy, or as she would put it...

To clarify, I do not stand before you as an expert on anything. You ask then, "Why am I here?" It is more because I am <u>not</u> an expert, but I did it anyway. I'd like to share my eleven years of full-time RVing experiences, and the lessons I've learned along the way (or not).

In that time, I have traveled 180,000 miles by RV, and countless miles by car, four-wheel machines, airplanes, helicopters, paraglider, ultra-light, trains, buses, dunebuggy, motorcycle, bicycle, raft, canoe, kayak, mule, horse, cross-country skis, and water skis. Let's see, what have I forgotten...oh...

These boots were made for walkin'
And walkin' they have done,
And I may not have expertise,
But boy, have I had fun!

NON-FICTION TITLES

by

Sharlene "Charlie" Minshall

Full-Time RVing
How to Make it Happen
(1997)

RVing Alaska!(and Canada)
(1997)

RVing North America
Silver, Single, and Solo

In Pursuit of a Dream

Freedom Unlimited:
The Fun and Facts of Fulltime RVing
Co-author, Bill Farlow
Published by Woodall's

Order Form and More Information
(Back of book)

DEDICATION

I dedicate this book to
my Producer,
who has given me all the special effects
in my travels,
the crash of the ocean waves against the rocks,
the gentle lapping on the sand,
the pine-needled path through majestic mountains,
the carpet of flowers outlining a stream,
the waving prairies,
the blossoms in an apple orchard,
and, on top of all this,
provides me with golden moments
of
pure joy and excitement.
Last,
but never least,
I thank Him for
healthy, caring daughters, sons-in-law, a granddaughter,
a grandson-to-be,
loving family,
and
precious friendships.

ACKNOWLEDGMENTS

My thanks to C. Jay Haynor, Technical Editor for Family Motor Coach magazine, and fellow FMCAer, who lent his considerable expertise to our knowledge of weight terms and how to weigh an RV, in Chapter 4. You helped me understand after eleven years!

Fellow SKPs, Barbara and Noel Kirkby, were kind enough to write about the solar electric experience in Chapter 5. Thanks.

Thanks to Steve Reyda for sharing his thoughts on choosing an RV in Chapter 2, and his personal budget in Chapter 3. Best wishes in your new lifestyle, Steve. It's the greatest.

Hugs to daughter, Tracey, for her encouragement when I am insane enough to write two books at once.

Special thanks to Janet for her computer expertise, bouncing ideas off the walls with me, bouncing off the walls with me, her sense-of-humor during trying moments, her hugs when the tears welled, and our shared triumph when the work was done.

Contents

Photography
Computer
Fairs and Festivals

Campgrounds, and boondocking   Life On Wheels Conference
Directories   RV Organizations
Membership Campgrounds   Singles
Volunteer Organizations   Maps and information!
Magazines

Mexico   Language
Is it safe to travel in Mexico?   Water
Firearms   Shopping
Pets   Canada
Insurance   Credit Cards and Cash
Roads   Firearms, pets, insurance,
"Angeles Verdes"   New law in BC as of April, 1997
Fuel   GTS

➔ **Contents**

➔ **Glossary**

➔ **Resources**

INTRODUCTION

Full-Time RVing: How to Make it Happen.

That is a serious title. It is a serious decision. It isn't one to be taken lightly. It sounds exciting; I agree. It is exciting; I know. Is Full-timing for everybody? Definitely not. No one should approach this lifestyle (or any other), with the misconception that everyone will love it, or that it is completely problem, or stress free.

I'll start this book with a disclaimer. I am not an expert at anything. I have been full-time RVing, since September, 1986. Except for a few instances, when I've stayed in one area for a few months, I've chosen to be "on the move." My expertise is only that I have experienced full-time RVing, survived it, enjoyed it, and I've loved it enough that I'm not ready to give it up yet.

Although my husband and I had an RV for several years before he died, he had the care of it. We used it for vacations and weekends. I did not find much information on full-time RVing in 1986. When I look back at how little I knew when I took off, it scares me. That's one of the reasons I wanted to write this book. I have RVed full-time, despite the lack of great knowledge or expertise; therefore, I know if it is something you really want to do, it's possible. The catch is that **you** have to make it happen.

If it is your dream, give it a good honest try. You don't have to do it forever. It isn't carved in rock. If this dream has taken you by storm, and you've never RVed before, please, please, **please**, rent one, and at least have some idea what you are getting into. I can't quite imagine anyone entering into the lifestyle on a full-time basis, without having had experience with vacationing in RVs, or owning one, somewhere along the line.

It is far better for anyone, even those who have RVed for some time, to try the full-timing lifestyle for four or six months, or a year, before selling the farm and leftover children. Living within the confines of an eight-foot wide (by whatever, up to forty feet) RV, is far different from living in a house, with 45,000 square miles of space in it. Get someone to house-sit your property while you travel, or rent or lease it for a year.

Another point of view, is that you **should** sell, and/or get rid of everything, before you go. Otherwise, it is too easy to back out when the first untoward thing happens. I fit into that category. I had so many problems with my first (used) motorhome, that by the end of a year and a half, I was seriously wondering if I could continue. Maybe if I had not burned my bridges, I wouldn't have had the amazing experiences I've had. I bought a new rig; the rest is history.

For me, keeping the house was not an option. I couldn't have kept it, and traveled, too. I didn't want the hassle of upkeep or renting. As it was, I sold it on land contract, and had to keep my eye on it for five years.

There are now many seminars, articles, and books on full-time RVing, and everything leading up to it. The basic information will be pretty much the same. Some books will be more technically oriented than others. Mine is not technical. As authors and full-timers, we each give you an opinion, from our own perspective. My perspective is that I am a woman traveling alone, with no more knowledge of mechanics, than would fit on the eyeball of a gnat. Regardless, my 180,000 miles have taken me on unparalleled adventures through Mexico, Canada, Alaska, and throughout the "lower 48."

In between informational chapters on the joys and woes of full-time RVing, I have written "Tween-Chapters." They will tell you where the yellow brick road has taken me, and will give you a tongue-in-cheek view of the RVing lifestyle.

Please take the time to read
Glossary and Resources
in the back pages. They are
comprehensive
(full of important information even).
The information and phone numbers were correct
at the time of publication

I'd ask you to sit back, relax, and read the book, but if you are as excited as I think you are, about the possibilities of joining the

FULL-TIME RVing
world,
you won't be able to sit still
until you know

How to Make it Happen.

God Bless

"Charlie"

IN THE BEGINNING...

Unless you have chosen to remain single all your life, or you are lucky enough to die previous to, or at the same time as your mate, you will, as sure as there is a tomorrow, through death or divorce, be alone. Your faith, physical health, and mental status, will determine whether you curl up on the porch and wither away in your rocking chair, or get up, dust yourself off, put a smile in your heart, and take off down a different path.

That "different path" was going to be my path, but I didn't know it. Jack, my late husband, and I, had daydreamed about RVing full-time. It was a good daydream, but as far as doing it together, it was only a daydream.

During vacations and weekends, we raised two daughters in a 9 X 9 tent (the rest of the time we let them in the house). Later, a truck camper disintegrated from innumerable trips. Our daughters, and their girlfriends, enjoyed fireworks from the overhead bed on the Fourth of July, or watched movies at the outdoor theatre. We always felt our RV cost too much to let it vegetate in the driveway.

We eventually bought a mini-motorhome. Regardless of whether the covering was canvas or fiberglass, we made lasting memories. We were hooked on traveling and planned our somedays.

Janet, our oldest daughter, graduated from Colorado Mountain College, married, and made her home west of the Mississippi. Tracey, the youngest, was about to start her senior year at Michigan State University. It was August when destiny knocked on our door. My husband manifested a heart condition, and died at the age of 47.

I thought my life was over, too, but it wasn't. I was 45. With maintenance on the house, property, and cars, plus a full-time job as a medical secretary, it took me a while to realize I had another whole life ahead of me.

Four years and many decisions later, I left Michigan to begin a second life as a full-time RV traveler and adventurer. Along the way, I communicated with old friends, made new ones, enjoyed a romance or two, embraced grandmotherhood, and savored life to the fullest.

When I say, "If I can live the RVing lifestyle, anybody can," that is not to belittle myself. It is to help you understand that I had no special talents, whatever, to think I could RV alone. Yes, I had talents, but they weren't even remotely connected to the mechanical end of life. The noisy, belt-dependent world under the "doghouse," whatever existed under the floors and tied the wheels together, and definitely the mysterious wires in the walls, were completely Greek to me. But, hey, nobody told me I couldn't do it.

In the following chapters, I will tell you about the Sprinter motorhome, his equipment, and our shared problems. Possibly what I tell you, will make your way smoother. If nothing else, it will give you insight into what it is really like to be a full-time RVer. We might even have a laugh or two.

I've traveled North America
I am woman, I can do it
Name a distant puddle
and I've probably driven through it

From a Mississippi barge trip
to a far Alaskan shore
I love this kind of livin'
with adventure near my door

Canoeing the Mighty Yukon
or exploring far-off Nome
When I return, I'm cozy
in my Sprinter Motorhome

Yessssss!

The Sprinter, returning from Inuvik, Northwest Territories, 1996

RV BUYING NEW?
or
RV BUYING USED?

Which type of RV should I buy?

I am often asked which is better, motorhome, trailer, fifth wheel, truck camper, or van. That is really a personal decision based on your research into what each offers and your personal needs.

Trailers have lots of room, without the driving space inside, and the tow vehicle can be driven. A trailer requires a proper hitch, and a tow vehicle heavy enough to pull it, but you would have more variety of tow vehicles from which to choose. Keep in mind that the stated trailer length includes the hitch. Actual living space would be 3' less.

Fifth wheels are my favorites, with the raised upstairs living room or bedroom. The entire length is living space, and the tow truck can be driven. From what I've observed, fifth wheels are easier to handle than trailers. It is easier to back them into a campsite, because of the forward-placed tongue weight. A fifth wheel trailer requires an adequate tow truck with a fifth wheel hitch mounted in the pickup bed. This leaves little room for using the truck bed for anything else.

Our truck camper was a great beginning RV, but I wouldn't feel comfortable putting one on and off by myself. They require an adequately heavy truck and springs. The truck can be used for a run-a-round vehicle. Many people use truck campers for trips into Mexico or Alaska, utilizing the higher clearance, and saving their bigger or newer RVs, the trip rigors and distances. Truck campers are as fancy or as plain as you desire.

I like a motorhome for safety reasons. If, for whatever reason, I decide to drive away, I don't have to "get out," to "get in." It's great during bad weather, if I'm parking late at night, or boondocking. I don't have to go outside unless I want to.

The down side to having a motorhome is that at least five feet of driving area, cuts down on living space. However, I utilize that space quite well. As a single, the navigator's side is storage. Couples wouldn't do that. It has been a mad scramble to re-arrange things whenever anyone travels with me for a few days. If I'm going to land for a while, the chairs can be turned around. This increases the living area somewhat.

If you have serious mechanical problems with a motorhome, it might mean having to move out until it is fixed. Unless you have insurance that covers it, staying in a motel until your RV gets fixed, is expensive, and all your possessions are left behind.

Some mini-motorhomes are no longer than a car or truck. A big advantage, is being able to park them nearly anywhere. Seldom do they have a problem being too big for campsites. The manufacturers are growing bigger and bigger mini-motorhomes, so if you like the style, there you go.

The Class B is a van-type camper. Fellow SKPs from The Netherlands, spent two years touring North America in a van camper, and continue traveling throughout Europe. They don't seem to mind the small quarters even though he is six-foot-six. I know a lady who has been full-timing out of a van for many, many years, and is quite happy with it.

I wouldn't recommend vans or truck campers for full-time RVers, only because of space limitations, but hey, whatever floats your boat. More power to people who want to live the lifestyle, and are willing to squeeze into more economical transportation.

So you don't want an RV that's forty feet long, but you could sure use some extra width. Not to worry. Slide-outs come in nearly any size. I even saw one that had been added to a school-bus conversion last summer. They come in kitchens, bathrooms, and living rooms, or you can have all three. When they are set up, even that few feet makes an amazing difference in the room. They are like being in a "real" house (I think that's what I escaped from!). Owners do not seem unhappy with the inconvenience of the slide-out inside the original width, for travel.

Some RV bodies are built up to 102", or eight-and-a-half feet, in width. I have seen motorhomes and fifth wheels that open up in the back, to allow carrying a car, or for a couple of favorite horses (and tack room). Why not, I take my favorite 454 horses, wherever I go.

I met a fellow in Mexico many years ago, who pulled an 8' by 15' trailer behind his 37' motorhome. He kept his regular-sized car in it when he was traveling. When he set up to stay for a while, he moved the car out, and made the trailer into a big living room. He was a big man and liked having a bigger space. It had a sofa, two easy chairs, lamps, magazine racks, the whole schmeer. When he was ready to leave, he pushed the household goods to one end, rolled up the rug, drove the car in, and took off.

I've dreamed of doing that with a portable office, but have never given in to it.

If you have enough money, you can get about anything. I had a reader from Seattle ask if "everyday" people lived this lifestyle, because all he saw in the magazines were the pricey bus-sized RVs. I wrote and said, "Hey, I'm doing it aren't I?"

The huge coaches are beautiful, miraculous almost, but the average Jill (or Joe) can't afford to live in them. It is great for those who can. You have to think in terms of what **you** can afford, or how much money you want to dance down the highways and byways.

Will it limit you in where you want to go? Will insurance cost more with one kind of rig over another? Are you going to have a tow vehicle, or drive your RV everywhere?

Trailer Life and MotorHome magazines publish an updated RV Buyers Guide every year. They get very specific with models, specifications, photographs, and floorplans. In 1997, it was selling for $7.95 including postage and handling. (Resources)

Honey, did we shrink the satellite dish?

Satellite dishes have shrunk through the years. You used to see this enormous satellite on top of an RV. Now dishes come as small as 18," with antennas that automatically locate and lock onto the satellite. Will you have a CD player, VCR? TVs come as big as 31" -- in the right unit.

Do you want a basement model? They're a little low slung, but how important is clearance? It will depend on where your new lifestyle takes you. Remember, the more storage you have, the more you will take with you, and the more likely you will surpass your GVWR. Basement models are nice, because the storage usually goes all the way through, and you can store long toys, like skis, fishing poles, and other outsized items. You can even have a computer desk built in for another kind of toy (maybe not in the basement).

When you go through the RV world, making notes about likes and dislikes, be sure to visualize yourself in the RV you are looking at. Sit in the living room chairs, the driver's seat, the booth. Are they all comfortable? Is the bathtub or shower or toilet area big enough to accommodate your size comfortably?

If my husband were still alive, we couldn't use the unit I have. The lavataory is extremely small. The bathtub and shower area would not be comfortable for a big man. I love a good hot tub bath. The one I have is a combination tub and shower, but the tub is about two-foot-square, with a seat to sit on. I cross my legs and slide down into the tub, but one of these days, I'm going to get stuck because I've eaten one too many bagels. By the time somebody finds me, well, it may be pretty embarrassing for my kids when I have to be buried in a bathtub.

Check for height, width, comfort, and specific needs.

It bugged me for a long time, because I had electrical outlets on only one side of the RV. You would think with the limited width and length, that wouldn't be a problem. My brother-in-law, George, installed an outlet on the other side. It doesn't matter if it is unreasonable in anyone else's eyes, you have to live with it. Look for what you want.

Check out the storage in the kitchen, bathroom, and outside. Eventually, you will make whatever RV you have, fit your needs. Why not start with a unit as close to what you need as possible. The options are endless.

What size do I need?

The first consideration is, how much money do you want to spend?

Next, the RV size will depend on whether you want to look into your mate's eyes because you love him, or her, or because you are forced into it.

Are you good friends, or do you just happen to be married to each other?

Do you practice the Marital Arts of Compromise, Communication, and Compassion?

Will you still love each other in the morning, or the fourth morning, after you've been cooped up because of super bad weather?

Are you patient, loving, kind, and generous, or do you blow up when "little" things happen?

Will you yell at your mate if something goes wrong, even if it isn't your mate's fault? If it is your mate's fault, can you be magnanimous, and pretend not to notice?

Our family of four had great trips in our 20' motorhome, but I wouldn't want to live full-time in that size. I live comfortably in a 27' length. I would have a smaller one, if it weren't for the office equipment.

Most full-timing couples should have at least 27' or more. A single probably could be happy with 22' or more, depending on their hobbies, interests, and the amount of junk they are going to carry on their backs. If your hobby is stamp collecting or flute playing, you don't need anything more than 20' and nimble fingers. If you train elephants as a sideline, I suggest a big hummer.

A couple from Michigan owned a motorhome, but found they didn't have room to practice their full-size hammered dulcimers. They bought a fifth wheel with a slide-out. The instruments fit behind the couch in the slide-out, and they have plenty of room for dallying with the dulcimers. Accommodate your interests.

Do you like to make crafts? Depending on the craft, it could take a lot of storage space. Sewing machine? Knife-sharpening tools? Wood-carving tools? Lawn mower? (Ah hah! We eliminated that one permanently!)

Think about your outside activities. Do you want to take folding bikes, kayaks, and boats; inflatable kayaks, canoes, and rafts; golf clubs; cross country or down-hill skis; fishing, scuba diving, backpacking, or gold mining gear? Where will you put this stuff? How heavy is it? Even if you can find a place to put it, is it easy to get out? Will you take the time to dig it out, if it isn't easily accessible?

My enterprising neighbor back in Michigan, solved the mystery of where to put my bike. I had creamed the one on the bike rack by backing into a palm tree in Mexico. The salt water also rusted it out there.

He put a quick release on the front wheel, so it could be taken off and put back on easily. He hung the bike, minus the front wheel, from the quick release he put up under the cupboard. The bike was situated between the office chair and the file cabinet (on the bed pedestal at that time). It was quite handy. It didn't take much to get it down or out, and the quick release for the front wheel was easy to use. I had it that way for a long time, then changed my office. Now I don't have a bike.

Other suggestions were to put it on the roof, but I was positive I would never use it, if I had to get it down from there. My husband used to keep the canoe and bikes on top of our mini, but he was big enough to wrestle it up, and down, with no problem.

I was recently looking at one-person, light-weight, plastic kayaks. I couldn't put it crossways across the back, because of the ladder and the spare tire. It was too long straight up. I couldn't put it on the roof because of the solar panels. I love the foldable kayaks, but they are really expensive. The new solid, molded kayak seems the answer, and someday I'll figure how to take it. Ah, well, back to the drawing board.

> **The size of your RV is gauged by what you can afford, the number of people traveling in it, your measure of claustrophobia, your temperament, and how much money you are willing to bounce down the highway.**

Gasoline or Diesel?

"Which is better diesel or gas?" I can only say, that when I put diesel in my gasoline engine in South Carolina, a couple of years ago, it wasn't the thing to do! Otherwise, whether you buy a diesel or a gas engine, it is more a personal choice.

I'll only mention a couple of differences, otherwise I know from nothin'. Gasoline engines are cheaper and quieter, and if you are traveling anywhere where there is a fuel station, they will have gasoline. Diesels are noisy, and not all stations have diesel fuel. Diesel owners will argue that while the original cost, and maintenance, on a diesel is higher, diesel engines will last longer than gasoline engines. I am replacing my gasoline engine, part by part, but after 145,000 miles, we are still doing okay.

Keep one thing in mind. Regardless of what you buy, stick with using diesel fuel in a diesel engine, and gasoline in a gasoline engine.

Scoping the RV scene

Buying an RV is a big decision (as if you didn't already know). It is likely you will attend RV shows once you get the bug for buying one. It is exciting to look, but it is confusing. The best way is to make up a chart. As you walk through RV shows, or visit dealerships, list the manufacturer, the model, and the features you like, or dislike. Pretty soon you will get a feel for what you really want in an RV.

Find out all you can. Don't decide on the price alone. Look at quality. If it falls apart after you live and travel in it a year, it wasn't inexpensive, it was cheap; **now** it will be expensive. If possible, take a tour of an RV manufacturing company. That can be an eye opener.

Check out the construction, frame, walls, insulation, floors, roof, and the underpinnings, suspension, tires, wheels, drums, and axles. In other words, **look at it all**.

Your new lifestyle should be flexible, not your RV.

Allow yourself plenty of time. **Buying an RV should not be an impulsive decision**. You wouldn't buy a house without doing plenty of looking (we hope). Treat buying an expensive RV the same way, with care and thought.

Talk to other RV people. Listen to the salespeople talk to other people (this tells me a lot.) They should be knowledgeable in their product, and not all are. Check out the manufacturer your dealership is representing. Make lists of questions. Look at older models of one you are interested in. How are they holding up after two years, five years, or ten?

Read, read, read. Read regional RV magazines, and buy Motorhome and Trailer Life off the rack. Go to a local campground and ask if you can look through their old magazines. FMCA, Good Sam, Escapees, Coast to Coast, Thousand Trails, Family Campers and RVers, all have their own magazines. If a regional magazine exists in your area, a copy will probably be there. Read books on RVing.

In the past, I have not had a great deal of luck finding information on RVing in the library, but I'm sure this is improving. I'll include a list of other RVing books in Resources. Also, surf the internet.

I bought the Class C from a newspaper ad. It had 23,000 miles on it. After major problems in my first year and a half of traveling, I knew I needed a new one, with warranties, or give up the lifestyle.

My brother-in-law, Jack, had bought an RV from Dennis Trailer Sales in Lansing, Michigan. He was pleased with his RV and their service. I looked at their only motorhome that fit my needs, a Class A.. I was skeptical. The salesman took me out for a drive in the Class A, and I was sort of hooked.

I went to Elkhart and Goshen, Indiana, thinking I could get a better deal where RVs were manufactured. Ha! First of all, I was ignored. I guess a woman alone isn't supposed to have such grandiose ideas, or else they thought I couldn't afford it. These "suits" were talking to each other, but not to me. When I finally got the attention of salespeople, I found their attitudes condescending. (Don't roll your eyes, guys, it was true!)

When I finally got the needed information from several dealerships, I found Dennis Trailer Sales was at least $5,000 cheaper. I bought that new 1987 Class A, and now I wouldn't have anything else. I like being up where the big boys are; I can see what is going on.

The Sprinter will soon celebrate his tenth birthday. One human year to seven chassis years makes him 63, just the right age traveling companion for a Silver Gypsy who celebrated the big "6-0" last November.

While I have seldom been in Lansing, Michigan, to take advantage of the expertise of the original dealership, I always find them to be knowledgeable, helpful, and not the least bit condescending.

The point is, be comfortable with whomever you are dealing. A whole lot of your money is involved. Be sure that the "sale is not the end of their serious involvement."

Know the reputation of the Service Department.
They'll be handling your warranty work. May God help you if they don't know what they are doing or don't do it in a timely manner.

I can't quite imagine anyone buying an expensive vehicle without test driving it. If you've never driven any RV before, this is quite an experience. It is certainly not one to be missed, if you are going to be an owner.

You need to be around your dealership a while to work out any kinks in your new RV. There are bound to be a few. Give it a good honest work out while you are still in the area, and your RV is under warranty.

Make sure you know what you are doing financially. Before getting into any serious discussions about an expensive item like an RV, this is a must. We'll get into ways to look at your finances in chapter three.

Buying a used RV

A reader wrote, "I'm concerned about buying a 'used' motorhome, but they are a lot cheaper." If you don't know your bellhousing from a ball joint, don't buy a used unit on the say so of "Honest John, the World's Greatest Salesman." I realize not all sales people fit into that category, but **you** need to do thorough research. It is a "buyer beware" world.

As an instructor for the Life on Wheels Conference at the University of Idaho, Moscow, last summer, I met a student who has a bigger desire to embrace this lifestyle than anyone I've ever met. While waiting for retirement, he has been scheming, planning, taking classes, reading everything he can get his hands on, and checking out new and used RVs. I can attest to the fact that he asks hundreds of questions. He rented motorhomes several times over the last few years, to give him an idea what RVing was like.

Steve Reyda is more adept in mechanics and other areas of RVing than the average person, plus he is very organized, and research conscious. After going to numerous RV shows, and checking out used RVs through ads in the newspaper, his list of RV needs and desires, grew. A picture of what he wanted took shape. He recently bought a 1985 Pace Arrow with 31,000 miles, for $25,000. As often happens, the owner's husband had died and she either couldn't, or had no desire, to continue traveling in the motorhome.

The motorhome had been in storage since 1993. Steve was impressed with it from the beginning; but for his peace of mind, he wanted a professional mechanic's opinion, before taking the plunge. He paid $140 for a Prospective Buyer's Check. Among other things, the engine compression, brakes, transmission, radiator, and exhaust system, were thoroughly checked. The Chevy 454 engine had a leaking manifold. The shocks needed replacing, and the front air bags had to be fixed. The cruise control, inside air conditioning, and refrigerator were checked out as well.

Steve, still on the sunny side of sixty, has another month before retirement, but I'm not sure he can last. He is raring to go. His "new" Pace Arrow motorhome fills the driveway, while he tinkers, and fixes, and fills it with not-to-be-left-behind treasures, and necessities.

He has kindly allowed me to include his proposed budget in chapter three. His extended computerized budget, using Cost-of-Living increases to gauge how much he will need to live on later, covers his new lifestyle until he is 105 years old. He says he has a lot of territory to explore, and it's going to take him that long. I've printed his one-month average predicted expenses. I averaged my 1996 RV expenses and included them as a comparison.

Now, Steve faces emptying his duplex. He said, "What do I do with fifteen empty margarine containers and lids?" I should remind him that he is now a full-time RVer. They would make terrific, light-weight bowls, for just about anything. He can use them for sewing supplies, leftover food, nuts and bolts, large breakfasts of cereal (after all, he is single), and to make giant ice cubes for giant margaritas.

And so,

Whether you are buying a new or used unit, don't be pressured into buying before you are ready, or buying what doesn't fit your needs. Talk to sales people, <u>after</u> you have an idea what you want. Don't let them influence you. Many of them have never traveled in an RV, let alone extensively. By the time you do any serious talking, you should already know your subject very well. You will be in a better position to ask questions and bargain.

If you're bent on a new unit, play with floor plans. Cut out refrigerators, beds, bathrooms, etc. and place them according to scale. See what you like best. If you have a computer, this game is duck soup. You may not be able to find exactly what you want, but again, perhaps you can find something close to it.

If you're buying a used unit, follow Steve's lead, and get a **Prospective Owner's Check**, **before you write out <u>your</u> check**.

Should I get a tow vehicle to pull behind the motorhome?

I didn't have a tow vehicle for several years. I put thought into the necessities before I parked. I didn't often have to break down and go into town. If I wanted to go somewhere special, I timed it to arriving or leaving. Using the motorhome as my main vehicle never stopped me from doing anything I wanted to do.

Eventually I bought a tow, thinking I might spend more time in one spot. That has been true to a degree. "Little Mercury Lynx, Bless His Heart" is his full name. He was born in 1981, and joined the entourage in 1993, with 94,000 miles registered on his odometer. He has a four-cylinder microheart.

A black umbilical cord with a plug on the end, dangles from the front grill, signifying he came from the very cold state of North Dakota.

If you are contemplating pulling a car or truck, look into the cost first. I didn't give it enough thought. I might have changed my mind.

You must have a **first class, safe,** means of towing a car. That cost me about $1,200 by the time I had paid to have the hitch, tow bar, and all the miscellaneous, attached. **Not all cars are towable.** Do your own research on this. Do not trust sales people to know. Coast to Coast magazine comes out once a year, with a long list of cars that are good, or not so good, for towing.

The tag will need registration, license, and insurance. Mine has only basic insurance, and if it is creamed, it will be a total loss. The insurance for the tag costs as much as the insurance for the motorhome (figure that!). It will require maintenance and repairs.

Unless you already own a tag you can pull, wait until you have traveled a while to make the decision. Have you missed having a car? They are often more convenient. Your need will depend a lot on what you are going to do. I have not taken the Little Lynx to either Alaska or Mexico. For Alaska, the clearance was better on the motorhome, than on the Lynx. With some of the places I chose to drive, I was better off without it. I rarely missed it.

You have to be much more aware when you are pulling a tag, or you might have to unhitch (which wouldn't be the end of the world -- just annoying). I have to think about length when I pull in for gasoline, propane, or shopping. If possible, I go to an outlying area that has a big parking lot.

Your tag needs Love, too

One morning I drove the Little Lynx up a long, steep grade. It shuddered. I thought, well, you deserve to shudder, that was a long haul. It didn't stop shuddering when it reached flat country. In the middle of nowhere (where else), I pulled off the road, opened the hood, and did the only thing I knew to do, I checked the oil. Though I check the Sprinter's oil frequently, at that time I wasn't used to the tag-a-long. I never seemed to remember to check its oil. I hung my head in shame when the poor Little Lynx gulped two quarts of oil, without stopping for air. I've since done a better job of remembering that Little Lynxes need their share of 10W30 and love, too.

This whole thing with checking the oil, at the first sign of a problem, whether it's the refrigerator going off, the printer getting stuck, or the front drapes refusing to come together, stems from an earlier motherhood frustration. "If you don't know what to do, at least do something." It is akin to always checking to see if the baby is hungry, dirty, or being stuck by a pin. By the time I've checked the oil, other things come to mind that I need to check.

Tow be or not tow be

I have a folding StowMASTER tow bar. The car travels on all fours. This means more tire wear, but I prefer more tire wear, to manhandling a dolly or trailer. The folding tow bar is very easy to use. I can have it on or off in five minutes. The bar is maneuverable. With that leeway, the Little Lynx is usually right on the mark, and everything lines up smoothly. I hook up the safety cables, and plug the electrical cord into the car and motorhome.

I put the car gear in neutral, the key in accessory position so that the steering wheel is moveable, release the emergency brake, lock the doors, and you can color us gone. I don't have a great deal of strength to wrestle equipment around, and this works great for me. With some tow vehicles, you have to disconnect the driveshaft.

When I drive off, the tow bar arms automatically extend, center, and self-lock. When I'm not using the tow bar, it folds easily and lives on the bumper. I keep a protective cover over it. It requires cleaning and spraying with silicone spray. I confess it doesn't get done often.

Occasionally, the coupler will bind when I try to take it off, but that only requires maneuvering the car a bit, or giving it a gentle reminder with a rubber mallet, to let go. Make sure your emergency brake is set when you take the coupler off the ball.

Several times when people have tried to help, they have gotten between the car and the RV. I don't let anyone do that. I am scared to death I will do something really stupid with the stick shift and crush someone's legs. Avoiding that possibility is worth two more minutes of maneuvering.

Another kind of tow bar has a rigid frame. It requires moving the car around to line it up with the ball. It can be removed from the tow car. Some people leave it on, pull it upright and fasten it.

An alternative to pulling with a hitch, is a dolly to hold the front wheels, or a trailer to carry the whole car.

After this last trip to Alaska, I discovered the long neck piece on the RV hitch that holds the ball, was actually bent upward. I can't imagine how I did that, unless I hit it coming out of a gas station or some other steep driveway. I don't recall ever hitting anything that hard (recently). Although the ball locked in tightly, I was uneasy about pulling with it. I had it replaced.

Good towing equipment is extremely important.

If you are going to tow a vehicle or trailer, you may want to have a mustache on the back of the RV. Protection for the tow car can be as simple as a piece of carpeting bungied over the hood, or a commercial car shield.

The Sprinter's facts

The Sprinter's water tank holds twenty-eight gallons of fresh water. That isn't a lot. Steve's unit has a seventy-five gallon capacity, and another friend, with a fifth wheel, has a hundred. It is great to have lots of water, if you are sitting still. If you are on the move, that is a lot of weight. Travel with enough for use that day, an emergency fire, or in case you have to boondock overnight unexpectedly.

The water tank, water pump, three in-house batteries, and a gauge for the solar inverter, are under the bed pedestal. I read it faithfully and pretend to know what it means. If it reads above twelve, I'm all right. Any less than that, and I can expect the computer to go bye-bye in the middle of an extremely important document. If I'm working on something that wouldn't matter if I lost it, the batteries will stay charged **until** I'm in the middle of an extremely important document.

I have a large electric fan that runs on solar. I also use it for drying my hair (everything has a double use).

A small electric vacuum cleaner works fine with the solar energy. When I visit my kids, I use their major-duty vacuum cleaners for an extra good job. I take my shoes off immediately when I walk in the door, to cut down on dirt being tracked through the RV, but I do have a carpet cleaning machine. A pair of slip-on shoes lives by the door, for short trips going in and out.

I rarely use the air conditioner, but since the heat and humidity gets me down in a hurry, it has been a lifesaver a few times. When the air conditioner was transferred from the old mini to the new Sprinter, it went in the space of a vent. That was a mistake, because I have no vent over the driver area or in the living area. Someday I will remedy that (if the Sprinter or I live long enough) with a vent that moves up and down with the temperature. I have three other vents.

An antenna did live on the roof, but I never used it. The space for the TV inside the cabinet, was not large enough to accommodate the right size TV. I never used the antenna. I had it taken off when the roof was refurbished.

Except for the very front over the driver area, the roof is solid and can be walked on without flexing. A permanent ladder is on the back along with the spare tire. The permanent ladder has a permanent crease from backing into a permanent brick wall somewhere in the permanent Maritimes.

An awning on my first RV was used once. I didn't buy one for the Sprinter. It would be handy on rare occasions but I haven't missed it that much. I have chosen to be more on the move than most people.

So there you have it. The Sprinter, the Little Lynx, and I. We aren't perfect, but we're a good team.

Revamping the Sprinter
If you have an older unit, it might spark some ideas for you

Heating

The Sprinter has survived many changes. I removed the forced-air furnace several years ago. That created a space to store my summer fan. The furnace fan used roughly 7.5 amps per hour. It zapped my batteries quicker'n lightning when I was boondocking, even using it only an hour or two, morning and evening.

A ceramic propane heater was installed. The manufacturer (Empire Comfort Systems) does not recommend use in an RV since it is not vented, but I have been pleased with its efficiency and the comfort zone it provides.

It MUST have a fresh air source because it will deplete the oxygen. I crack a window or two, but I do that more for the condensation than worrying about asphyxiation. The heater is next to the outside door that has become so warped over the years, I could throw twenty-five well-fed, overgrown, gi-gantic mice through it (and I have!).

It is an excellent heater. I don't like being cold. When I have all three tiles lit, it is toasty within a few minutes. I maintain the warmth using only one tile, unless it is extremely cold outside. It has no connection to the batteries.

A small twelve-volt fan, near the ceiling, blows warm air back toward my bedroom and office. Changing the direction of the heat can also be done by mounting the heater on a piano hinge, to allow some leeway in aiming it.

I seldom leave the heater on through the night. I prefer a cold room for sleeping. When it is on all night, I open the window a ½" near my head.

Another option is a catalytic heater. These are propane fueled. I have had two in the past and didn't care for them. They can also be mounted on a piano hinge, to direct the heat in various directions.

I have a small electric (Maxi-Heat™) 5200 BTU ceramic electric heater for when I have shore power. Extreme caution should be used regarding where you put any heater, and what you put near it. The electric heater shuts off if it is accidentally knocked over.

The "home" office

When I left Michigan, I installed the office equipment along one side of the living room. I was never happy with that because I couldn't "go home from the office."

I stored the RV mattress. My brother, Ted, put ½" plywood over the bed pedestal, and carpeted it. This made a good base and I could stand on it without hitting my head. He put in boards and legs to make a desk on two sides of the office chair. Behind that was my two-drawer file cabinet with the copier on top. Voila! The home office.

That was fine for several years, until I tired of climbing in and out of the narrow bunk bed above the driver's seat. I had the vanity torn out of the bed-room, and had specific-sized spaces built in for the computer, printer, and other necessities. The office was growing. I had a ¾ size mattress created to fit the bed pedestal, leaving a space along the edge for me to sit on and work on the computer. This has worked fairly well.

Another idea I read about, and maybe will institute one day, is taking out one-half of the booth area, and building in a computer workstation.

Each "improvement" required ways to fasten the equipment down. I have lips on the shelves, and a bar across the computer monitor. I use a bungy-cord across the printer front. It is so heavy it never moves, but I don't take chances.

Other changes

When the unit was five-years-old, I had new carpeting, upholstery, and drapes put in. The original material wore out fast considering most RVs aren't built for living in. The carpeting was extended up the motorhome walls, lending insulation against the cold and heat. I also like the look of it.

In 1995, my brother-in-law, George, built shelves in half of the hanging closet, and put a bar across the top of the shower to hang clothes on for drying. He built a shelf with a three-inch lip across the bathroom under the medicine chest. George did a lot of engine work, including replacing the timing chain and gears. He stripped the roof, made any repairs, recovered the seams with gauze-like repair material, and painted the whole roof with rubber reflective paint, and fastened a third solar panel on the roof. That reflective paint made a big difference in the heat. Even sitting in the desert in the middle of the day, the Sprinter doesn't get nearly as hot it would normally.

His wife, Lorna, made drapes cutting off the driving area from the living area. When I pull the drapes, I have more of a living room, and I don't have to close the front sliding drapes across the windshield. When I'm boondocking, I like to keep the motorhome ready for driving away. They replaced the faucet in the kitchen sink with a "goose-neck" faucet that allows me to wash my hair or get a bucket of water.

Over the years I have removed the doors to the bathroom, shower, and between the kitchen, bedroom, and bathroom area. The four doors in so small a place, were constantly banging into each other. I replaced one with a shower curtain, and the two between rooms, with drapes. It is quieter and less hazardous.

Before leaving for Alaska last year, I took out the couch. A friend built a folding shelf on the end of my countertop, next to the sink, which gives me much-needed space, on rare occasions, when I do something so dastardly as cooking (or washing dishes).

After taking the motorhome out of storage (after house-sitting), Janet made new drapes, and revamped new bedspreads to fit. The carpet was professionally cleaned. I put down new runners, over the tops of the others, for warmth. I use "Miracle Hold™," by Vantage Industries, between layers of carpet. It is the only product I have ever used that works to keep rugs on rugs from moving.

"Scoot-Gard™," is another product by Vantage Industries. I have the lacy kind and I love it. It can be used for placemats, coasters, or like a scarf. The best thing about it is, it holds--then it is practical--then it is pretty. I use it under my computer keyboard and mouse. They stay put when I take off.

It is easily cut with scissors. It lines my drawers and cupboards. It cuts down the noise in my "whatnot" drawer, and I no longer find black bottoms on objects from their sliding around while the Sprinter is moving.

The blinds for the bathroom, bedroom, and kitchen windows were replaced with frosted Contact® paper. I have drapes to hook over them if I want it totally dark. Janet used Velcro® to fasten my power surge unit to the wall. Now, the cords don't tangle and it stays in place.

I re-wallpapered the bedroom and kitchen. The kitchen is a plain pinkish, mauvish color. I put a border of lighthouses across it. I refurbished worn places on the cupboards and walls with the same wood-design covering it had. Eventually, I will redo the bathroom walls.

Several years ago, I removed the table in the booth area. I had a cabinet built in along the back wall between the booth seats. It holds boxes of photographs. I made the booth up as a bed. Janet made a new quilt into a sack and I slid an egg crate into it. It is now more of a lounge seat. I bought big bed pillows, with pillowcases, to match all the colors for both the lounge and my bed. On the rare occasion when anyone might stay with me, the lounge can be used as a bed, as it has been in the past.

It isn't often that I miss having a table. When I need one, I have a plastic round table, or we eat on our laps.

I say it is "eclectic." Janet says, "I like it, Mom, but if a decorator walked in, they would turn puce." It's bright, cheerful with blues, greens, purples, aquas, mauves, pinks, and whatever. In close quarters, you need to like your surroundings. With all the colorful fabric and carpeted walls I've surrounded myself with, I find most other motorhomes seem cold and dull, even the new ones.

I have light-weight hanging wall files on my bedroom wall, and inside the closet door. The four drawers underneath the closet are files and office supplies. Empty spaces lurked under the drawers, with no access. I take out the drawers and fill the space with extra paper towels, TP, and other light stuff.

I am not into lots of clothes. What I have fits into the upper cupboards. If clothes are seasonal (or another range of weights), I put them in a big suit-case in the car. The Little Lynx is my mobile garage. Among other things, it carries boxes of books, cross country skis, boots, and anything else I can't fit into the motorhome. You have to be aware of the weight you are pulling, as well as the weight of the RV.

Janet and Bill removed the bunk above the driving area. It had bowed through the years. I stored only light stuff up there, but everything sags with age, sooner or later (Unfortunately, she says, looking in the mirror.) Now I have more headroom. Janet stapled leftover carpeting that matches what is already there, on the side walls, covering the bad spots where the bunk had been.

I take good care of my home, just as I would if I were land bound. Sometimes it is frustrating because when I get one thing fixed, something else falls apart, but that, too, is the same as it would be, if I were land bound.

After I took it out of storage this year, I took the Sprinter to Kelly at All Seasons RV in Wenatchee, Washington. With his expertise, the refrigerator works better than it has in years. The water heater seems to have taken a new lease on life, and we buried the poor step that I creamed in Alaska, with honors. Dan, at Leavenworth Auto, had his mechanic install a new emergency brake, and two horns.

I am truly ready for "getting on down the road again." Little by little I am replacing the entire RV. When the Sprinter and I roll into the Twenty-first Century, I'll have a whole new motorhome.

If you want to make drastic changes in your RV, research it, and give it a lot of thought. Your "improvements" could make it more salable, or it might make it a very poor buy for the next guy. I finally decided I would drive the

Sprinter until the wheels fall off. It doesn't matter what I do to it. It is now "uniquely mine," and personalized.

Something else to think about, with revamping, is whether you are adding extra weight. I have added some, but I have also eliminated rather heavy pieces.

Watch the RV magazines. They carry articles and ideas about what others have done to create their own special spaces, for whatever reasons.

Whew! Hey, don't give up yet. You need to know what's in the next chapter.

"Charlie," in the home office

The ABC's of RVing

Anxiety, Budget, and Cost

Consider the costs you will give up when you no longer have a permanent home, mortgage payments, rent, property taxes, utilities, furnishings and equipment, household operations, and house and yard maintenance.

You will have more gasoline, and vehicle maintenance, plus mail-forwarding, and campgrounds. You will still have medical, dental, and prescription expenses; insurances; registrations and licenses; contributions, and taxes. Some costs will remain roughly the same, depending on your personal decisions, i.e., food, clothing (this might go down as you take on "casual"), and miscellaneous.

Finances will be affected by personal decisions; eat in or out, stay in campgrounds or boondock, park for a week or keep driving, volunteer for a summer and let the investments pile up.

Let's talk about mileage. The total mileage I have traveled with the Sprinter and his predecessor, is 180,000 miles, or roughly 16,300 miles a year. When you consider I've been in sixteen Mexican states, fifteen United States (forty-nine with the RV), and all the provinces and territories of Canada except Newfoundland, that isn't bad. Still, my gasoline expenditure, especially at 6 mpg, for any given year, has been high. That was my choice. You don't have to go that far, or spend that much, to enjoy RVing.

You aren't going back and forth to work, but more in a circuitous, meandering fashion around the country. You may not put on as many miles as you did when you were landbound.

Cards from specific fuel companies are issued by the RV organizations as perks for joining. They offer discounts on gasoline, diesel, and propane at certain stations, or they offer money back after you have bought a certain amount. In addition, they offer long distance calling card service, or other discounts. I bought into one of them at an RV show. The main reason was to get their laminated Atlas. I never did use the fuel card.

The laminated Atlas has been priceless. Until I bought that, I was replacing my torn, worn, and weary Atlas, every year.

The problem I have with going to specific fueling stations, rather than just go where it is easy driving in, or cheapest, is probably more being a single. By the time I realize there is a station around, I have already gone by it. I have a "thing" against "going back" unless it is extremely convenient. With an RV pulling a car, it is seldom convenient enough to find my way back. With a co-pilot watching, it would be easier. (It would, wouldn't it?)

I don't eat out a lot. If I see a quaint little cafe, or I'm just plain tired of my own company, I'll eat out. Most of the time I eat out only when I am with friends or family. I prefer to eat in. Since I'm allergic to cooking, my meals are simple and food is not a high expenditure.

If you do "dine" out, there are lots of ways to cut costs. How about going for lunch, instead of dinner? It is often the same meal for less cost. Eat in the late afternoon or early evening, and take advantage of the "earlybird" specials. Don't forget to ask for the senior citizen discount.

If you'll be in one area long enough to go back to the same place several times, some restaurants give punch cards for an eventual free meal. Senior Centers are in almost every town. Their meals are inexpensive, nutritious, and it is a great way to make new local friends.

I went to a "Farmer's Market" in Fairbanks, Alaska, last summer. Yummy. We used to have a terrific one on Saturday mornings in South Bend, Indiana. We lived in Michigan, and it meant getting up mighty early to get there when it opened, but that was the best time. Fresh donut holes were reason enough for getting up that early. The sights and smells were incredible. It will excite your palate and palette. Markets are open only certain days of the week. It is a great way to get fresh **everything**.

Most of the time my clothes are embarrassingly casual. Sunday morning is about the only time I make an attempt to dress up. I didn't realize how casual my comfortable shoes were though, until the church people took up a collection for me (Honest! I'm kidding).

Only when I give seminars or fly somewhere, do I take a good honest look at my wardrobe. It's frightening. Keep a few good clothes hanging in the closet for special occasions. This depends on your lifestyle. If you are parked at an RV resort with lots of evening activities, or you go out a lot, clothes might cost you more.

Even casual clothes and shoes must be replaced sometime. Linens, drapes, carpeting, and upholstery, will eventually have to be upgraded.

Entertainment is also a personal choice. I don't go out to movies, and I don't play golf, tennis, ski, or gamble. I spend my money on the unusual, like paragliding in Colorado, ultralight flying in Arizona, playing with the grizzlies at Katmai, or canoeing the Yukon River. Those activities are expensive. That is my choice. You don't have to spend a lot of money on entertainment to enjoy the RV lifestyle.

Daily miscellaneous expenses will cost you a little. After all, you're going full-timing, you are not becoming a monk (I suppose you could. You'd have time for it now). You may want a newspaper once a week, or maybe every day. If you love to read, you'll have the time for it. Why not go to the book exchange stores or yard sales? They are great places to find book treasures. Be careful of those yard sales. You can't buy a bunch of "stuff," (unless, of course, it's something to send to your grandchildren). Watch that weight.

I belong to Coast to Coast, a membership campground. I only stay in them if they are in my path, unless I'm going to stay for a week, or in my home park for two weeks. My home park is free. Other parks have gone up to $4 a night with a few places charging for extras I don't use. This is getting to be a bigger bargain every day with the costs of private parks going up.

I travel where I can boondock, stay in National Forest, BLM or Core of Engineer campgrounds. I visit with my kids on either end of the country, or other family in Michigan or Arizona, and occasionally, with friends. I prefer having my own space even when I'm visiting.

Many people pay by the week, month, or season, because it is cheaper. They visit family or friends more often. The various passes for National Parks and Monuments, Golden Eagle, Golden Access, and Golden Age, are explained in the Glossary. A book on "free" camping is in Resources. We'll talk more about ways to save money camping in Chapter 11.

I use propane for the water heater, cook stove, the ceramic heater, and exclusively, for the refrigerator. Sixteen gallons lasted me three weeks this last time, and that included using the heater all but during mid-afternoon. If you are really cutting costs, you can shut off your water heater when you've completed your ablutions (let's give this action some class) and dishes for the day.

We've already talked about phone calls and mail. When you settle for a few days, let your kids or friends call you for a change. My oldest brother gave me his credit card (what trust) so I would call him more often. When I thought of it, I used his card every other time. Now the rates are heavenly, but the distance is too far.

Because my repair expertise is sadly lacking, the more miles I put on, the more maintenance costs I pay. Again, that is a matter of choice. If I would marry a mechanic again, it would cut expenses. But then I suppose I would spend more for Excedrin, so there you have it. Choices.

When you stop for a while in one place you've always wanted to see, you aren't moving; therefore, you aren't paying for gasoline; you aren't racking up maintenance bills; and if you're lucky, you aren't paying for camping. Your investments will have a chance to pile up, or re-cooperate, until you are ready to "hit the road again."

Steve's Projected Budget

Here is Steve's budget. He reminded me this is an **estimate**. He will not start his full-time RVing adventure for a couple of months. He based the budget on his state of residence, age, health, lifestyle, interests, and personal preferences.

I must quality my larger expenses in Entertainment, RV Maintenance and Fuel costs. I drove over 9,000 miles in a five-month trip to Alaska and Canada last summer. (The Little Lynx stayed home.) I paid a high price for a two-week canoe trip on the Yukon River, and playing with the grizzlies at Katmai National Park. Major expenses cropped up in a complete brake job, four new tires, and a rebuilt transmission. Steve elaborated more fully in some areas, where I had combined expenses. Your expenses could be much lower, or much higher. It all depends on your choices.

RV MONTHLY BUDGET		
	Steve	Charlie
HOUSEHOLD		
Groceries	115.00	183.00
Laundry	10.00	11.00
Miscellaneous	28.00	41.00
PERSONAL		
Clothing	8.50	24.00
Haircut	10.00	0
Medical & Dental Insurance	181.08	176.00
Long Term Care Insurance	142.00	0
Prescriptions	33.87	0
Toiletries	9.28	(Inc/Msc)
MISCELLANEOUS		
Bank Charges	2.50	3.00
Dues	16.83	13.00
Gift Expenses	22.47	21.00
Newspaper	4.00	(Inc/Msc)
Other	18.07	(Inc/Msc)
Postage	20.00	13.00
Subscriptions	5.25	(Inc/ Med)
Telephone	60.82	61.00
TRANSPORTATION		
Campground fees	180.00	76.00
RV Fuel + Oil	360.00	231.00
RV Insurance	75.00	57.00
RV License	12.75	9.00
RV Maintenance & Service	125.00	359.00
Propane	15.00	35.00
Ferries and Parking tolls		14.00
DISCRETIONARY		
Contributions		66.00
Dining Out	60.00	(inc/Food)
Entertainment	55.00	289.00
Recreation	65.00	(Inc/Ent)
TOTAL EXPENSES	**1,635.42**	**1,682.00**
TOW CAR		
Fuel	40.00	14.00
Service	125.00	12.00
Insurance	54.83	34.00
Ferries and Parking tolls		2.00
TOW CAR TOTAL EXPENSES	**219.83**	**62.00**
TOTAL MONTHLY EXPENSES, RV AND TOW	**1,855.25**	**1,744.00**

Thanks, Steve.

Volunteering

Some of you may be like I was, too young to retire. Others may want to fill their time , supplement income, or curb costs for a while. Later on, I'll tell you how to find paying or volunteer work. Right now, I'll tell you a story about volunteering that I wrote in 1995.

Murphy, "A wimp who is scared of everything" and Garp, as "In the World According to," two eighty and ninety pound Labrador retrievers, live in a 1995 37' Holiday Rambler. In 1995, Murphy and Garp pulled campground guard duty at Snowmass-Maroon Bells Wilderness, near Aspen, Colorado. They shared this fresh air and magnificent scenery with their parents, Ronni and George Hoover.

Ah, well, the air wasn't always fresh. One late night the propane sensor alarm rang in the bedroom. Murphy and Garp weren't talking but the conclusion was that one of them was not so fragrant as flatulent. They were forever exiled from the Hoover bedroom.

Previous to full-time RVing, the Hoovers lived in Ellicotte, Maryland, and worked for the government. The offer of an "early out," as well as the premature deaths of George's parents, prompted them to forego the hassle of the working world to savor whatever awaited them "on the open road."

Through the Good Sam Campground Host program, they received information about a volunteer position at "Some place called Maroon Bells." Being familiar with this Rocky Mountain paradise, their response was, "Let's go." For two summers, the Hoovers hosted in the White River National Forest at Weller, Difficult and Maroon Bells Campgrounds.

While Ronni is the chief cook in the family, George is in charge of fish. He loves this new avocation and caught his limit regularly. He wrapped them in tin foil with butter, onion, seasonings, lots of garlic and cooked them over the open fire, much to the delight of this co-host.

One early evening George was past due long enough to worry Ronni. He limped in with two fish and a boot full of blood. While crossing a rock slide, he had steadied himself on "a perfectly stable-looking rock." It moved. He caught himself but not without gashing his shin. He didn't realize immediately that his pantleg was receiving a blood transfusion and his brand new insulated boots were fast filling. George was in stitches for several days, but Ronni didn't find it humorous; thereafter, he took a two-way radio with him.

Ronni had a special relationship with her "Hummingchildren." The tiny birds zoomed in and around the host RVs, finding the feeder she filled often with a combination of boiled four-to-one water and sugar. When it emptied, they flew within inches of her face, demanding their daily allotment of goodies. She put her finger on the wire landing strip; and in trust, they sipped while clamped to her finger.

The males are fiercely territorial. George found two males who might have survived fighting each other but not with Plexiglas. One was already dead of a broken neck. He picked them up in his huge hand, and tenderly held them both, until the second tiny creature breathed its last.

With non-electricity campgrounds, the Hoovers appreciated their two solar panels, inverter and generator. A small satellite dish provided enough TV reception to know what was happening in the outside world. Ronni, a former Computer Systems Analyst, cross-stitches, and uses the solar electric to sew and keep a daily journal of their adventures, via the computer. They are both computer buffs. George, was an engineer and sometimes wood-carver, who now spends his extra time solving RV problems for the less mechanically fortunate (like me).

"One little mistake, just one little mistake," was George's favorite expression to interject levity into tense situations. There were many such aggravations hosting forty-four campsites. Some days it seemed everybody switched campsites without benefit of host knowledge or guidance, causing unbelievable snafus in site assignments. The Hoovers took it all in stride.

They moved into their RV during the iciest season in Maryland's recorded history, according to Ronni. "We were still working and George forgot his briefcase. By the time he turned around to unlock the RV door, it was already frozen shut. The wind chill was thirty below zero."

When you live in a tin tent, following the sun becomes a habit but the Hoovers didn't entirely miss winter the summer of '95. Maroon Lake Campground was picturesque with one and a half inches of snow on the Fourth of July. That kind of picturesque didn't interest them.

I ran into the Hoovers again in 1996, in Surprise, Arizona, where George was volunteering at Westside Food Bank, an organization that distributes extra farm crops to the needy. Ronni was catching up on news with two daughters and a grandson by phone, one of the privileges she missed at Maroon Bells. Although they have a cellular phone in their RV, it wasn't workable in the high mountains.

Since their hosting experience in Colorado, Garp has gone on to that Great Campground in the Sky, survived by sweet Murphy. While they loved the full-time RV lifestyle, work once again beckoned George, and he succumbed. They bought a house in Arizona, and I'll bet they are still volunteering one way or another.

This was my experience at Snowmass-Maroon Bells Wilderness

So that politicians can pour more of Middle America's tax money into more needy areas, like ratholes, more and more volunteers are needed in every phase of life.

The United States Forest Service is not an exception, and according to the rangers, "We couldn't run the parks without volunteers." Consequently, in enjoying the panoramic beauty of the Snowmass-Maroon Bells Wilderness near Aspen, Colorado, I hadn't any more than said, "This is magnificent, I wish I could stay longer," when a mop, bucket and sponge magically appeared in my hand.

As I backed into this summer hosting job due to someone's illness, I didn't have the usual training. When I received the complimentary USFS long-sleeved Tee-shirt, baseball cap, and jacket, I was admonished by Joe

Chavez, Manager of Development Recreation, "It is very important that the campground host present the image that the U. S. Forest Service is striving to achieve. Our main purpose is to see that guests have an enjoyable time and are treated by all volunteers in a friendly, courteous, responsive, and professional manner." We were to be patient and diplomatic regardless of the situation. That was not always easy.

It was a learning experience. A few years ago I volunteered for two weeks in a very small campground. The duties were minimal. This time the campground had forty-four sites and a three-night limit, an entirely different story. All money deposited in "the green pipe" had to match a campsite, the number of days, the vehicle license, and be double-checked with a khaki-colored "Compliance Officer" each morning.

This area was also excessively busy because of the roughly 1600 day-use hikers and lookers arriving by bus, necessitating two sets of hosts. I was the second temporary "set." Duties included cleaning firepits; scooting visitors out of no-parking zones; and diplomatically persuading dog owners that the "leash your dog" signs really did mean Brutus "who always stays at my heels" but who at that moment was streaking after a terrified marmot.

A good argument for leashing was the Alaskan husky whose owner let him off the leash on the trail. He returned asking the whereabouts of a vet. The dog ran to investigate a porcupine and acquired several quills in his cheeks before his owner could restrain him.

Sites were checked several times a day in a Kawasaki utility runabout. If campers were on a hike, beyond the 11 a.m. check-out, by several hours, and sites were at a premium, they were apt to find their tent and belongings at the host site when they returned. RVs were a little more difficult to gather in your arms and remove from a site. Tickets were sometimes issued for overstaying time limits. From 8:30 a.m. to 5 p.m., the USFS personnel assigned sites. Before and after those times, sites were host assigned.

Nobody likes a free night of camping more than I do, but camping fees are one of the few fees the government collects, that I don't mind paying. Aside from the messy toilets, the site switching, and the leashless dogs, I resented most those who posted tags but didn't deposit the fee. In my estimation, we needed to track the culprits down by their license numbers and fine them.

To keep everybody smiling, we helped people switch to "just the right campsite" with a view or near the stream or next to friends. Often they changed campsites without checking with hosts, causing elevated temperatures when occupied sites were assigned a second time.

We handed out instructions on wilderness ethics; what to do if confronted by wildlife; how to be safe in a storm; topographical trail maps; trail conditions; city maps for finding food, churches, licenses; and information on gas stations, dump stations, shower facilities, and buying wood.

We were in charge of Lost and Found. When I left we had two cameras, a hammer, two pairs of men's shorts, and keys to a Saab, a Hyundai and a Toyota.

Campfires were sometimes left unattended with flames merrily crackling in the pit. It was amazing. It takes all of two minutes to put a fire out. It's just as easy to be an "I'm sure glad I did it the right way" camper as an "I regret what I did" camper surveying scorched acreage or loss of life.

The benefits of hosting far outweighed the woes. One benefit promised was to "Work with an enthusiastic staff and summer crew." So true. If anyone had a problem, the staff was there to help almost before the words were out of our mouths. They were so grateful for any extra courtesy you extended them. One day I stopped at the entrance station to say hello. The ranger in charge was stranded. Someone had taken off with his keys. I said I would go back to Aspen to get him a second set. "Really?" he asked, "You would do that for me?" Actually, I don't know of a volunteer who wouldn't have done anything for those people.

My co-hosts were out and Pat Collins, the head Wilderness Ranger finished up his paper work. He seemed reluctant to leave me alone on a Saturday night with an overflowing campground. I assured him it wasn't a problem.

He said, "If anybody gives you trouble, go inside, lock your doors, and call the Pitkin County Sheriff on the two-way radio."

I said, "I travel all over North America by myself, I'm not afraid."

He said, "You may have other angels watching after you in other places but here, we are your angels." This USFS earth angel and his big heart didn't realize the One who built the Maroon Bells was looking after me.

Twice a month the staff planned picnic lunches or evening barbecues for the roughly thirty hosts in the White River National Forest. These were paid for by money gleaned from aluminum can recycling. Everybody brought a dish to pass. Conversations touched on the bear that ransacked a campsite the night before to "remember when" stories.

One such story came out of host orientation. They were told, "Explain the rules to visitors. Remind them if they are breaking those rules but don't argue with them, call for a Compliance Officer." One lady said she had reminded a wilderness visitor of a rule he was breaking and he pulled a gun. As quick as a wink she said, "I got to pee" and took off. It worked. He was too thunderstruck to follow.

Another story was about a new host who didn't know the terminology. On the two-way radio that is often garbled, she heard that Pulaski was lost. She passed on the information that a visitor was missing. After the story was checked and everything quieted down, it was explained that Pulaski was a ten-pound wilderness ax. It had been misplaced.

We also had drama. A concerned husband reported to the host that he had left his wife "somewhere near the falls" because she was having a "breathing problem" and needed help. When they went to find her, she was gone. The host immediately contacted the Wilderness Ranger, Pat Collins, who was hiking the trails at Crater Lake, with Linda, a Volunteer Wilderness Ranger, a mile and a quarter away.

Pat handed Linda his Pulaski ,and ran all the way down the mountain. Linda carried the ten-pound ax that was "sharp enough to slice tomatoes with" and fielded questions from visitors she passed on her way down, "Where is the ranger going in such a hurry?" and "Where in the hell are you going with that?" pointing to the ax. "It's bigger than you are."

Pat set up a command center and briefed both volunteers and rangers as to the situation and the description of the lady in distress. Rangers hiked the trails to find her, and questioned hikers returning from the wilderness trail. Suddenly the host realized the lady in question, was boarding the bus to Aspen with her husband. He had found his wife and assisted her back, but had failed to tell anyone they no longer needed assistance.

After the emergency was over, it was relief time. Linda said, "When Pat gave the lady's description as "An elderly woman, about 55,' I nearly decked him. I'm turning 55 this year and there's no way I'm elderly."

Our host sites had sewer and water. Gasoline was provided for a USFS generator or for using our own. We could make phone calls from a ranch five miles away or travel another five miles to the "Bunkhouse" in Aspen, where the single volunteers and rangers lived. We also did laundry and took showers at the bunkhouse.

While most hikers, tenters, and RVers leave their surroundings more clean and pristine than they found them, a minute percentage leave trashed campsites and disgusting toilets. I will never take the cleanliness of an outside toilet for granted. In addition to providing TP, every piece of paper dropped, dirt tracked, smudge left on a seat or wall, the host swept, picked up, mopped up, or washed off in the seven "necessaries." This translated into fourteen necessaries if you counted them as "his" and "hers."

The consensus is that most of us wouldn't do that kind of work for money. One of the favorite stories floating around Maroon Bells was about Jim Adams. He and his wife, Vada, from Illinois, have hosted at Maroon Bells for many years. He was swabbing a toilet and remarked, "I used to own a railroad, and now I'm cleaning toilets as a volunteer."

As hosts in the wilderness, we sometimes had unwelcome visitors inside our RVs. A motorhome seems particularly vulnerable to rodents who crawl in almost any-sized hole. With a mouse-born killer virus in the news, I expressed my paranoia to Peggy Lyons, one of the rangers.

She said her USFS Hanta Virus seminar, proclaimed the virus "a problem with only 'aged poop,' such as when someone opens a cabin that has been closed all winter and sweeps up the dusty 'remains.' This gets into the air, is breathed, and can be dangerous."

I tried my big brother's theory that mothballs would keep the mice at bay. I spread them liberally throughout the ground under the MH. I nearly died from the fumes as I watched the mice go in and out of the motorhome, having snowball fights with the mothballs. That went on for a week. I set three traps every night and caught a mouse a night. Finally, their reunion was over.

Joanne, at 64, had answered an ad in the paper and became a Volunteer Wilderness Ranger. She loved it and was losing an average of a pound of weight a week, not that she needed to. She said of her trail hiking, "I'm having so much fun doing it, I feel guilty."

Joanne and her husband are both health-conscious. One day she arrived back at the parking lot at the same time that her husband finished riding his bike up the narrow, steep road to the bells which he does three times a week. She said he kissed her and said, "I love kissing Forest Rangers." With her sense of humor and warm smile, she is a natural for the PR she does on the trail while counting all those noses. Her philosophy, "Enjoy life, and do some good for others along the way."

After the first month, I moved down the mountain a ways to host two much smaller campgrounds. It took me two hours a day to take care of my duties. The rest of the time I was hiking, writing, or listening to the stream down below me. It was an incredible two months.

As I said, I practically backed into that volunteer hosting job. It was hard work but I loved the area and all the people with whom I worked.

Interested people usually start months before the season, sending in resumes, filling out papers, etc. Even if you haven't applied ahead of time, if you find an area you really love being in, check to see if they have an opening. You might find the same situation I did. People have to leave volunteer positions for all kinds of reason, and the powers that be might be delighted to find a responsible replacement on their doorstep.

It can be hard work and frustrating; but on the other hand, you make great friends. You're doing something worthwhile, and you get to park in a free RV spot in some of our country's most scenic places.

Three publications come to mind when people ask how to find volunteer or short-term paying jobs, or trading...wait, just read the article below. It tells all.

Work Resources

"Work" by some RVers is considered a four-letter word. Other RVers either have a need, or a desire, to keep their hand in the working world, to supplement investments or social security. Others want to be of service as volunteers. Still others are looking for interesting places to spend time, and want to trade services for parking spots. The following are three publications that list an amazing number of job, volunteer, and caretaking possibilities in North America and overseas.

Three major considerations make RVers perfect candidates for employers who need part-time help. RVers pull their housing with them. They have unscheduled chunks of time. They are extremely dependable. Those same reasons make RVers valuable volunteers and caretakers.

Since August of 1987, Debbie and Greg Robus have published the WORKAMPER NEWS. It is published for all working ages, but mostly their "Workampers" are retirees who can't resist a bit of extra dough to enjoy a full loaf of the RV lifestyle. The newsletter has two objectives. The first is to help readers find interesting and rewarding work opportunities. The second is to help employers find just the right couple or single, to fit their situation.

Even with a circulation of 30,000+ RV owners and employers, WORKAMPER NEWS can't keep up with all the employers who say, "We hired someone through your newsletter and they worked out great..."

A typical issue of WORKAMPER NEWS has classified ads listing business and income opportunities, with everybody from the Bureau of Land Management to theme parks, to Kampgrounds of America, and American Guide Services. In addition to a Situations Wanted column, there are articles on how to find a job; how to recruit Workampers; information on volunteering with the Core of Engineers, county, state, national parks and private campgrounds; plus addresses and phone numbers.

The Workamper Bookstore sheet lists various publications about full-time RVing, retiring, travel writing, RV adventures, cookbooks, places to visit, and making your paycheck last, written by experts who are living the RV lifestyle (Yesss!).

Through the Workamper Referral System, resumes on active job-seekers, are kept on file. When an employer calls in with specific needs, the resumes are scanned for a match. A photocopied resume is sent and the employer takes it from there. If this results in employment, the resume is pulled.

To sum up the philosophy of WORKAMPER NEWS, Greg Robus explains, "WORKAMPER NEWS has been created to help those who seek a real change of pace, and a rewarding new lifestyle." Amen!

WORKERS ON WHEELS (WOW) is written and published by Coleen Sykora and her husband, Bob Nilles, who are full-time RVers. This publication is "A mixture of information for anyone desiring to operate an RV based business, or for those seeking outside employment." It includes interviews and personal accounts of those who are actually on the job.

The "Free Guide to State Tax Laws" and "Follow Construction Booms" articles were in one issue. "The Why and What of a Resume" article presented resume and cover letter samples. Another article discussed "Selling Arts and Crafts" and the "Arts and Craft Shows." This newsletter gives encouragement, and sometimes a kick in the gluteus maximum, as with this thought, "Some people wear their wishbone where their backbone ought to be."

The motto of THE CARETAKER GAZETTE is "Living the good life, rent-free." Who could argue with that? Thea Dunn, editor of THE CARETAKER GAZETTE, says, "Many RVers are discovering that caretaking can be an interesting and varied profession, offering unique rewards. People desiring a lifestyle change, retirees seeking a second career, and downsized corporate employees searching for new job opportunities, have discovered caretaking."

As I travel, I hear of more and more RVers parking on commercial and private property, school grounds, and other places, that need that little bit of presence to discourage robberies, vandalism and other malicious intent. It doesn't seem to matter these days whether property is "out in the boonies," in a city, in a village, or whether the company or digs are in the "best neighborhoods," they are at risk. Having caretakers makes a great deal of sense.

The packed pages of caretaker job listings are fascinating. Needs range from a caretaker for "My remote and beautiful fifty-acre homestead"; to a manager for a B and B in Nashville, Indiana; to a nanny in Hutchinson, Kansas; to a public greeter on an island in Lake Erie, Ohio.

Not limited to households, caretaking can be as varied as working in nature retreats, ecological preserves or fisheries. Horse groomers and guards were requested, as well as one "very nice old 'Blue Bib Overalls'" type rancher who wanted a grandmotherly type to relocate "back to the land," in Oregon. Hmmm. Dunn says an increasing number of farmers are turning to caretakers to help them maintain their land. What a revelation it would be to go from city living, to the rural life, and experience nature first hand.

These three bi-monthly publications complement each other and I heartily recommend all of them. Who knows, you may decide to try a new type of adventure. Writing and full-time traveling keeps me busy, but I might give it all up for maintaining and restoring an offshore lighthouse at Sequin Island, Georgetown, Maine...or maybe one of the three jobs listed in Australia. AAAAGH! So much to see and do, so little time!

Why don't you go look at Resources, then let's take a break with Tween Chapter #1 on CRS, before we meet in the chapter 4 for some extremely weighty information.

Major Toys for Girls and Boys

Giganticus CRSicus

Been There, Done That, but Can't Remember It

For those of you who might read this who are not advanced RVers, Giganticus CRSicus is the scientific term for a formidable case of CRS, a.k.a., Can't Remember Sugar. It is of epidemic proportions and highly contagious, but unfortunately, not too communicable in terms of making someone understand.

For instance, if a group of six RVers are standing in one spot, four are being thoughtful, trying not to notice the lapse in conversation. The speaker is embarrassed beyond words, desperately searching his (or her) mental compartments for the right punch line to a hilarious joke, or various information which by this time is totally irrelevant to the conversation. Number six is confusing the speaker even more by supplying one hundred possible endings, words, or phrases in ten seconds or less.

In a community of peers, this CRS is understood and easily forgiven, but not if you are in a group of people younger than thirty-five who are relatives, namely children, who just happen to be your offspring. They do not, I repeat, do not, understand why you can't remember their Social Security numbers, kindergarten teachers, whether or not they have a belly button big enough to harbor Cincinnati, or which sister is which. God forbid you should mix one of them up with a sibling.

Actually I think everyone who has only two children should combine names. When I am visiting Tracey, I always call her JanTra, and likewise, when I am with Janet, she is called TraJan. By this time they figure I am getting senile, so they answer to whatever name I tag them with, put their arms around me and say, "It's o.k. Mom, I still love you." I'm never sure that is a comfort.

Just this last year I was talking on the phone to my youngest daughter. As I usually do, I call my girls on their birthdays, during prime time, to prove how much I really love them. "Hi Mom!" she said eagerly, delighted to hear my voice so early in the morning. I sang happy birthday to her and said with great joy, "This is almost exactly the moment you were born, Sweetheart." It was truly phenominal how quickly long jagged icicles froze my ear to the phone. Simultaneously, as the warmth drained from the lines, I went from "Mom" to "Mother!."

"I thought I was born at night, Mother!." When you transform from Mom to Mother, they talk in exclamation points.

"My darling daughter, once that precious baby is in your arms, you don't care what time it is."

"Quick recovery, Mother!."

My oldest daughter just squeezed into thirty-nine and she has this not necessarily genetic disease. She calls her daughter "Sarah" about half the time. Sarah is a lovely name but it belongs to the lovely cat. Dear Lord, please let me live long enough for my youngest to have her child, and *puleeze* let me hear her call it Roxie or Patches by mistake.

Full-time RVers never know where they are, or what day it is, because they are on the move all the time. When you see someone who looks familiar, it takes a session of "Twenty Questions" to ascertain where you met previously. I ran into a couple yesterday. It took ten minutes to realize we had shared Christmas dinner at a SKP park last year. Usually the revelation of a name matched to the face comes prancing into your subconscious in the wee hours of sleep. Yes! You finally have the name, but you're wide awake for the rest of the night.

Our memories are getting so bad that campgrounds are putting up not so discreet signs at the end of the driveway, "Antenna down? Step up? Wife aboard?" They need another, "Computer off?" I stopped in a rest area, and turned on the computer to find information before making a phone call. I was in a hurry, so I left it printing something else. Ninety miles later, at another rest area, I wondered what was humming. The computer was still on.

How many of you have walked from the bathroom of your RV to the kitchen, or from the driver's seat to the living room, and forgotten why you were there? I mean, how long does it take to travel ten steps or less? And how often have you returned to get an item you *know* you put there five minutes before, only to find it gone. The minehunes hide items under flat-looking newspapers, behind salt shakers, or if the lost item is a pair of glasses, on your forehead.

The one thing good about a fading memory is saving money. If you buy two movies, two books, and two magazines, you are set for life. By the time you get through reading the second one, the first one is only vaguely familiar, and it is a pleasure to read it again. If editors weren't getting younger and younger, I could get away with writing only two columns a year. Younger people have memories like elephants.

Now that I've come to the end of this "Tween Chapter," I probably should tell you to turn the page for "The rest of the story" but I forgot what it was and by the way, tell me again, just who are you? God Bless.

WEIGHT!
LET'S BITE THE BULLET
TOGETHER

Weighty Problems

Somewhere in the dim, dark, recesses of your mind, you will recall hearing about Gross Vehicle Weight Ratings (**GVWR**). We don't like to think about it, because it puts restraints on our pack-rat tendencies, and we think of full-time RVing, as having no restraints. 'Tain't so.

When you add "improvements" to your RV, or stuff all the cupboards, nooks and crannies, and outside holds, you must be aware of your **GVWR**. Also, keep an eye to <u>where</u> you are stuffing it. If the front of the RV is lifting off the ground at a precarious angle, you can be certain your rear end is too heavy (If you want to take that personally, read Chapter 9).

Where is the refrigerator located? Where are the water and sewer tanks? Sink and stove? Bathtub? Tools? Know where the heavy weight is, and pack everything else accordingly, with an eye to **weight distribution,** as well as **weight**.

Some items are not absolutely necessary, but they make life more comfortable. Think about whether you really need it. How often is it used? Does it have a dual purpose? How often will you wear it?

We think we can take some things because they don't weigh **very much**. The problem is that <u>weight adds up quickly</u>. <u>Think twice</u>, (or more) on <u>everything</u> you drag inside (or put in your hold). Remember, the necessities come first.

Let's start with definitions. This basic information came from the Recreational Vehicle Tire Care and Safety Guide, but I liked the way C. Jay Haynor, Technical Editor for Family Motor Coaching magazine, made the information even more understandable. With his permission, I have used his explanations.

♦ **GVWR**: **G**ross **V**ehicle **W**eight **R**ating is the weight specified by the *chassis* manufacturer as the maximum loaded weight of the vehicle (including driver and passengers). **Sometimes a tag axle--a non-**

powered rear axle--is added to a chassis. This usually is done to increase the GVWR of the chassis, and, becomes the responsibility of that party to post and certify the new GVWR.

♦ **GAWR:** Gross Axle Weight Rating is specified by the chassis manufacturer as the **load carrying capacity of a single-axle system** as measured at the **tire-ground interface** (in other words, at the place where the tire meets the ground). It is important to note that the **GAWR is limited to the lowest individual rating of the tires, the wheels, the springs, or the axle**--in other words, whichever component is **the weakest link in the chain**. Therefore, changing from load range D to load range E or F tires, may or may not, increase the GAWR, since this rating could be dependent upon other (weaker) components. The GAWR assumes the weight is evenly distributed over the axle, with 50% on the right, and 50% on the left side--not 70/30. In other words, in the case of an axle with a GAWR of 6,000 pounds, the load distribution should be 3,000 pounds on one side and 3,000 pounds on the other.

♦ **Axle weight** is both the **weight carried by a single axle**, and the **weight transmitted to the highway by one axle**.

♦ **Shipping weight** is the **average weight of a specific vehicle** as it leaves the assembly plant, **including grease and oil**, plus regular production options, but **without any gasoline or diesel fuel.**

♦ **Empty weight** is the **shipping weight plus the maximum weight of gasoline or diesel fuel.**

♦ **Curb weight**, is the **weight of the vehicle empty** (without carrying capacity and driver) but **including engine fuel, coolant, engine oil, tools, spare tire, and all other standard equipment**. This **excludes water in the tanks, water heater, with empty LP-gas containers**. (Note: This definition, may differ from governmental regulatory agency definitions.)

♦ **Wet weight** is the **empty weight with the fresh water tanks, water heater, and LP-gas containers full but with waste water holding tanks empty.** This weight is particularly significant to motorhome owners, **because when you subtract this figure from the GVWR**, you have a <u>fairly accurate indication of the weight that can be added to the vehicle, including driver and passengers, clothing, foodstuffs,</u> etc.

♦ **Carrying capacity** is the **average weight** that can be **added** to a specific vehicle **without exceeding the GVWR**. Carrying capacity is **computed by subtracting the empty weight** of the vehicle **from the GVWR** figure. The **addition of other equipment or cargo and passengers, adds to the vehicle weight, and subtracts from the allowable carrying capacity**. It is important to **remember that the limiting factor in this rating could be the axles, springs, tires, transmission parking pawl, or any other equipment.**

♦ **Center of gravity** is the **point where the weight of the chassis and/or body and carrying capacity** is concentrated, and **if suspended** at that point, **would balance front-to-rear and side-to-side**. Cornering, acceleration, and other forces are considered as acting on a vehicle's center of gravity. Thus, it has a great influence on body lean and other handling characteristics. Even **if all within specifications, if** they are **not distributed properly**, the coach **could** still **suffer** from **excessive body lean or substandard handling characteristics**. Note: The center of gravity of a basement model coach, will be higher than a traditionally designed motorhome.

♦ **Weight distribution** is **the arrangement of body and carrying capacity on a vehicle's chassis**. It has a **definite bearing on the life of tires, axles, springs, frame, and other parts. The fact that the total vehicle weight does not exceed the recommended maximum GVWR, does not insure that the coach is not overloaded. Overloading can be due to improperly positioning** heavy materials so the load is centered over one rear tire, or so far forward on the body, that the front axle and tires, are overloaded.

♦ <u>GCWR:</u> <u>G</u>ross <u>C</u>ombination <u>W</u>eight <u>R</u>ating is the value specified by the chassis manufacturer as the **maximum allowable total loaded weight of the tow vehicle and trailer combination** (For our purposes the tow vehicle is the motorhome and a towed car). **Subtract the actual motorhome weight** (must be less than the GVWR), **from the GCWR**. (Towed car combination includes the trailer, dolly, or tow bar.) **Weigh the tow car as you normally tow it**, and if it is overloaded, remove any weight necessary to bring it into specifications.

I admit that's a lot to assimilate but hey, if I can do it, you can do it. And you say, "What do you mean? Don't you know, and do all this stuff?" After all these years, I am just now, as I delve into the details of RVing for the sake of giving accurate information, realize that the problems with my first minimotorhome, were probably more associated with weight, than anything else. I had every space filled. **Just because the space is there, doesn't mean you can fill it**. That poor little 350 Chevy engine in that 25' motorhome, didn't have a chance, and obviously, the tires struggled too. But you don't have to make the same mistakes I did. Listen up, we aren't through yet.

Jay gets into how to weigh a motorhome, and with some abbreviation, I am again using his words. Although you can sometimes weigh your vehicle on a truck scales along a major highway, if they aren't busy, this kind of weighing is detailed, and lengthy (at least thirty minutes). It would be better to go to a certified public commercial scales at a truck stop, grain elevator, gravel pit, or moving company. With that said, a" weigh" we go...

- The level side area is very important.
- It is necessary to have 50% of the left and right sides of the coach off the scale during some of the weighing. If the side area is not level, the side weights will be incorrect.
- Before weighing, load it as you normally would for travel, including food, clothing, fuel, water, propane, etc. This is not the time to be conservative!
- Divide the coach into four sections. Use axles as reference points.
- Find halfway point between front and rear tires (axles). Mark with tape on both sides of coach.
- Find halfway point between front tires. Mark with tape on bumper.
- Find halfway point between rear tires. Mark with tape on bumper.
- Drive coach onto scale to point the front-to-rear tapes indicate 1/2 of wheelbase is on scale and 1/2 is off. (Label coach section W1)
- Drive entire motorhome onto scale. (Label section W2)
- Drive off scale so side tape indicates that rear half of chassis remains on. (Label section W3.)
- Important: one-half of chassis, not the coach, rests on the scale during weighing.
- Weight W1 should not exceed the GAWR for the front axle.
- Weight W2 should not exceed the total GVWR.
- Weight W3 should not exceed the rear axle GAWR.
- Use the side-to-side and front-to-rear tapes to divide chassis into quarters
- Front left (Label zone W4)
- Rear left (Label zone W6)
- Front right (Label zone W5)
- Rear right (Label zone W7)
- Weights for zone W4 and zone W5 should be about equal.
- Weights for zone W6 and zone W7 should be about equal.
- If not, move items within the coach to bring the weights close.
- When you compare the total weight of the two front quarters, and the weights of the two rear quarters, with their total axle weights, the figures probably will not be exactly equal, but they will be close.
- Use the front and rear axle weights to determine the proper air pressure by consulting the tire manufacturer's tire manual.
- If the weight of the vehicle is over the GVWR, remove some weight and weigh again.

**"The importance of weight and weight distribution,
in terms of safety,
and
your motorhome's overall health,
cannot be over-emphasized."
C. Jay Haynor**

There you have it. Thanks Jay, for your invaluable contribution to our knowledge and safety.

A special Tire Care Kit is available through the Tire Industry Safety Council that includes a thirty-page brochure giving all the above information, weighing diagrams, and more. (Resources)

Height

At the same time you are weighing your advantages, keep your tape in hand, and measure the height of your vehicle. Include the air conditioner or anything else that adds to the height. Overpasses have clearance figures marked on them, but it is comforting to know exactly how high you are riding (That doesn't include the personal high you get from being a full-time RVer). It is especially necessary when you are traveling the back roads. Those overpasses aren't always marked, and I can vouch for a few that I had to go around.

In Mexico, a few years ago, where they seldom have overpasses marked with clearances, I started on to a major autopista. Thankfully, I realized I wasn't going to fit under the bridge before I hit, but it meant getting a lot of people behind me to back up, until I could get out of the situation. Know your vehicle's height.

Suggested tools, parts, and supplies

Don't let the list scare you. These are only suggestions. I must have started my full-time RVing years with at least five of these items. If you can't replace the parts yourself, you might find someone who can, easier than you can find the needed parts. It is best to have the proper tools to replace and repair, as well. Most of these are plain everyday things that you need to run a household...or a garage. Use a plastic (it's lighter) tool box for tools.

Suggested handy items to carry with you		
Extra light-bulbs: brakes, 12-volt lights, turn signal, etc.	Filters: Gasoline and air	Tire Pressure Gauge: Find out what your tires are supposed to hold. Have them checked often. It makes a difference in your mileage.
Air cleaner	Wire	Battery-operated screwdriver
Bolts	Hammer	Batteries: Keep extras for everything in frig or freezer
Bungy cords	3-IN ONE oil	Compass: fastened in front where driver can see it
C-clamps	Flares	Tape: Duct and masking
Crimping tool, connectors	Can of foam: For filling holes	Jack and tire changing tools: Big enough and heavy enough for your RV
Extra wind-shield wipers	Emergency re-flectors	WD-40: A product to solve a multitude of problems, removing tar, rusted bolts, and squeaks (except mice)
Fuses: All amps to fit anything including tow vehicle.	Water hose: Two 25-foot lengths	Receptacle adapters: Many older campgrounds do not have 30 amp power. Carry adapters to connect with 20 amp powers (and between extra cords???)
Glue	Roof repair kit	Come-a-long: Attach it to a tree and pull yourself out of trouble.
Headlights	Antifreeze	Flashlights (Working)
Nuts	Wrenches	Fluids: Power-steering and brake

Suggested handy items to carry with you		
Plastic (Throw-a-way) gloves for nasty jobs	**Shower curtain or rug and rags:** For keeping clothes clean(er)	**Silicone Spray**: For spraying stubborn window tracks, hold locks, and sliding tow bar, among other things. **Silicone sealant**
Rope	**Water pump**	**Multimeter:** Electricity-solving problems
Screws	**Pliers**	**Oil:** Engine and transmission
Sharp hatchet	**Water bucket**	**Screwdrivers**: Phillips, regular, square, all lengths
Small shovel	**Fuel pump**	**Hoses:** Radiator, heat, A/C
Voltmeters and test lights	**Indoor-outdoor carpeting**	**Jumper Cables:** I keep mine in the tag. If my battery goes dead on the motorhome, I have a button to push that connects me to the in-house batteries.
Windshield cleaner	**Compact: For checking water in your batteries**	**30 amp-rated electrical cord:** Two 25-foot lengths of no less than 12 gauge, This allows you to use a shorter cord. The longer the cord, the greater the resistance, resulting in power loss.
Wooden mallet	**Belts:** Air-conditioning, alter-nator, fan	**Water Pressure Regulator:** To keep campground water pressure under control

Things I carry in the Little Lynx:

Shovel	Folding chairs
Extra Atlas	Portable outside table
Paper towels	Hand wipes
Space blanket	Jumper cables
Extra oil	A jug of water (and thou?)

Household items to take

I use a vegetable brush for cleaning dishes and vegetables. Recently I read about another use for a vegetable brush, to clean the toilet bowl. It's a great idea. I wouldn't have thought of it. The thing is, use a different one for the toilet, and never get them mixed up!!

In the kitchen, I keep a spray bottle of water and Clorox for squirting in the drains, and disinfecting my dish cloth when I'm through cleaning the kitchen.

Over the years, my reasons for buying things have changed. My eyes light up when I see a big peanut butter jar, if its plastic. When it is empty, I can use it for shaking up pancakes or dried milk. I use plastic plates rather than heavier ceramic. I rarely use paper plates. I'd rather wash dishes. I don't like eating on cardboard (Maybe it's because it reminds me too much of my cooking). I do use paper cups and towels.

I rarely entertain. I keep dishes and cooking pans to a minimum. When I need them, I get creative. I like big soup bowls. I use them for everything. I have two casserole dishes, a small one for me, and a big size for the multi-tudinous potluck dinners that I rarely attend.

Thoughts to consider

♥ Update your address book with current doctor, dentist, and insurance phone numbers.

♥ Use plastic instead of glass. Glass is heavier, more easily broken.

- Wrap foam or other non-slip material around hangers to keep clothes in place while moving. I have hangers that my mother-in-law crocheted around (two at a time) for just such a purpose. I'm not sure she realized they would be traveling so far.
- Spread extra bedding under mattress cover or mattress.
- Extra rolls of paper towels are great for stuffing in places where you have a rattle, or you want to protect something fragile. I also save the "popcorn" from packages I receive, for this purpose.
- Use coffee grounds to eliminate odors in the refrigerator.
- Daughter, Janet, taught me this. Vegetable cooking oil removes tree sap from your hands. It works for removing the stubborn glue left behind from taking stickers off plastic, bathtubs, etc. WD-40 and peanut butter also work.

What clothes should I take?

As a full-time RVer, you will need clothes for every season. I keep clothes in the closet for the season I'm in. The rest I pack in my big suitcase, and put it in my mobile garage (The Little Lynx). Unless you are in really hot country, it will be cool in the evenings and early mornings. It is wise to have clothes you can layer. Most RVers dress casually.

What other "stuff" should I take?

You probably have everything you'll need in your medicine chest already. I carry a few basics, Pepto Bismol, Vanquish, Bag Balm, Hydrogen Peroxide, and Alka Seltzer for the sewer tank. While collecting items for your medicine chest, make sure you throw out, or replace any expired or old medications.

You know what you and your spouse (or your family) have on hand to keep plugging along (or perhaps unplugging). These are only suggestions. Your list will depend on the type of activities you will be involved in.

Glasses & Repair kit	Extra glasses with a copy of your prescription
Sunglasses	Sleeping remedies, a mask
Eye drops	Anti-diarrhea medicine
Sunscreen	Mosquito netting (for the bugged)
Laxatives	Something for motion sickness
Aspirin (painkiller)	Antihistamines
Ace bandages	Allergy medicine

Eyeglasses

A hard cover holder for glasses that I bought through one of the mail-order catalogues, is fastened to the wall just inside the door. I try to remember to always put my glasses in them, so I don't forget where I laid them down. Don't even entertain the thought that you couldn't possibly lose things in a small RV.

I don't need glasses for close-up jobs so I frequently lay them down where they shouldn't be. One day I was checking the oil on the Little Lynx, I laid the glasses near the radiator. When I finished, I slammed the hood and walked away. Later, I looked for my glasses. Sure enough, they were still near the radiator. They weren't broken, but they were certainly bent out of shape, and after searching for them for a half day, I was, too.

Another time I laid them on the car roof while I did something else, and promptly forgot them. I couldn't find them when I went to town so I found another pair (always a good idea to have two pair of prescription glasses). On the way back to my campsite, I spied them on the gravel. Someone, probably me, had driven over them. I colored them beyond prayer or repair.

Maybe in my third life, I'll get contacts.

Possessions: How do you get rid of them?

In my case, getting rid of possessions was a progression. Nine months before I went on the road, I moved out of my home. My daughters reclaimed their belongings, and went through my large pile of "must leave behinds." I moved the remainder into an apartment and rental shed. I tossed out collections of favorite magazines and miscellaneous other "things" I could live without (but hadn't been able to for the previous thirty years).

After a few months in an apartment, and the decision to make a drastic lifestyle change, I was down to bare bones. The children chose what they wanted, once again. I sold larger items through the local paper and bulletin boards. I participated in one yard sale with a friend. It was more work than resolution. What I didn't physically take in the motorhome, went to the Salvation Army, one of my favorite charities.

On the day I moved into the motorhome, it was packed solid with the last of a lifetime accumulation of memories and basic junk. I lived for six weeks in the parking lot of the hospital where I worked. That gave me time to weed through everything, and either pack it or eliminate it.

As most full-timers do, I found nooks and crannies for what I really wanted to take, like about two hundred paperbacks. The rest was office equipment and bottom-line necessities. I had far too many dress-up clothes. Eventually, they went to a grateful lady in Mexico. Except for my cross country skis at one daughter's, and a small box of mementos (which I haven't been able to find for years) at the other daughter's, I eliminated everything.

I gathered more tools as I needed them, and figured out how to use them. Repair necessities and spare parts fill the holds. I have enough belts, filters, hoses, C-clamps, and fuses to start my own NAPA store. Before I went on the road, I didn't know what a C-clamp was.

Since I am not mechanically adept (to say the least), I don't carry nearly as much as my late husband would have, but then he was a mechanic. I would fit into an old saying of his, "He doesn't stock enough parts to overhaul a yoyo."

Many people store lots of "stuff" the first year or two, then realize they really don't want it. Store anything you have a question about. Don't sell or get rid of possessions until you have given full-timing a good honest try.

> **Fulltiming RVer's rules**
> **If you haven't used it for a year, throw it out**
> **When in doubt,**
> **throw it out**

We made choices over the years to "go and do." Instead of accumulating materials, we accumulated memories. When it came time for me to eliminate the household, it wasn't loaded with precious antiques or valuable china. My children became the proud possessors of Early American Holloween.

By all means, take a few sentimental, can't-give-up-treasures with you, keeping within weight and space. When you are making a major break with a former lifestyle, it is comforting to have familiar objects where you can enjoy them. I took some major projects with me "to do in my spare time." Ha!

One project included taking all the family photographs. I had the equipment to take pictures of pictures. I made montages of various family activities, photographed them, and put copies into two albums, one for each daughter. That took me about six years.

A large number of photographs no longer had meaning after the death of my husband. Many scenery photos were tossed. I made copies of family photographs, from generations back. I labeled them from old family records, or from information gleaned from relatives. Copies of those went to Jack's siblings, my siblings, and my kids.

> **This advice has nothing to do with RVing. Take the time to label photographs. Some of the really old ones we had were so neat, but with all the older folks gone, we haven't a clue as to who they are. What a shame to lose our identities so easily.**

Again, remember

Keep the weight down. Remember that all things you take from your home, to the motorhome, are just that, things. If it isn't a necessity, store it for a while, then decide if you want to keep it. **If you give it to your kids, you can visit it whenever you go to see them**. I take a nap in the warm arms of Janet's waterbed every so often, just to remember how comfortable it was.

At any rate, people are more important than things, and we'll discuss relationships in another chapter. Come on, let's see what happens to fulltimers in a phone booth in Tween Chapter #2, then we'll get on with Chapter 5 and find some energy.

Soul-Searching

Have you considered the eventual disposition of your soul? Think about it. Surely in Heaven, there are no telephones. If you go the opposite direction, you may spend eternity in a small red box with a telephone glued to your ear, listening forever and ever to a nasal recording, "Thank you for your patience. Your call is important to us. Please wait for the next available analyst."

Telephone. This word should be shortened to "fone" so it can be labeled for what it really is, a four-letter word (which of course you wouldn't use in Heaven).

At five p.m., when the rates change, RVers line up at phone booths everywhere. If several phone booths are present, they are fastened together. If the next person in line ate garlic for dinner, you can depend on curly hair for that night's great date.

Phone booths are built as close as possible to constant noise, i.e., diesel trucks, Interstates, airport landing strips. If per chance, a booth is in a quiet alcove, it is the only one available for five hundred miles, and expected to service one thousand callers. They are all behind you, conversing, laughing, or arguing to be sure you can't hear any better than in the booth beside the fireworks testing factory. Indeed, why shouldn't they enjoy the days and months it takes to complete your call. They have become bosom buddies, discussed their last three operations in minute detail, and have the world situation well in hand.

I am ever so grateful for my cup of A T & T, but invariably the phone I'm using is serviced by another company. I dial the six digits to reach A T & T. A monotonous voice lists five choices. I push, "If you wish to make a credit card call, dial one." After that, I dial ten digits to reach my party, then fourteen digits including my "pin" number. When I have dialed the required thirty-one digits, the phone rings and I breathe a sigh of relief. Then I hear a click. A Lily Tomlin impostor gives me one of several messages, "This number is not valid; Please dial your calling card number again; This number is no longer in service; or Please hang up and dial again."

On the outside chance I actually get through, it is tricky avoiding an expensive conversation with a machine announcing, "This is the Starship Enterprise. We have boldly gone where no one has ever gone before. If you'll leave a number, we'll...."

Full-time RVers can't leave numbers. We don't have permanent phones hanging in the saguaro cactus or resting on the backside of an alligator in the Everglades. Frustrations reach an all time high, knowing you must go through it all again another day. I mean if God had wanted us to live in a phone booth, we wouldn't have RVs, right?

But on to the next problem. I'm standing in either the blazing sun or a raging typhoon, cradling the phone between my ear and shoulder, dialing the number from my address book, or if there is one present (rarely), the phone book. Have you noticed, the bigger the phone book, the smaller the print? To bring it close enough to read, I crouch to cradle the swiveling book on its two-inch cord, and scramble for a pen and pad.

You ask, "Why don't you have everything laid out first?" Don't be silly. Booths are designed with cute little shelves under the phone. The shelves are slanted. My quarter and materials slide to the ground while I struggle with the two-inch phone-book cord that yanks me unceremoniously backward if I go too far.

The quarter is finally deposited. I dial the number, but I can't let go of the phone book. With no place to write, and my advanced CRS, it is a foregone conclusion, I will have to look it up again. I juggle everything, trying to get my stuff to stay on the slanted shelf with one of my knees. Unfortunately, my second knee holding up the leg that is balancing my body. By this time my neck, which is anchoring the phone without benefit of my already busy hands, has a giant kink in it.

Some shelves are flat but only five inches across. Either side of the shelf is open. The address book pushes the quarters and pen to the ground. Some have "slotted" round bars which hold even more nothing.

Telephoning obviously requires the mental stability and physical agility for which I am not universally known. My parents raised me to respect private and public property. I think it was the 11th commandment. I wouldn't want my sainted Mama to know how close I've come to annihilating public property. I wonder. Perhaps the vandalism of phone booths isn't necessarily teenagers bent on an evening of "fun." It is entirely possible, that these dastardly deeds are done by none other than frustrated RVers.

I advise two solutions. Number one, chew Valium. When it takes so long to reach your grandkids that they have grown up, married, and moved to a difference area code, you'll take it calmly in stride. Number two, definitely do some soul-searching. If you repeatedly hear, "Please wait for the next available analyst," it may be too late and too hot.

May God Bless all His RVing children...and telephone companies everywhere.

SO MUCH TO LEARN
SO LITTLE TIME

Solar Energy

Three solar panels are fastened permanently to the roof. I can just see tilting them toward the sun as it crosses the sky each day, then forgetting to put them down, when I drive off. I know me pretty well. The 2,000-watt inverter is in a small outside hold.

Having solar energy gives me a great deal of freedom to boondock. I use the solar to run my computer and printer, as well as the vacuum, radio, VCR, and TV. It is virtually maintenance free, but the initial outlay is expensive. Unless you have special needs, or you are going to boondock extensively, you probably won't need more than one panel to help keep the batteries up.

Noel and Barbara Kirkby are fellow SKPs. They sell solar products and can explain it much better than I.

Sunlight into Electricity
By Noel and Barbara Kirkby

The purpose of SOLAR ELECTRICITY is to charge 12 volt batteries for RV lighting, stereo, TV, water pump and other 12 volt appliances. An INVERTER allows for the operation of appliances like a blender, toaster, vacuum cleaner, microwave oven or any item that draws up to 2500 watts of energy from the RV battery. Note we did not mention air conditioners or electric refrigerators as they <u>run for long periods</u> of time and are best run from propane or generators when utility hook-ups are not available.

BATTERIES are the heart and soul of an RV that is electrically independent. A large and rapidly growing majority of RVers are opting for solar power to keep their batteries fully charged. Others have built-in generators or occasionally stop for RV park accommodations.

The number of solar panels you select is not a critical matter when your RV already has an effective alternator. Add panels and batteries as your lifestyle dictates. An ALTERNATIVE POWER SOURCE is a consideration for those who "dry camp" for three days or longer. With proper planning and the right equipment you can keep your batteries fully charged and live comfortably without hookups.

The process of changing sunlight to electricity seems very scientific and many assume it to be technical. Just the opposite. Adding a solar system to your RV may be simpler than having an extra light fixture or 12 volt outlet installed. There are considerations: cost, space and efficiency -- just as with light fixtures. We encourage you to read and talk with other RVers who are using solar.

When shopping for appliances, always read the label. Some color TV sets (9") use only 2 amps, while others draw up to 5 amps at 12 volts. There are "hidden" power loads like AES refrigerators that use 12 volt even while on 120 volts AC to operate the electronic "brain."

Also, "digital" TV and stereo sets use some 12 volt power to maintain the memory circuits, even while turned off. Gas detectors use 12 volt power, too.

Whether or not you choose to install a solar system, you should look closely at your energy requirements. Based on the thousands of systems we've been involved with, the average dry camping RVer, one without unusual needs, generally finds that ONE PANEL PER BATTERY PER PERSON provides an adequate system. An extra battery or solar panel provides insurance during bad weather or to handle unexpected needs. Frequently, where an extra panel is used, panels can be mounted flat -- even in winter. The SOLAR GUARD regulator/meter has a trickle charge outlet, where excess power can be automatically directed to maintain the vehicle starting battery, as well.

To determine your solar power needs, you must measure your daily consumption and add the power you recharge daily, while driving or operating the generator. A solar panel generates a predictable amount of power each day. A typical 40-50 watt panel, in full sun, can produce up to 20 AHs (Amp Hours) per day. This power is stored in your battery until used. If you use more power than produced, you can cut back on consumption (conserve) or produce more power by adding a solar panel, driving or running your generator.

CALCULATION: Amps at 12V X Hrs/Day = AmpHours. Add up the AHs from all the appliances you typically use per day. Divide that amount by 20. This provides an estimate of how many panels should meet your needs, if ALL electrical energy needs were met by solar panels.

Our book, **RVers Guide to Solar**...has received favorable reviews and is listed as a "must have" reference by many RVing authorities.

Our newsletter, "**Solar Electric Update**," is available free. (Resources) Thanks, Noel and Barbara.

Generator

A 4,000-watt Onan generator came with the Sprinter. If I'm not connected to shore power, it supplies 120-volt electricity for the microwave, and the air-conditioner. It takes hours for this generator to recharge low in-house batteries. Newer generators restore batteries much quicker. I generally find shore power for recharging low batteries, or if I'm going to be traveling, the engine alternator recharges them fairly quickly.

If it is a traveling day, and I want to use the microwave for only a few minutes, I use the solar to run it rather than run the noisy generator. The microwave takes a lot of energy, and I wouldn't use the microwave on solar while I'm boondocking.

One morning, while I was boondocking in Death Valley, California, I tried to start the generator. It wouldn't even cough. I checked the oil, wiggled a few wires, probed, and pushed, to no avail. A neighbor heard me rattling around, and came to look into the Onan's deep recesses. The tray that holds the generator was designed to slide out, but it had never been pulled out before. We sprayed verything with WD-40, to loosen years of rust and dirt. The RV body was installed a half-inch in front of the sliding tray.

My rescuer cut a small slit in the frame to pull the tray out, and proceeded to get very dirty, oily and sweaty. About the time we decided a professional Onan technician was needed, I asked, "What's this little red switch on the side?"

He said, "Let's try it." Wouldn't you know, one flip of the **"circuit breaker,"** and the generator fired right up. Neither of us realized it was there, but you'd better believe it is engraved in both our memories now. Of course, with taking three hours to clean up, my neighbor will probably never respond to an ailing generator again. People are good-hearted.

My big generator works great, but it is terribly noisy. Now they have "quiet" generators, with reduced noise and less vibration. They have top-mounted switches and easy access for filling the oil. Where did I go wrong?

Batteries

Be sure you have good batteries, both in-house and engine starter. In-house batteries should be deep-cycle batteries. You have a choice whether to get maintenance-free batteries, which you shouldn't have to add water to, or the open-cell types, with removable caps. I have four Marine-RV, deep cycle, open-cell batteries. Three in-house batteries are under the bed pedestal, and another is in the front with the engine battery.

For me, it is a problem remembering to add water to them, and often I have let them go far too long without checking. The ones under the bed pedestal are difficult to reach. It is also hard for me to see into the cells, so I use a compact mirror. I use a long, narrow, flexible, plastic hose to fill them. You can also use a big meat baster.

The open-cell batteries last somewhat longer than the maintenance-free batteries. Even though they are maintenance-free, they will eventually lose water. I have known people to force their way into them and fill them, as a way of making them last, but I wouldn't try it.

There are also sealed, gel-cell batteries. The gel-cell batteries are very expensive, but are completely sealed, and have a life of around ten years.

I bought the Sprinter's four batteries new in December of 1992. They will soon be five years old. They have never corroded, but it is wise to clean batteries off at least once a year, regardless. The Sprinter engine "starting" battery is the same age, and is also an open-cell battery.

My car battery must be checked often. The battery was new a couple of years ago, but the corrosion gets bad on it quickly.

After I brush the excess corrosion off the battery with a wire brush, I pour a mixture of Arm and Hammer Soda (or sometimes regular soda pop) over the battery. They both neutralize the battery acid. I pour water over the battery to clean that off. After the terminals are dry, I spray a red battery corrosion preventative on them. Dire warnings accompany this product. Don't breathe the fumes.

At the same time, check for cracks. If it is an open-cell battery, see if it needs water.

When I replace in-house batteries, I replace all of them at once. With my lack of expertise, I probably over-do maintenance. I don't cotton to the idea of being stuck out in the hinterlands with a dead battery.

Be sure your battery storage area is well ventilated. Keep sparks, flames, and cigarettes, away from batteries. They produce explosive gases. Always shield your eyes when you are working near them.

According to a press release I received from PulseTech Products Corporation, they have something called a Solargizer™ Battery Maintenance System, that is supposed to keep batteries in "optimum working condition, help reduce downtime, battery maintenance, and replacement costs."

"Solargizer™ is small, weatherproof, and easy to install. It emits pulsating DC current into the battery, to remove sulfates from the plates. It keeps the sulfates from returning. With the plates clean, the battery starts every time, and keeps them running at 100% efficiency."

In case you didn't know, like I didn't know, "Sulfation is where sulfur molecules in the battery acid, coat the battery's positive and negative lead plates during energy discharge. The more the plates are coated, the less energy they can accept." When they become too coated, they expire. (Resources)

Leveling

The Sprinter doesn't have attached leveling jacks. I have two wooden blocks, made of three, two by six boards nailed together, and cut diagonally. I use them to level the Sprinter and for chocks, if I feel the necessity. To relieve strain on the axle, if I need blocking under the back end, I put the leveler under the inside dual. Their other purpose, when not being used for leveling, is to hold down my indoor-outdoor carpeting so it doesn't fly off to Oz with Dorothy.

Don't do as I do, do as I say. Whether you are using home-made levelers or commercial ones, they should be long enough to easily drive up on, and gradual enough, that it doesn't mess up your transmission. When leveling dual tires, both tires should be on the leveler and fully supported. The levelers should be as wide as the tires.

Park in a level parking lot. When the RV and refrigerator freezer are level, fasten one bubble level indicator to the front of your fifth wheel, trailer, or inside your motorhome, for side-to-side leveling. Another should be attached somewhere, for front-to-rear leveling.

Refrigerators are not as sensitive about being level as they once were, but for your own comfort, it is better to have your RV "reasonably" level. You wouldn't want anyone to call you "Tiltin' Milton." More expensive and newer units have attached leveling jacks. Leveling jacks can be installed, but they are expensive.

If campground people would do one thing for me, I would be forever grateful. So often, their sites are not level. It really annoys me to pay the price to stay in a private campground, then have to run the Sprinter up on blocks. Most RVing sites on public lands, are level. That always amazes me. They are usually way out in the boonies where I wouldn't expect to find level sites. I never expect a government agency to have anything, anywhere, "On the level." They do site-leveling really well.

Sewer

A sewer hose compartment was built into the body of the Sprinter. I'm sure you have one somewhere on yours. Once the sewer hose had been used, and was no longer two-feet long, there was no way it would ever fit back into that space. I had a large PVC pipe and cap attached the full width, above my back bumper. It works nicely.

There are commercial holders to hold your sewer hose off the ground, while it is being used. You can also make one by cutting PVC pipe in half.

In my other RV, the sewer hose was stored in the bumper. The inside of the bumper rusted, and grated against the hose when I pushed it in or pulled it out. I've learned only recently that two coin-sized holes in the front on one side, and two on the other end on the back side, would have eliminated the moisture that was causing it to rust. You never quit learning.

On older units, the designers must have thought it would be fun to stand on your head to connect, and disconnect, the sewer hose. 'Tain't so. Some of the newer RVs have easy-to-reach, easy-to-attach sewer connections, behind neat and clean closed doors.

A lot of you won't have new units. You'll have to do repair jobs like I have had to do from time to time. A leak had developed in the sewer system, an embarrassing drip, drip, drip, that I couldn't eradicate by tightening the clamp, or retaping the hose. I bought a new wastewater valve. The valve had never been replaced on the Sprinter. I had to coax the nuts and bolts to let go of years and years, of rust, dust, road oil, tar, and whatever else accumulates on the underside of RVs.

After spraying it repeatedly with WD-40, bruising a knuckle or two on the unusual angles required to keep the wrenches in place, getting a crick in my neck from lying directly under the aforementioned gunky valve, and two hours of calling upon a complete inventory of newly learned CB words, I got the old blackwater valve off. The replacement went slightly faster, but I don't often work with my arms overhead for hours at a time, matching O rings and screw holes from an old product to a new one. Everything had to be held in place, while I pretzeled my back into all those positions that scrapped my knuckles, when I removed the old one.

My despicable language had reached the level of wishing a pox on the whole RV industry, before the deed was finally done, and the blackwater valve was replaced. You know what, it didn't leak anymore. As tired and as dirty as I was (and we're talking filthy here), it was a terrific feeling. I had actually fixed it myself. That was three years ago and it still doesn't leak. Wonder of wonders.

I have every kind of sewer connector there is, plus a rubber donut. Different campgrounds have different rules. Sometimes, they only require pushing the hose into a donut. Others allow the hose to go directly into their sewer pipe. Still others require the hose to be screwed in. There are at least eight different-sized sewer pipe openings.

Not to worry, Prest-O-Fit® came to the rescue. I complained to them about needing gargantuan hands, and strength, to change parts or fasten pieces together. They sent hoses and various connectors. The "Universal Elbow" fits every common RV park sewer opening without any additional threaded adapters." The "Pushover Quick Connector" connects to the universal elbow, or to any of the other adapters.

I won't go into all of it, but if I had had that complete set to start with, I would not have needed a hold full of odd sewer hose parts. It would have eliminated the many screaming sessions in the middle of the campsite, using screwdrivers to get one piece to fit over the end of the other, with one end squeezed between my knees, and the other end held down with my foot...or broken nails. If I were ever to compose a song about my favorite things, it would not include wrestling with a stinky, slinky, aqua blue sewer hose.

Another product I read about, but haven't tried -- is the Camco's Easy Slip RV sewer hose. The universal-fit hose has a built-in clamp, that slips over the adapter. Once it is tightened, your problems are over. (Right!) (Resources)

It never hurts to have an extra section of sewer hose. I have been in campgrounds where there was one base for four hookups, and it took a lot of hose. By the way, leave your gray water tank valve open (unless you are in Mexico, where sometimes you get cockroaches crawling inside).

Now for the real poop. Close your black water tank valve after you have emptied it. Empty it again any time after it is at least half full. This prevents all the liquids from draining out and leaving only solids. If you leave that valve open all the time, you will soon have an impressive case of sewer constipation.

Another thing to remember, it is better to push your hose into a donut, rather than directly into the campground sewer opening. Sometimes they slip too far inside, and cause backups. Caution, no matter how hungry you are, do not chew on the donut.

I was driving behind a motorhome last summer, and saw an open sewer valve. I don't know if it was gray water, black water, or both, but the one responsible, was making us all look bad. The line of wet pavement was obvious, and the liquid poured out while he waited for a light. I tried to get his attention on the CB, but he either didn't have his ears on, or he didn't want to talk with me.

**Yukoners have signs, "Bears dump in the woods,
RVers don't have to."
One could add,
"Clods dribble on the highway,
Responsible RVers wouldn't think of it."**

Many of the rest area sewer dumps have been closed because of the messes left behind by the "clods." However, some remain open, and are listed on highway signs. Sometimes gas stations offer free sewer dump and water with a fuel fill-up.

The area around Virginia, where my youngest daughter lives, is not particularly RV oriented. In desperation, I called a mobile home court, and they were kind enough to let me dump my sewer, in the sewer pipe on one of their empty lots. Later, I discovered the city would let me dump at their sewage treatment plant. I have called the city in other places, and have only run into a couple that had no way for a private individual to dump sewage.

How do you take care of the sewer tanks?

If I am going to be sitting in one place for several weeks, I use a commercial product (non-toxic with no dangerous chemicals or formaldehyde). There are many on the market. When I am on the road, I use a couple spoonsful of Rid-X. I find it doesn't do quite as well breaking down solids, unless the solids are being moved around. It is available in hardwares or Wal-Mart.

Sometimes, when the weather is extremely hot, it doesn't control the odor as well as it does under normal conditions. Otherwise, Rid-X works great, and it is cheaper than regular RV products. It won't hurt the seals in the stool, nor does it have dangerous chemicals or formaldehyde to hurt campground sewer facilities.

Use some kind of odor control in both gray and blackwater tanks. The gray water sometimes smells worse than the black water.

The KISS method

No, this isn't the section on romance. **K**eep **I**t **S**imple **S**tupid is the best way to handle problems (Actually, that's not a bad way to handle romance, either!).

My lack of talent for fixing mechanical difficulties frustrates me. I've been known to utter such profanities as "For crying tears in a bucket" or "Jeeze peez and blood clots" (from my medical secretarial days). Having done that, I cry, stomp a little more (depending on the seriousness of the problem), and do what I should have done in the first place, pray for help.

The answer is always the same. I have already been given the knowledge to fix it (If I think about it calmly) or I have the ability to find somebody who can. See, it's really quite **S**imple.

To get started, three very important thoughts come to mind, whether you are an RVer or not. If you do these three things, it will help you avoid crisis conditions, being broken down on the road, and being at the mercy of whomever is nearby to fix it, instead of someone you know and trust.

1. **Keep your vehicle in good mechanical shape so you WON'T break down on the road.**
2. **LISTEN to your vehicle. You drive it nearly every day. If the sounds change, it may signify a problem. Analyze it and fix it or get it fixed.**
3. **Give your vehicle daily TLC (Tender Loving Care).**

I can be driving along without a care in the world, enjoying the scenery, and then I'll smell or hear something unusual. Suddenly, all senses are alerted. What is it? Usually, sounds are a change in the highway surface, or a nearby vehicle. Odors turn out to be burning trash in a village I'm passing, or a smelly bus.

Coming north on Highway 87 out of Phoenix, Arizona, I saw smoke near the back of the Sprinter. I looked around quickly to see if it was coming from something along the road (I was hoping), but it was floating between the RV and the Little Lynx. Major quick stop.

It was one of those rare but fortunate times when a friend was riding with me. He crawled underneath, and found two bolts on the transmission pan loose, and slowly dripping oil. It was splattering against the hot exhaust pipe and smoking (I usually like the smell of a pipe). He tightened each bolt 1-1/2 turns. It was a minor miracle that I had the right tool to tighten it.

If I had been alone, I would have crawled under the rig to check it out. If I hadn't found the loose bolts, I would have called my mechanic in Congress (Not everybody has a mechanic in Congress!), and ask what I should do. With some problems, I would nurse the Sprinter along to the next town and have it checked. With a fire potential, I wouldn't have moved it.

Two months before starting for Alaska last year, I was going down a long mountain grade into Death Valley, California. As usual, I put the Sprinter into second gear to save on the brakes. I kept going faster and faster and the sound wasn't right. I slowed down and put it in first gear. That gear worked fine and sounded normal. I tried second gear again and the same thing happened. The second gear manual transmission shift had gone on vacation.

After getting several opinions and estimates, I opted to nurse the RV through the mountains until I got to Leavenworth, Washington, and one of my "stashed" mechanics at Leavenworth Auto. The transmission had

130,000 miles on it. It would have cost nearly as much to repair the second gear, as to get a rebuilt transmission. They took it out, rebuilt it, and put in an Alisson style converter. I drove it in the area for two weeks, before crossing into Canada. Everything was working fine

If possible, major problems always wait until I get to a place where I know the mechanic. I didn't realize how much money I had spent at B & B Auto in Congress, Arizona, until I returned the following year. When I pulled in to get propane, both mechanics came out and hugged me! My blessings are mixed.

I watch closely to what is being done to my vehicles. The mechanics to whom I return (I have at least four favorite mechanics stashed in various parts of the country) have gotten used to my crawling underneath, to look at the problem, or peering intently into the mysterious recesses under the dog-house, while they explain something.

Once I know what's happening, I don't bother them. When they finish, they explain what they did. It helps me learn, so the next mechanic doesn't give me a snow job. As long as I don't keep them away from their work, they don't have a problem with my questions. That's one of the reasons I don't go to dealerships very often now that the Sprinter is out of warranty.

My husband was a mechanic. I know why dealerships keep customers at bay. They don't want them looking over the mechanic's shoulder, and asking stupid questions. However, since I pay them handsomely for my "stupid" questions, I feel I should have the right to ask them, either before or after.

I once had an editor refuse a story about having a flat tire, because he didn't want people to read about the negative side of RVing. Hey, this is life we are talking about, kids. Nobody said it was all perfect. Let's be realistic, tires go flat, motors freeze up, belts squeak or break, and a whole myriad of other things can go wrong. As with a landbound home, equipment wears out or breaks down sooner or later. Experts can fix them (if you can't) and most mechanics are fair (or more than fair).

You can't shake, rattle, and roll <u>anything</u> down the highway month after month, year after year, and not have problems at some point. If you drive the rough back-road miles as some of us do, it takes a toll.

A couple of things I do for the Sprinter, on the advice of another RVer I consider to be far more "in the know" than I am. I use Lubri-gas in the gas tank. I don't remember to use it every time. It lubricates the top cylinders, rings, and valves. They also have lubri-diesel. (Resources) I add a quart of "Slick 50" to the oil change every 50,000 miles.

I figure there are a lot of "without-a-clue" male and female types out there, who don't know any more than I do. As you might have guessed, I really get a kick out of learning something new about how to take care of my RV. I think others do to. Every time we solve a problem, we grow a little.

I read an article about being a "Dipstick Detective." It told what to see, smell, and feel, on your oil dipstick to tell you about the health of your engine. I could understand it! Amazing! I might not be able to fix any problems the detective work unearthed, but I might save myself a bigger bill with a little preventative medicine.

At the end of the article, was an address for "Nutz & Boltz," a monthly publication for $36. I put the address in Resources. I think I'll send for it. If the author can write so I understand it, he must be good.

Let's talk about some everyday "stuff."

Locks

Good advice for the hold locks, is to replace them. The ones that come with the RV, usually can be opened with almost anything that will fit into the keyhole. I have opened them with thin rocks, sharp sticks, and nail files, when I didn't want to hunt for the keys. One day another RVer was standing there when I was trying to unlock one of them. He reached into his pocket and brought out the keys to his RV, and unlocked my hold lock. That tells you how secure they are.

If your RV doesn't have a deadbolt lock on the entry door, put one in. I always use it. Seriously consider having the deadbolt lock in your new RV, and definitely in your used RV, "Re-keyed." Re-keying might eliminate the strange keys that fit your deadbolt.

Another type of lock to consider, is a "hitch lock." It might keep someone from stealing your towed vehicle or trailer, when you are not fastened to it.

Carry heavy locks, and some light cable, to lock up your outside toys at night, and when you are leaving them behind.

Water hoses

Whenever you put your hose into the RV hold, fasten the ends together to keep out nasty beasties. A good way to clean hose is to put some water and Clorox in it. It takes a heap of flushing with water to take out the taste, but it's worth it.

If you get water from a gas station or park or anywhere else, use your own hose. You won't know where theirs has been and I'll guarantee they didn't just flush it out with disinfectant.

It is best to get one of the white and blue water hoses. I have a round one but they come flat as well. I admit on cold mornings, when I try to coil a belligerent hose, it nearly does me in. My hands are small, and I have a hard time getting it to bend to my will. I use a wet wipe or a damp towel, and wipe it off as I roll it up. Some people prefer the flat hoses for that reason.

I have two lengths, 50' and 25'. If need be, I can fasten them together.

I use a water pressure regulator to prevent any high pressure systems from rupturing my hose, or the RV plumbing. I also use a 90-degree connector, so the hose will hang vertically.

Use a "Y" valve on the campground faucet, one to your RV, and another for a separate hose to wash your vehicle, for other water needs, or to have it handy if there is a fire.

Drinking Water

Filtering drinking water has become the thing to do. We travel from place to place, always with different drinking water, rarely knowing its quality. Be sure the filter is capable of taking out most of the bugs. I have a filter that hooks to my kitchen faucet (or under the sink) that requires filter replacements. The carbon filter and replacements are easily installed (If I can do it, you know it is). It "reduces greater than 99.9% giardia and cryptosporidium cysts, reduces many foul tastes and odors including chlorine." I've been drinking that?

Outside filters are also available. They filter your water before it comes inside. Whatever bugs are there, aren't contaminating your water tank or inside lines. Come to think of it, why don't I have one? It's great writing this book. It gives me all kinds of ideas.

Many filtering systems are on the market. Read what they offer. The unit I have, warns of using the assembly with water pressure under or over 125 psi, another case for using a pressure regulator. (Resources)

Electrical Systems

I could almost stop with the title, to let you in on what I know, but these are a few of the things I've learned.

If an entire lighting system fails, check your fuses. Put in a good fuse (same rating, never higher) and see if it fixes the problem.

Vibration can cause all kinds of problems in an RV (and sometimes the tag), especially in the electrical system.

I had a real headache with my electrical system, before I went to Alaska last year. I took it in to be fixed several times. The problem was sporadic. They jiggled a few wires, tightened something, and it worked again. I left the area thinking the problem was solved. The mechanic replaced a frayed wire, but that wasn't the main problem.

A friend of mine took the problem in hand. He followed the wiring through the car, through the connection to the RV, and through the RV. Between the two of us, my expertise as a watcher of the tail lights, head lights, etc., and his as a Sunday mechanic, he found the problem. The diode adapter, and connection near the right rear light on the car, were bad. To make matters even more frustrating, that was the time a fuse went out on the RV four-way flasher. We had both checked all the fuses, and that one was fine before we started working.

I haven't had a lick of trouble with the lights since. (Did I really tempt fate by saying that?)

Being Towed About Radiator Problems

I was in Colorado, towing the Little Lynx for the first time in high mountains. When my power was drastically cut, well-meaning old pros said I should expect a cut in power, when I started towing a car. I nursed it along, thinking it really should have more power, but what did I know.

The campground attendant directed me straight up the mountain. The closer I got to the campsite, the slower the Sprinter went. Suddenly, the

Sprinter stopped dead in his tracks. Panic city! I pulled the emergency brake on, put the gear in park, and prayed everything would hold. I had to work directly behind the motorhome, to get the car unhitched.

The manufacturers are adamant about your not backing up against a StowMaster tow bar. I put the car in first gear, and the emergency brake on, but couldn't get the coupler off the ball. I asked for help from the only other couple in the campground. He climbed in, and moved the car forward, to take the tension off the ball. I unhooked it. He backed the car down the hill, and I backed the Sprinter into a different campsite.

Eventually, I drove south over Raton Pass, into New Mexico, at five mph. When I got to Arizona, and one of my trusted mechanics, not one, but several factors, entered into my power problem. A sparkplug wire was reattached. A distributor rotor, and an "inline" fuel filter, were replaced. At that time I had been full-time RVing for eight years, and I was totally unaware of any filter, other than the gas filter under the rig. To my knowledge, it had never been changed. The sparkplugs and gas filter were also changed.

Although the power improved, the Sprinter ran hotter than normal, over the next couple of months. Those, "in the know," didn't seem alarmed, so I eventually headed for Mexico. When the RV gauge registered in the hot-now-wow zone, I coasted into a rest area (It is always prudent to break down near a rest area). I unhitched the car, and drove into town for help.

You can't get much farther away from anywhere, than Gila Bend, Arizona, but the guys at Bill Henry's Service Center, towed the Sprinter to their shop, removed, recored, and replaced my radiator within forty-eight hours. It was Saturday, President's Day weekend.

The radiator recoring was the final touch to bringing the Sprinter up to power, and making it run like a real cool cat. Until then, my expertise on radiators was limited to my big brother's warning, **"Don't touch that cap, or try to take it off when it is hot."** I never did.

So what did I learn? I learned to trust my instincts more. Someone else may have more expertise, but they don't have my ears, or my feel of my wheels. I drive this unit all the time. I know what it sounds like, and when it needs a little Castor oil or hot tea. I added another piece of mechanical knowledge to my growing list; an in-line filter should be changed every 40,000 to 50,000 miles. A radiator builds up chemical deposits that eventually restrict the fluid from passing through, and keeps the heat from escaping.

According to Henry's, a radiator lasts about 100,000 miles. That was about the mileage the Sprinter had, when it gave up the ghost. I was long overdue for a recoring. This should be done at approximately 60,000 miles. A big RV engine needs all the cooling power it can get, and the poor Sprinter was gasping. Nobody was paying attention.

I wanted a new radiator. The mechanic said after all he did to it, I didn't need a new one.

Coming through the mountains in British Columbia, on my return from Alaska last fall, I kept hearing a roaring noise that sounded like I was constantly in second gear, but the gears worked fine. When I reached Washington, the clutch fan in front of the radiator, that increases its speed when the engine loses its cool, had to be replaced.

The hoses should be checked often, and replaced about every 50,000 miles. I probably have the hoses, and belts replaced more often than necessary, but then I've never had a problem with them either. With going into the hinterlands, like I do, I don't take chances. I carry replacements for all of them.

The thermostat is important, too. Thank Heaven, everything didn't go out all at once. The thermostat committed suicide, while I was traveling south of Tucson, Arizona, several years before the radiator "incident." The Sprinter was steamed, the radiator screamed, the antifreeze flooded, and I wanted to go home to mother. My rescuer threw cold water on the radiator to cool it down. I followed him to his shop, and within short order, he put a new thermostat in.

The Sprinter always perks along again after these mishaps. It takes me a while to recover, and my VISA even longer.

Another time, snow-dribbled mountains drifted in and out of the fog on a magnificent mountain morning. The breeze tousled my hair. Music blended with other sounds and wafted into the blue. I was headed down I-90 East, in Washington State, at Snoqualmie Pass. A tall, tough, young muscled hunk named Bart was beside me, for what more could I ask.

Perhaps only little things, like that I be driving, not a passenger in a tow truck, vintage 1954 cab, on a 1973 chassis. The music was rock and roll, and its beat, combined with the sound of a workhorse 350 Cummins Diesel engine, was Excedrin Headache #460. The stiff breeze was coming through the floorboard. We were comin' around the mountain, sans seat belts, pulling a strangely silent Sprinter.

To digress, I was driving I-5 near Seattle, when the engine started revving like it had gone out of gear. It was my first clue to get off the road. After parking overnight in a business parking lot, and trying unsuccessfully to get help from a dealership the next morning, I called my stashed mechanics in Leavenworth, Washington.

Dan agreed the problem was probably the transmission. He said, "I'm sorry, but it'll take me at least two or three days to fix it." Two or three days! I expected him to say two or three weeks. As usual, the problem was not as big as it loomed in my eyes. It was a stripped governor, an external transmission problem, and fixed by the next evening.

The only thing that remained big was the towing bill, and that was my fault for wanting to take the Sprinter to a mechanic I trusted. Insurance paid a fourth of it. I needed to diet anyway.

The refrigerator

I have had repairmen work on the Norcold refrigerator over the years, but it never seemed to work right with new circuit boards, wiring, dusting, or whatever they did to it. A hundred miles down the road, it would get temperamental again.

In the middle of the night while boondocking on a beach in Puerto Penasco, Mexico, I heard a "click, click, click" which meant the refrigerator wasn't lighting. I am tuned in to sounds, especially when I am boondocking. I turned the propane off for a few seconds. For whatever reason, it will sometimes light when I turn it back on. The magic formula didn't work.

Since I'm not into rummaging around in the dead of night, on a Mexican beach, to fix an expired refrigerator, I waited until morning. I dug out a Phillips screwdriver, an ice pick, a toothbrush, and a fingernail file. I cleaned six months worth of grime from anything reachable, with the toothbrush. All the little gismos, whatchamacallits, and connections were secured. I peered through the window where the pilot light lives. It had a yucky nose.

With the ice pick, I knocked off the residue. The fingernail file was thin, and flexible enough, to get in and clean it off even better. With all this accomplished, I blew in its ear and whispered "Light up my life and you can travel with me forever." It lit. I'm not sure whether it was my great expertise at fixing things, the whispers, or the prayer I said before I turned on the propane.

An RV repairman told me recently, that sometimes problems wouldn't be as bad, if "people" didn't "mess around" with trying to fix things, on their own. I can relate to that. I understand that without proper knowledge, sometimes we Monday-morning quarter-mechanics can make matters worse. Another way to look at it, is that we also don't learn anything, if we don't try.

I don't usually mess with serious refrigerator problems, but last summer when I was in Hope, Alaska, my refrigerator was giving me fits (again). It worked sporadically. I couldn't count on it. It finally quit altogether. It was a weekend. Where do you find anyone to work on a weekend? It was 88 miles into Anchorage, and I didn't think it would do me much good to go there anyway.

The friend of a friend of a friend, was a mobile RV technician. He cleaned everything out, wiggled a few wires, pinched a couple of wires together, and got it going. The next morning it quit again. I had an electronic board, given to me by another technician in Virginia years before. He wasn't sure the board was the problem, so he told me to keep it on hand...just in case.

This was the "in case." With the help of a friend, the two of us put the electronic board in. It couldn't hurt. It worked. Wow! Well, let's say it went back to working sporadically. At least it worked long enough to get the refrigerator cold, then it would quit, then it would work long enough to get it cold again. I had to be very careful what I kept in it. The electric hadn't worked for years so it didn't help to find a place to plug in.

When I returned to Washington, I had it repaired by Kelly at All-Seasons RV in Wenatchee, Washington, who obviously knew what he was doing. It is working better (and longer) than it has since the unit was new.

In-house Water Pump

When I first stopped on the above-mentioned Mexican beach, I admired my scenery for a few minutes, then proceeded to get lunch in that magnificent spot. No water. The pump wouldn't work. I had just come across five miles of absolutely awful, washboard and sand road. The fuses were fine. I knew the battery wasn't down.

Process of elimination took me to the pump itself. I drug everything off the bed pedestal and checked it out. Sure enough, a wire had jiggled out. This happened after I drove the RV back over it the day I left, also. Amazingly, it has not happened since, and I've been over some gruesome roads.

I've mentioned before that when you take someone with you who is not an RVer, they don't understand about "limited water" consumption. I was in Nova Scotia, Canada, a few years ago, and took a friend with me around the Cabot Trail. It was so nice to have some "girl-talk" kind of company. We were boondocking late in the fall. I hadn't a clue if we would find facilities anywhere.

She must have thought I was less than hygienic after a while. I kept cautioning her against letting the water run for half hour, while she cleaned vegetables, or washed her hands. Trust me, these things can be done with a minimum of water usage, and still maintain cleanliness.

Within a day and a half, I noticed the water pump was not shutting off. It gurgled. I was really upset, because something was wrong with that stupid water pump. Of course it had to happen when I had someone with me. Oh me of little faith. The water tank was so close to empty that the water pump wasn't getting any water. You'd gurgle too, if you were dying of thirst.

I have taken the water pump apart. It was coming on when the faucets weren't open. A couple of times I did that and it seemed fine, but since the problem resurfaced within a couple of weeks, I deducted that the tightened screws were loosening for a reason.

Eventually, I got a new water pump, a Whisper King™ Shurflo, that I can barely hear. I've always had a Shurflo. They are really workhorses. I kept the old water pump and when I was at Quartzsite, Arizona, the last time, Shurflo had a booth. They were fixing old pumps for free. Now the old pump has retired under the front seat of the Little Lynx, awaiting the next emergency. Next best thing to being quiet, is the fact I could install it myself. When I can install something myself, it makes my day.

How are your driving skills?

Falling Asleep

A few times I have driven when I was sleepy. I was usually in a place where I couldn't pull off, or I would have. I don't like to drive when I am sleepy, and I have no reason to. Neither should you. Remember, if you take the chance, you may not have to live with the result (unless you kill somebody else), but your loved ones will. You (or your mate) may be killed, or maimed, and you won't reach your destination "on time" anyhow. Drowsiness at the wheel causes 100,000 crashes, and 10,000 deaths a year. It isn't worth it.

It is wise to stop every couple of hours for a drink, bathroom break, do a "walk-a-bout," walk or water the animals, make love not war, nap, read, anything to break the sleepiness. It doesn't necessarily work to drink something with caffeine in it. If you are sleepy, you are sleepy, and you never know when you will nod off--then it is too late.

Most highway accidents due to drowsiness, happen between 2 and 5 p.m. The other high time is between 12 midnight and 7 a.m. You will be off the roads and snoozing in a campground by then, won't you?

If you are drifting between lanes, yawning excessively, your head is nodding, or you are not aware of having driven the last few miles, you have a problem. If you hit another vehicle head on, you are causing someone else a headache, too.

I've always been really frightened of driving when I am sleepy because I use the cruise control. If I nod off in a "micro-nap," which might only last a few seconds, the Sprinter is still going down the highway at 55 miles an hour. Scary!

Don't drive when you are on medication that causes drowsiness. If you don't know if drowsiness is a side effect, ask your doctor or pharmacist.

Back to the subject, how are you driving skills? I think mine are pretty good. One time I backed in too close to the amenities. When I pulled out to regroup, I hooked the water spigot with my big back end (no comments please). I reported it to the manager but he didn't even come to look at the slightly creamed water pipe.

If you don't know how to drive well, take lessons. Check the local high school or college for driving lessons. If you are lucky, an RV driving school may be nearby.

If not, make haste to your first FMCA, Escapee, Good Sam, Coast to Coast national meeting or a Life on Wheels Conference, to take advance of Defensive Driving Courses. In some states, a driving course taken by those over age 55, makes them eligible for a discount on auto insurance premiums. (Resources)

Classroom hours include talks on safety, braking, road emergencies, and how to cope with them. The rest of the course is in the parking lot, learning operational techniques.

When I drove the new Sprinter off the lot, by myself, it was scary. It wouldn't have been so bad, if I hadn't been in a rain storm, in four lanes of traffic, during rush hour. I didn't know where I was within the driving lane. I finally realized, if I lined up the yellow line in the center of the pavement, with the vinyl button holding down the corner of the dashboard, I was in the center of the lane where I belonged. Even now, when I get into a crunch during highway construction, I line something up with that vinyl button and know I have room to spare. If that button ever flips, so will I.

I was already used to using side mirrors when I got my motorhome. We had them on our family mini and the school bus we used for the Girl Scouts.

It didn't take me long to put convex mirrors in the corner of the side mirrors. It helps you see what is along-side. Magnifying plastic stick-ons can be used in the back window to help you see directly behind you. You can get TV monitors to show you what's going on back there, too. Newer units have back-up warnings like construction trucks.

Backing an RV

Please don't ever stand around watching people maneuvering an RV into a campsite, or anywhere else. When it goes smooth as clockwork, it is a pleasure to behold. Too often, screams between the husband at the wheel, and the wife in the back (or the other way around), resound through the campground.

I witnessed such a tirade last year. I could see them from inside my RV because they were in the next row behind me. Two guys, who shall remain nameless (because I don't know who they were), stood there watching every move, and making wisecracks. If I had been the driver, I would run over them!

Just for fun, let's run through these backward thoughts

♦ Have a friend or spouse outside the trailer on your side, to direct you

♦ **Agree ahead of time on your signals** and identifying words (Not **those** words, nice ones!)

♦ In the driver's seat, **put your hand at the bottom of the steering wheel.**

♦ **Move it in the direction you want your trailer to move.** (The trailer will turn in the opposite direction of where you are steering your truck)

♦ **Move slowly until you have your RV where you want it.**

♦ **Ignore the clowns who are watching you.**

Simple, right? I couldn't do that if my life depended on it. That's why I drive a motorhome, pure and simple.

If you have a hard time backing, or maneuvering your RV, ask when you register in the campground, if they have a pull-through site. Sometimes they save these for extra-long rigs, or people who have problems backing, or for those who don't want to unhook because they are leaving the next morning.

Winterizing your motorhome

I am in my motorhome most of the time and usually following the sun. I seldom have to winterize the RV. Once I had an RV service do it, but last winter, I did it myself. That tells you it can't be too hard. A "bypass" kit had already been attached to the waterheater. I shut off the heater, opened the valve to drain it, and turned the bypass valves under the sink so the RV anti-freeze didn't have to go through them.

I emtpied the sewer tanks, and drained the freshwater tank, via the valve under the bed pedestal. I added a gallon of RV antifreeze into all the drains.

The motorhome radiator had proper antifreeze. I filled the gasoline tank, to prevent condensation. The windshield washer reservoir was already drained (don't forget that). It hadn't had water in it for the past year. (All the powers that be in the Chevrolet Company and various RV Service Centers have never been able to find a replacement and I can't seem to repair it. (I have felt a whole lot like I was getting the run-around!)

Places where you can get specific, step-by-step information on "the rest of the story" about winterizing, are listed in Resources. The Sprinter was not in storage very long, so I didn't take batteries out. I unplugged everything, and fastened the door of the clean refrigerator and freezer, open.

For anything that is outside vented (water heater, refrigerator, furnace), you may want to put cardboard covers inside to prevent nastie beasties (four-, six-, or eight-legged) from creating hearth and home.

I drove the motorhome onto boards, about eight inches off the ground, to keep the front high enough that water would not settle on top. I fastened a huge blue tarp all around the upper part of the Sprinter, to cover vents, air conditioning, and solar panels. I shut off the inverter, and closed all drapes, to keep the sun off the upholstery and carpeting.

In the spring, I closed the fresh-water valve, filled with water, and ran water through the lines until it no longer ran pink. I tightened the waterheater valve outside, and turned the inside valves the opposite to what they were, opening the lines to the waterheater. Nothing was cracked, and I breathed a sign of relief when everything worked.

The engine battery was dead. When I pushed the button for some juice from the in-house batteries, it fired right up. I fully expected to find the house batteries dead when I returned. They were already over four years old and I tend to forget to water them until they need about three quarts of water. They were not only alive and well, I only added a cup of water to the four of them altogether.

I loved house-sitting for the winter, and having all that room, but it was so great to get behind the wheel again. It definitely felt like home.

OK, just so we don't get paranoid here. All these problems happened to me over **eleven years**, not bad considering my expertise in repairing, or lack thereof.

Now,

BUCKLE UP!

---

before we get to the Nitty Gritty Down N' Dirty. That's pretty heavy stuff though, maybe we ought to take a detour, a little like you might do if you were out traveling.

Hub of the Universe

Full-time RVers pride themselves on getting off the Interstates and traveling the "Blue highways." You can find the most delightful places quite unexpectedly. It might be a scenic vista or it might be a charming town such as

Boswell, Indiana

If you get off the beaten path, you'll find places like this. If you mirror friendliness, and take the time to scratch the surface, you'll find real, honest-to-goodness, down-home people. If you don't find Boswell, you'll likely find another little town with character.

When a stranger car drives through town or along the narrow country roads, neighbors notice. Neighbors watch out for neighbors in Boswell, because they still occasionally leave their doors unlocked. Grain elevators stand tall against the horizon. Moews Seed Company is emblazoned on the side of a big building. The IGA Store and Tastee Treet provide sustenance. A car lot exists among the always-healthy dandelions. Flags fly high over the Armory and the Volunteer Fire Department.

An abandoned mansion with broken windows and blackened chimneys is ripe for a *Murder She Wrote* episode, should Angela decide on a Midwest setting. It is a Norman Rockwell painting of yesterday.

The population is around 700 but they think big in Boswell. Painted across the water tower is, "Boswell, Hub of the Universe." The principal of the high school challenged locals to prove that it is not. In a place where home made pie and Mom remain high on the list, who indeed, can prove it is not, or should not be...

Through reader mail, Jennie and Bob Cox invited me to "Drop by any time," prompting me to do just that when I found them in my path. Birds, pear and apple trees, Iris, mushrooms, and life in general, were blooming at their lush paradise in the midst of the Indiana flatlands. The farm has been in Jennie's family for a hundred years, and she is rooted in its history.

The farmhouse, a weathered barn, a windmill, and a fat silo are intermingled with pine and dogwood trees and lilac bushes. Jennie, a budding writer, does her best composing on the front porch swing. Her grandfather helped build the family church of several generations, that sits on a hilltop a few miles down the road.

She met Bob, a WWII pilot, while getting their cars serviced a few years ago and they joined forces for life. He grew up in nearby Danville, Illinois.

Like I said, they think big in Boswell. Everywhere we went people told me about the local pizza, "The greatest in the world." The world being such a big place and all, I wanted to check it out. As fate would have it, the pizza place wasn't open Mondays. Instead, we consumed the Monday Night Special at The Farmer's Table Restaurant, corn muffins, navy bean soup, fried potatoes, coffee, and topped it off with honest-to-goodness home-made pie.

Making the rounds Tuesday morning, Bob claimed the bright red geranium plant in the Johnson TV Store window was the "Liveliest thing in Boswell."

According to a native, "The antique store at one end of the town has good junk, and the other end just has junk." I didn't ask which was which. There are more antique stores per block than most towns. Of course that's where its history lies, in the dust-covered cream separators, rusted cook stoves, and once-adored, one-eyed, china-faced dolls with yellowed cloth arms, an avalanche of junk in some eyes, treasures in others.

We sat next to the window in the "Hometown Cafe" for breakfast. Colorful oil cloths, practical as the biscuits and gravy that come from the kitchen, covered the unmatched tables. "Dood" brought eggs over easy, crisp bacon, perfect hash browns, wheat toast and delicious coffee for a whopping $3.98. For a moment, I thought I had gone "One Step Beyond."

Jennie said when she and Bob have been gone for a week or so, they always stop at the Hometown Cafe for a meal before returning home. "It's like the theme song from *Cheers*, you want to touch bases, '*Where everybody knows your name.*'"

The whole population of Boswell checks into the Hometown Cafe during the day, that included the "Pizza Man." Bob Dallas sported a gray beard and wore a white cap with "Dallas Pizza" printed on it. Bob is into woodcarving when he isn't making dough. He gave me a small walnut dove as a remembrance of his faith and Boswell, and suggested I stay for evening pizza.

I asked Paul at the "Toys, Tools, and Antiques" store if anybody would mind if I parked overnight in the street. He said, "You can do almost anything in Boswell and nobody will mind." He re-iterated, "People come from miles around for that pizza."

I felt comfortable under the "Loud and boisterous behavior will be kept to a minimum," sign, listening to, according to Bob Cox, "Nice music, not that ya-ya stuff."

The pizza emporium, a refurbished gas station, was clean as a whistle, cozy, and smelled delicious. A brown and wrinkled "Roosevelt for president and Charles Fairbanks of Indiana for vice president" poster graced a wall along with dozens of pictures of family and friends. Curtains and dried flower arrangements made by Debbie, Bob's assistant, added to the homelines of the room. Everybody knows everybody in Boswell, and they were all there to celebrate TGIF.

Boswell is on US-41 NW of Lafayette, IN. Within a short drive, you can reach Tippecanoe Battlefield at Lafayette, the Ernie Pyle Museum in Dana, and the Possum Bottom Covered Bridge.

The pizza, well, it was just as good as the Boswellians claimed. I get warm fuzzies when I visualize the warmth and friendliness I found in that little burg called Boswell.

Some day, when I'm traveling through the Midwest, I'll go back for more of that pizza.

THE NITTY-GRITTY DOWN N' DIRTY

Direct Deposit and Paying Bills

If you have Social Security or other income, it can be deposited directly into your bank account.

You probably won't have many bills. Escapees and FMCA have my VISA number, for paying mail-forwarding, postage, and telephone bills. My health insurance premiums are also taken directly out of my VISA account. The only bills I receive in hand, are vehicle insurance, that come once or twice a year. Unless you are going to be traveling really far into the hinterlands, you'll have your mail in time to pay any bills you receive directly.

Credit Cards and Cash

I don't carry much cash with me, unless I am going into Canada or Mexico, and then I get their money at a bank (Borders and Barriers Chapter). I choose to get advances on my VISA in a bank. ATM machines are open twenty-four hours a day, and have cropped up just about everywhere. I know, without a doubt, that somewhere, somehow, one of them would chew up my card. I don't trust machines. What a curse in a Technological Age.

It isn't always technology to blame either. An over-zealous clerk took my son-in-law's card. Even though he protested she had made an error, she persisted. It was a mistake, but a great deal of inconvenience to him.

Hopefully, you won't have my paranoia, and you will use your Credit cards at one of the national ATMs. When you get your special card from your bank, you will also get a directory that shows you where the affiliated banks are. If you turn your card over, you'll see symbols for Plus, Cirrus, Exchange, or other ATM machines. When you see a corresponding symbol on an ATM machine, you can get funds. There is usually a fee involved on the machine end, and perhaps at your bank. My VISA is through Merrill Lynch, and has Exchange and Plus symbols on the back.

I never get a bill. They take my expenditures out of my account at the end of each month. Advances are subtracted immediately. If you have a charge-card bill at the end of the month, pay it off promptly to avoid charges.

If you're carrying cash, don't let anyone see into your billfold or purse. It is better to stash a few larger bills, somewhere inside the RV, or in a different compartment.

There are various ways to hide money, all of which are probably familiar to anyone who might break in -- especially if he (or she) reads this book. I used to have a hollow book where I kept extra money. That really makes me wonder, because I have no idea where the book is. I probably gave it away to a white elephant sale somewhere. No wonder my riches are slipping away so quickly.

It pays to remember where you put money. This really happened to me. I stashed three $50 bills in a book above my work station. Since I didn't need them, I completely forgot about them. Months later, I was thumbing through the book, looking for something, and found them. That was fun. It was like "found" money. I guess it was. Others put money in pop cans with removable lids made for that purpose.

Jewels are hidden in the ice cube trays. Friends of mine have a safe built into their step. I have a heavy-duty, lockable, fireproof, steel box for important documents. My daughters have copies or the originals of important papers.

Telephone

A variety of answering services are available. I use Family Motor Coach Association's 800 number. This is free with the $25/year (renewal) membership. I may leave thirty messages a month, and retrieve thirty messages a month.

Escapees, Good Sam, and Coast to Coast all have message services, but they charge a monthly fee. Ads for other voice mail and message services are in the back of the RV magazines.

I have an AT&T calling card through Escapees. Dealing with local phone companies had caused me to contemplate suicide. I now access AT&T through an 800 number. Using a calling card is expensive. Another option is pre-paid calling cards.

I have received several prepaid calling cards as gifts, either from companies or friends. They make a great gift to an RVer by the way. They are handy, and are on sale in supermarkets, among other places. I tend not to use them when I am making long distance business calls, because I like getting itemized proof, but it is cheaper than my calling card rates for making personal calls.

People ask me if I have a cellular phone. No. I find the cost prohibitive, but recently someone put the high cost of a cell phone in a different light. They figure it into their budget, like they would emergency towing service. They think of it as insurance. Depending on your reasons for having one, the cost may not be prohibitive. Don't forget, it isn't just the basic monthly charge, there are roaming fees, and you pay for each call that is put through to you, as well.

New technology in the works, will no doubt lower the cost, and improve the means over the next couple of years.

Most RVers have a CB. When you call for help on a CB, you are letting everybody know you are stranded along the road somewhere. With a cellular phone, you are supposedly only letting the one you are calling, in on your problems. Although it is illegal to listen, cellular phone calls can be picked up by CB scanner. My other reason for not getting a cellular phone is that I couldn't get connected in many of the areas I choose to travel. That, too, will change.

> Use disinfectant pads to wipe the telephone mouthpiece
> before and after using.

Mail-forwarding

For the first couple of years, I used my daughter's address in Virginia for my mail-forwarding. Something happened that made me change to an organizational box number.

On one of my forays into Mexico, I met a man who was very nice; but for various reasons, I didn't wish to continue the association. He acquired my business card through mutual friends, and wound up on Tracey's doorstep trying to find me. She fielded the situation quite well (Staunchly protecting me and my privacy all the way, bless her heart. She is WOMAN, too!). I decided with answering reader mail, and meeting many people in my travels, I needed a post office box.

With my FMCA membership, I have free mail-forwarding. I pay only for the postage. They send Priority Mail, according to last name, and send it only on that day. The inflexibility has been a problem a few times, but the service is free. I am still using that excellent service.

In roughly eight years, they have never (that I recall) screwed up on anything, except on rare occasions when I have received someone else's letter, or one of mine has strayed for a while. That's pretty good considering where I've been.

I managed to go looking for mail in the wrong place in Pennsylvania. I inadvertently sent it to a town a hundred miles up the Susquehanna River. Because of a similarity in names, and my advanced CRS, I went to pick it up in the wrong town. Be careful.

For business reasons, I recently joined the Escapee mail-forwarding service. They send priority (or overnight if I pay for it) mail whenever I want it sent. I pay $62 a year, and they send all mail, including third class. They have three different rates, depending on what you want sent. They are all reasonable.

You do have to plan ahead, just a bit, for getting mail. You can't rely on Priority Mail reaching you in three days. Even in the lower 48, I have had it take up to a week. At holiday time, this is to be expected, but I resent paying for priority mail that doesn't get to me in less than seven days!

In Canada, always allow at least two weeks. In Alaska, it depends on where you are. In some outlying towns, they only get mail twice a week. If you are near Anchorage or Fairbanks, you will probably have it in three days.

In Mexico, allow forever, just in case. Don't have anything you can't live without, sent through the mail. When I lived on the beach at Santispak, my mail was delivered to a post office box in Mulege. At San Carlos, the mail was delivered directly to the office of the RV park. I have had it sent to post offices when I was roaming in old Mexico but gave it plenty of time to get there.

When I have gone to Mexico for two weeks or a month, I have had my mail delivered to my daughters. They open anything that looks important and give me the scoop. It is expensive to telephone from Canada or Mexico. I limited my calls to once a week for phone or mail messages.

As far as sending mail from Mexico, most people send it out with another traveler heading for the border.

When you are sending for anything, remember you are dealing with the time it takes for it to be physically put into the mail, and the time it takes mail-forwarding to get it to you.

Get a zip code book. You have to have a specific name and address, or have it sent general delivery. You'll need the zip code.

Residency, Vehicle Registration, and Voting

Reasons for choosing a particular state for registration, licenses, and insurance, are many. States are usually chosen because of cheaper insurance or license rates, a lack of sales tax or income tax. Alaska, Washington, Texas, Florida, Nevada, and Wyoming have no income tax.

It is wise to check the laws of any state before you leap into residency. I was a resident of Oregon when I first started full-time RVing. I used the address of a resident, who shall remain nameless. After doing this, I realized what deep do-do I could get into. Basically, I try to follow life's rules whether I like them or not. I then worked and lived in Oregon for six months to establish residency.

I had my vehicle and voter registration, driver's license, RV and health insurance, lawyer (will), and paid taxes through the State of Oregon. In the last three years, I moved my residency to the State of Texas, and learned "Bubba" language. All the above are now through my residency in Livingston, Texas, the Escapee National Headquarters address.

Estate taxes might also be a reason to use a certain residency. Check them out because those things change. Watch for county and city taxes, as well. I liked the lack of income tax in Texas, but health insurance is more expensive.

Whatever state you choose, make sure you sever all ties with your previous state, and make as much of a dent in your new state as possible. Leave no doubts that you are a resident of your new state.

When I bought my licenses, and changed my vehicle registrations, I made sure I could renew by mail. This is important. In some places you have to have a yearly vehicle inspection, and must be physically present to renew your license. It never hurts to go through a lawyer to learn your best options.

I paid $128.70 for the Sprinter and $78.80 for the Lynx to change from Oregon to Texas licenses and registration in 1996, and a total of $150 renewal for both in 1997.

Voting

I am registered to vote and make sure I vote absentee ballot. The freedom to live on the open road, does not mean we should shirk our responsibilities. Besides, I want to know that somebody else helped put those guys in office. I don't want the blame for the whole mess (whichever party)!

Taxes

My accountant, Barbara, is in Michigan, and in my prayers every night. She helps keep my sanity intact. The first winter, my mail wasn't forwarded in a timely fashion, from the hospital where I used to work. I was living a carefree, sun-warmed, palapa-shaded life, on a Mexican beach. The mail reached me three months late. A letter from the IRS claimed I owed them $200. The deadline had long passed.

Barbara wrote them a letter of explanation, and I sent a check. I didn't owe it, and when I got back to the US and my records, I proved it, but it nearly gave me a heart attack on the sand, I can tell you. Since then, I have carried at least two year's worth of income tax reports with me in the motorhome, and I keep Barbara's phone number, taped to the steering wheel.

She held my hand through a tax audit a few years ago. I wasn't sure whether the auditor's great interest in my daily log, book manuscript, and tales of the open road, were for me, or against me. Her interest was genuine. She said, "You certainly lead an interesting life."

I went in thoroughly prepared, and didn't "dump" receipts on her desk, as she said so many do. It went well.

Thanks to the computer, I keep accurate records for both business and pleasure. I keep all receipts. It helps me sleep at night, knowing I can prove, that expenses eat up the entire $300,000 a year I take in as a writer. Let's see, where is that membership receipt for the Liar's Club?

By the way, if (when?) you sell your house, keep all the records documenting your house purchase, improvements, and sale, to prove or disprove long-term Capital Gains.

Last Will and Testament

Check with a lawyer and see if your will is valid in the state of residency you choose. When I changed my residency from Oregon to Texas, I changed my will as well.

Encouraging Wives

I was fortunate that I had driven Bessie Bus (Sixty-passenger school bus we carted our Girl Scouts in all over the country), and the mini-motorhome we had for several years. I was also fortunate in that my husband encouraged me to drive.

I, in turn, encourage wives to learn not only how to drive, but to breakdown, set-up, empty sewers, fill water tanks, get propane, and anything else that has to do with RVing. I didn't know how to do anything but drive it. When my husband was in the hospital, he instructed me from his bed. I lived in the motorhome in the parking lot until he died. I had never even filled the RV with gasoline or checked the oil.

In my travels, I have met so many woman whose husbands were taken unexpectedly ill, or perhaps even died. Suddenly wives were faced with a big rig they didn't know how to drive or live in. Friends or relatives bailed them out, but why not avoid that terrible helpless feeling. Learn the ropes, women. I have seen women who have had to take over the wheel because the husband became disabled but they still wanted to travel. Like I said, learn the ropes.

It helps if husbands are not threatened by the wife wanting to learn. It is even more helpful if he is a patient teacher. Best of all, learn from a neighbor!!

Of course it wouldn't hurt you men to learn the art of cooking, cleaning, balancing the books, writing checks, thank you notes, and the gamut of "woman's work" either. I've met some men who were pretty lost in those areas.

Vehicle Insurance

All RV organizations have RV and/or tag, as well as road emergency insurance, available through their memberships. I have RV Emergency Road Service for $69 a year. It covers the motorhome and the Little Lynx. I have not had an occasion to use it. I was attracted to its promise to provide service "24 hours a day, 365 days a year, **anywhere** in the United States and Canada."

I was on my way to Alaska, and knew I would be traveling Top of the World, Denali, and the Dempster Highways. Although I was perfectly happy I didn't slide off the Dempster when I was pushing a foot of snow, it certainly was a possibility. Hello, Road Service?

Weigh the insurance options offered. Be sure the insurance company you choose, will insure you as a full-timer living in a motorhome.

Full-time RVers are pretty much an unknown subculture to most of the world. If your insurance company doesn't understand what you are talking about, chances are they will not cover you in an accident, if you are living, and traveling, full-time in an RV. There are only five companies who do. I have listed addresses in Resources. If they don't advertise full-time RV coverage, be suspicious.

It is important to know if you have <u>Replacement Cost Coverage</u>. If you have a fire, flood, or accident, and you have to pay to replace your RV out of your pocket, it could very well destroy your dream. When you are full-timing, the RV is your home. Think in those terms. The age of your rig will also determine your type of coverage.

Are your personal effects covered? It may not seem like you have a lot at quick glance, but replacing personal effects is costly.

Do you have <u>Emergency Expenses Coverage</u>? If you are living in your RV, it would be expensive to find other accommodations while your RV is being fixed.

My insurance on the Sprinter is Progressive Northwest Insurance Companies through Miller Insurance Agency, Inc. It is $487 a year with $1,000 deductible. Because of the motorhome's age, it does not have replacement insurance.

The Little Lynx is Sweet Sixteen (he has been kissed--by a sneaky little Toyota in the next site). It is insured by National General through Good Sam. It has only the basic coverage because of its age. If I cream it, it's a lost cause. Strangely enough, the cost is $425 a year, almost the same as a much newer, more expensive, recreational vehicle. No one ever said life was fair or logical. Sigh!

For at least a minimum of insurance savings, consider the size of your deductible (You are a good driver, aren't you?), the age of your vehicle (and tag), reducing deductible, etc.

Most insurance companies offer Driver Training, Renewal, Alcohol and Drug Awareness Course, and Anti-theft Device Discounts.

Inventory

It is just as important to keep an inventory of your full-time rolling igloo, as it was your landbound home. God forbid you should ever have to make a claim, but if you do, this is the place to start.

When I seriously figure the value of my inventory, it is much higher than I realize. My computer equipment alone would be worth at least $25 (that's after I have "booted" it up a few times with accompanying anguished screams of frustration).

What kind of insurance coverage do you have on your personal belongings? Exactly what is covered? Is it <u>Actual Cash Value</u> (Replacement cost less depreciation) or <u>Replacement Cost Coverage</u> (Replacing with same kind and quality). What are the deductibles?

Even if you don't have a computer, a table format might be easiest. Arrange it according to categories, i.e., clothing, cameras, TV. Start at one end of the RV, and list everything that didn't come with the RV. Remember the contents behind doors, inside drawers (Don't forget that secret drawer in Aunt Grace's antique music box where you have your $150,000 diamonds), and outside holds. If you use your tag as a mobile garage, write down what's in it, too.

Item	Purchase Date	Original Cost	Estimated Present Value	Cost Of Replacement	Serial Or Model Number

Got that done? Now go back through, and videotape or photograph it. You do have a camera to record all the adventures you're going to have, haven't you? When you're done with that, find your receipts.

Some would say it is unnecessary baggage, but I keep every receipt in a recycled manila envelope. At the end of the year, I put them in a big priority bag (you'll get many of these from your mail-forwarding) for the year. I use receipts for tax purposes, refunds, warranties, just plain interest, and once I used a twenty-year-old receipt as proof in a Court of Law.

Now you have a great graph, receipts for special items, and pictures or videos of your treasures. What do you do with them? Send a copy or the original to your children, safe deposit box, **or wherever you can retrieve a copy, should yours be destroyed**. Remember to add or delete items as you make changes.

You might save yourself some work by getting an inventory brochure from your insurance company.

Before you make your record permanent, scan it thoroughly. Is there a way to lighten the load? Maybe you don't absolutely need that antique jewelry box with the secret drawer. Besides, wouldn't you have more fun spending that $150,000, than wearing it? Always keep the weight of your rig foremost in mind. **Weight affects gas mileage and vehicle wear, greatly**.

You could get a cardboard box (or cardboard file drawers from Wal-Mart or K-Mart), to keep medical records, insurance papers, bank statements, owner's manuals, household accounts, etc. You may need nothing more than an expandable file or a small fireproof box.

Because of my CRS, I have tried keeping an inventory (clothes, linen, appliances, food) of each drawer, cupboard, and cubby hole, especially the ones that are harder to get into, like the ones below the booth. It is helpful to have a list of the outside hold contents, too. Being that organized shouldn't be that hard with my computer, but I find I stick to it religiously for about two weeks..

Information Sheet

Each January, I update an Information Sheet, and send it to each of my daughters. If anything should happen to me, they have the information they need. It includes:

♦ Name, address, phone number
♦ Description and licenses of the motorhome and tag
♦ Motorhome, car, life, and hospital insurance, name and phone numbers of people to contact
♦ Accountant and attorney's names and addresses
♦ Investments, bank accounts, and contacts

- ◆ Any other pertinent information they would need to know if I were incapacitated, or dead. (I guess I would be incapacitated if I were dead!)

Health Insurance

Count yourself fortunate, if you have continued insurance through the company where you worked. When I quit working at the hospital, I was on my own, and it is expensive.

Check with your insurance company, before you go on the road. Are you restricted by HMOs or PPOs, to doctors and hospitals in a specific geographic area? You may have problems getting the bills paid. Until recently, I had Blue-Cross-Blue Shield of Oregon and my policy covered me anywhere.

Because rates continued to go up drastically, and I already had $1,000 deductible, I changed to a company through Escapees, Inc., John Aldon. I have not had occasion to use this yet. I still have the $1,000 deductible. I am not restricted to a specific area. A $10,000 life insurance benefit was offered with this package but I discovered they don't cover anyone after the age of sixty.

Veterans are eligible for treatment at Veteran's Hospitals. It is helpful that most towns now have emergency clinics open twenty-four hours a day.

Because you have become a full-timer, doesn't mean you should skip that yearly physical or dental check-up. I haven't exactly adhered to that, but in the last couple of years, I have established relationships with medical and dental offices in the towns where my children live. My reasoning is that I will most likely be visiting one or the other of them, more often than going back to Michigan, to my original doctors.

If you have had baseline medical or dental x-rays, or mammograms, have copies sent to your new physicians or dentists. In this day of computers, you might also want to save yourself time by making up an information sheet on your personal history, information (names, addresses, DOB, SS#, etc.); past history (surgeries, surgeons); and current medical history (prescriptions, allergies). Include names of your physicians, dentists, ophthalmologists, along with their addresses and phone numbers. Make copies of your medical insurance cards as well.

If you going into a hospital situation, it is also a good idea to give them written instructions as far as a Living Will, and whom to notify as next of kin (besides your mate).

Let's face it, when you are visiting a new physician, or going into any hospital (new or familiar), you or your mate are not well, or you wouldn't be there. Under pressure, it is often difficult to keep your mind on answering the questions medical personnel ask.

Life Insurance

The RV organizations have various offers of life insurance along with their memberships.

Conserving

On rare occasions, I have had guests with me for a couple of weeks who were not RVers. If we were in campgrounds, it was no problem but with my penchant for recreation areas or places with no amenities, this was soon a problem. Education time.

I've often talked about a "bath in a teacup." A bit facetious perhaps but I have an old unit with a twenty-eight gallon fresh water capacity. This is a very small amount of water even for one person, let alone two or three. I never let the water run, whether I'm rinsing dishes, washing vegetables, my hands, brushing my teeth, taking a shower, or whatever. The shower head temporarily shuts off with a twist so I can lather up, then rinse.

Using less water means you won't fill up the gray water tank so quickly and you won't use as much hot water. The hot water, if you plan your day right, can be turned on for only a couple of hours, long enough to do dishes, shower, then turned off. That saves propane.

A lot of people use campground lavatories and showers but I rarely do that. Even though most of them are clean and acceptable, I like the convenience of my own bathroom. That's why I have an RV, the convenience. Each to his own.

I have found that disposable wipes are extremely handy around the RV. I use them to do a rough clean up after I have played with the sewer hose (so I don't have to come inside with dirty hands). I keep a container in the car, in the RV bathroom, and on the doghouse. Sometimes if my hands aren't overly dirty, I use the wipe again to dust out the window sills, dusty cupboard doors, or wipe up the bathroom floor (always enough hair to start a large cat).

If I have slightly damp paper towels, I clean the mirrors or the face of the TV or computer monitor.

I promised to get "Down n" dirty," so we'll end with a word about

Laundry

I keep two large net bags hanging on a hook in the shower area. The purple one I use for dark dirty clothes. The white one I use for white or light dirty clothes. Air can get to the clothes while they are waiting to be washed, and I can throw the bags into the wash machine with the dirty clothes. I've seen people use folding plastic baskets, and plastic garbage bags. I like the nets better.

I fill a small jar with enough soap for however many loads of laundry I will be doing, rather than drag the whole container. According to the washer repairman, you need use only half the soap it says to use, on the side of the soap container. He says it is better for the machine to use less soap. Unless I've been playing around in the engine compartment or underneath the RV or car, I don't get that dirty anyway.

I take only the number of non-cling sheets I need for the dryer. I collect quarters in a small change purse for washday. I've also kept them in film containers.

Unless you are going to be traveling in the boonies, most small towns or villages have Laundromats. It is easier to go some place that has a big parking lot. Most places are clean and well cared for, but I've run into some that were terrible. Look it over, if you don't like it and can wait, go to the next town.

One clue, don't go on Friday night, or any time on the weekend. They are crowded with working people who don't have a choice of time as you do. Wait until a weekday morning.

This tip has been around since the beginning of time. It works. Put small, hand-washable items in a large bucket or container with a lid. Fill with water and adequate laundry soap, cover tightly and put in the shower or bathtub. Your clothes will be jostled and swished around enough to come clean by the time you reach your destination. Rinse and hang up.

With that said, I'll hang my close on this chapter and go on to the chapter on Relationships.

This statue isn't! This is a man painted completely gray. He stood along the walk on the Inner Harbour at Victoria, British Columbia. People would pass him, not realizing he was a statue. He stood perfectly still until after they got beyond him, then he followed them with his eyes, and stuck out his very red tongue. For someone who was doing absolutely nothing, he drew a crowd.

RELATIONSHIPS

Death of Spouse

In Chapter I, I told about starting my second life "four years and many decisions" after my husband died. We had a very good friendship built up over the 28 years from the time we met, until he died, after nearly 26 years of marriage. His dying was like cutting me in half. I felt dangly and awkward, like I was living in an incomplete body.

We each had individual interests we sometimes shared, sports and arts. We had even more interests that we shared all the time, traveling and camping. We did almost anything we could share with our two daughters, that took us outdoors. We both had families we were close to, and we were all active in church.

Yes, I know, almost fifteen years later, I am remembering all the good parts, but we really didn't fight and have arguments. Sometimes that was a problem in itself, but we managed pretty darn good. It didn't take a rocket scientist, to know when one of us was angry with the other. We both settled ruffled feathers by walking in the woods.

One time I was upset with all three of them. The kids were fighting about whose turn it was to do dishes. Jack was never a disciplinarian. His heart was too soft. That day I got tired of being the "bad guy." I grabbed my coat and keys, and took off in the car. In my hurry, I broke my glasses, but I didn't let that stop me. I needed them for distance, but I figured with the snow, I couldn't see very far anyway.

I drove to Lake Michigan, and stopped to watch the wave action on that cold winter day. I was still mad. In the meantime, I dredged up all the things I had been mad about for thirty years. I continued north, and the farther I went, the more I realized I really didn't have any place to go. What a revelation. I couldn't go home to Mom and Dad. They had been dead since I was in my twenties.

Next in line was my father-in-law, whom I considered to be my Dad, as well as Jack's, but I certainly couldn't go to the enemy's father and grandfather. I knew my four brothers would send me packing. I knew, without a doubt, that the Lord loved me; but at that moment in time, I wasn't talking to Him either!

Within a few hours, I returned home. It was quiet. Nobody said anything. Life continued.

After Jack died, I took my dinners outside, and sat in the family swing during those beautiful Michigan fall evenings. I could eat little of it. I went down to 116 pounds for the first time since I was born. I stayed that way until I found my life again (Perhaps I shouldn't have done quite such a good job of finding my life again!).

I felt guilty because I was alive, and he wasn't. I thought ahead with great sadness to Tracey's college graduation, or when she would walk down the matrimonial aisle, or when either of the girls would have made him a grandfather. Every month that went by, I felt guilty because I was leaving him further and further behind. I was betraying him by going on with my life.

People were kind, but except for very close friends, within a much shorter time than I was ready for it, they didn't want to see tears. They were uncomfortable discussing my dead husband at all. They forgot that what he and I shared was the focus of my life, for twenty-five years. The memories, and the pain of loss, couldn't be put out of my mind and heart overnight.

It is often said that, "It takes a year" to get your life in order again. Ha! It is different for different people, but it took me a lot longer than that. I thought I had my act together; but after two years, I saw the hospital counselor. Instead of beating myself for still sorrowing, she helped me see my grief for what it was, let it out, and begin healing.

Fifteen years hence, those who have lost spouses within the last few years (men and women), ask me, "When does it stop hurting?" I'm sorry to say that it doesn't, but you stop thinking about it so much. You put the sorrow in the back of your mind, where it pops out occasionally, at weird times, bringing the pain back again for a second, or a few minutes. It flies in on a snatch of song, a fragrance, something remembered, something once shared, a look-a-like, a photograph, a feeling, or a dream. Then it disappears, sometimes for months at a time.

Selling the house and going on the road brought the thought I was betraying him, because I was selling all we had worked so hard to get. Then I realized, if he were alive, we would probably be going about it with great excitement.

I took a part of him with me, a tan, canvas hat. Over the years it disappeared, when I no longer needed that crutch. It doesn't matter how silly it was. For whatever reason, I needed it. As I grew, I apparently I outgrew my need to carry it with me.

The only thing I have with me of Jack's, is a "mind-bender." It has a dual purpose (literally). It is a two-foot long, inch-in-diameter piece of hard wood, that I beat my duals with, to see if they have met their demise. Sometimes I take it with me, if I'm hiking in a strange place. It has been used as a wedge, a hammer, and a tool to dislodge a plugged toilet (how romantic can you get!). Obviously it gets a bath once in a while.

My curious lifestyle, and my willingness to put my emotions on paper, have brought laughter from some people and disapproval from others. One lady whom I barely know, after reading my books, commented to a former neighbor about my frequent dating, "She shouldn't be doing that!" My question is, I am single, why not?

Lonely or alone?

Everybody asks if I'm lonely, because I travel alone. To begin with, being alone has nothing to do with being lonely. Although I'm almost always alone, I'm seldom lonely.

At first, I could not go into a restaurant by myself. It took a long time to build up my self-confidence. I finally said to myself, *"You are not alone; you are unique."* Now I hold my head up and walk in with a smile. Sometimes I take a book, sometimes a notebook, sometimes just me, and that is enough. I am a wonderful person. Just ask me, I'll tell you. God loves me, so how can I be otherwise?

I can't say I've conquered walking into a party with the same attitude. That terrifies me. If they are close friends, and people I know very well, it is no problem. It is much easier walking into a room with 300 strangers in it, to give a seminar, because I have a specific purpose, something to do, a function. I am not much of a party person, even with a partner.

If you are going to travel alone, you will first have to like yourself, and your company. Even if you join singles or other organizations, you will spend a certain amount of time alone. In a later chapter, we'll talk about organizations.

I have gotten so in tune with full-time RVing over the years, and truthfully, most of the time I like being by myself, that I don't get lonely. More than likely, I get "restless." All of a sudden, nothing quite pleases me. I am normally content to sit and watch the stream rush by, or birds flitting from tree to tree (when I am not trapped by the computer). Then suddenly, I don't feel like working. I'll read the paper or go for a walk, but nothing satisfies this "restlessness."

That's when I call my kids, or call an old friend. I realize I am missing human contact. I do not always have telephone access, and I may not be in a campground where there are other people. Then I am more apt to switch on the TV and a VCR tape.

After the kids left home, and especially after Jack died, I hated Sunday afternoons, and workdays from 5:30 until 7:30. I'm not sure why, but those were always hard times for me, not sorrow, but that strange restlessness. Perhaps that was more family time than I realized. I also find that writing letters helps. My "to be answered" priority bag is always overflowing.

"How do you make friends?"

That's an easy one. You talk to someone. Walk around the campground. Ask your neighbor, or the people in the site four doors down, about something obvious, his hat, her cat, their license plate. Ask where they are from, where they've been, where they're going. Start a conversation about generators Vs solar, and I guarantee you'll be there for an hour or two. Reflect friendliness; it will come back to you. This is true whether you are in a campground, visiting a tourist attraction, or anywhere else.

Children

There are a whole lot of good points and bad points to being parents. Given my personal experiences, I feel as though I wouldn't have anything worthwhile in this world, if I didn't have Janet and Tracey. I don't live my life in their shadow, but *they do keep the shadows away*. Of all the people who are assured I am crazy for quitting my "regular" job and taking to the somewhat strange life of a full-time RVer, "all my children" back me to the hilt.

It's funny how life turns around. I like to think we encouraged them in what they wanted to do (probably the reason they wound up on opposite sides of the country -- we showed it to them first!) and now I feel their approval.

I hear stories about travelers whose children gripe and moan, because they are gone several months of the year. My children are delighted that I have my own life. They feel fortunate that I am healthy enough to do it until such time as I can't.

I loved their growing up years (mostly), remembering specifically the cuddling after bathtime, bedtime stories, teenagers climbing into bed during electrical storms, and pillowfights in our bed on Sundays before church. I admit I was happy when they were beyond dirty diapers, projectile vomiting, and new teeth (I breastfed both kids).

One of the happiest times I've had since I've been on the road, was when both girls took ten days away from their mates, and went with me to Florida. We talked and laughed our way through beachcombing and sightseeing, from St. Augustine, Florida, through Jekyll Island, a rare Bed and Breakfast stop in Georgia, and back through North Carolina.

Quality time as Grandma

Janet and I were on our way to see her sister in Virginia, when granddaughter, Rebecca, lost her first tooth. She stuck it under her pillow, which was going down the highway at fifty-five miles an hour. During the wee hours, Janet asked if I was sneaky enough to make the exchange. Silly girl! This silver-haired, old-hand, tooth fairy, carefully extracted the precious first tooth from beneath the sleeping Rebecca, and replaced it with Mom's shiny dime. I asked Janet what she wanted me to do with the tooth.

"What did you do with ours when we were little?" I gave her a blank look. Old tooth fairies never give up their secrets!!!

Rebecca and I had a day together during our Colorado family gathering, when she was six. I had no idea where we were going, but we packed up and took off in the car. Would you believe we saw wallabies, reindeer, llamas, and sled dogs?

She fed hundreds of dandelions to the llamas, and went horseback riding. The cowboy who led the horse, showed her how to make the horse go left and right and whoa, and then let her do it. What a magical day it was.

Most of the time, we do what we probably would have done if I were a grandmother back in Michigan. We bake cookies, cut, paste, and draw pictures; have campfires, roast hot-dogs, and stuff ourselves with s'mores.

This last winter when I was house-sitting in her town working on books, we dug a 17' by 7' snowhouse out of the 5' snowdrift on the chalet deck. After it collapsed, we created an anatomically-correct snowlady that guarded the deck, and peeked in the window, to watch me work until she melted into eternity.

Once we played photographer and model. We pretended we were in a beauty shop. I combed her hair and put lipstick, powder, and eyebrow pencil on her. She put on ear-rings, and changed from one of grandma's outfits to another, while I snapped pictures. A couple of the finished photos discomfited her father a bit. She will be quite a beauty as a teenager. We don't see each other often, but it is quality time.

Our family awaits, with great excitement, the August arrival of a grandson in Virginia. More memories to be made.

There are many ways to help your grandchildren take part in your adventure. A few months after Rebecca was born, I made a tape recording. I read my favorite fairy tales and Bible stories to her, and sang songs. Janet said she listened to it long before she understood what the words were, or that it was her grandma's voice.

I have sent her envelopes with goodies in them from wherever I happened to be. I took her a small block of salt from the salt evaporating ponds at Guerrero Negro in Baja, Mexico, (with permission). From Prince Edward Island, Canada, I sent her a set of Lucy Maude Montgomery's "Anne of Green Gables." I don't think she has read them yet, but one day she will be old enough to pick them up.

Sometimes when I call her house, I ask for her first. She loves getting phone calls. She also loves getting mail. I left a stack of self-addressed, stamped post cards with my address on them. Now that she can write, she sends me one every once in a while. I love to get mail, too.

When my mother and father-in-law were still alive, I left a North America map with them, so they could follow my travels. The same can be done with grandchildren. It is a lesson in geography. By the way, it's nice to use a marker for you to keep track of where you've been. I have a family map that we used while the kids were growing up. It is so marked, it can hardly be read, and it is falling apart. I'm not ready to give it up yet. I have my own map, recording all of my travels since I went on the road alone. It is goes even farther afield.

Other Family

Things happen when you're on the road full time, but if it is important, you find a way to get back. In books and articles, I've mentioned my oldest brother, Ted, and his wife, Mary. Ted was fifteen years older and more like my dad than my brother, and he spent a lot of time helping me with the RV. Heaven knows we had our moments. I didn't always agree with his advice, but I will miss it, and him, tremendously.

I flew back to spend four days with him during the middle of February this year. He died February 28, and I didn't go back. It pays to say, "I love you" when you leave people you love, or end a phone conversation. That way you won't regret that you didn't.

My second oldest brother, Dick, and his wife, Vivian, celebrated their fiftieth wedding anniversary in 1995, with a huge party with friends and family, some of whom I hadn't seen in years.

Third brother, Leo, and his wife, Pat, had a family reunion from my Dad's side of the family. That involved a three-day campout, with over-the-open-fire roasted sausage and other mouth-watering unmentionables. Brother four, Dean, and wife, Dorothy, were there from Arizona for two weeks. My four siblings, plus their spouses, and I, were together on several occasions for activities. I took photographs of the couples, and later sent them each an album. Now I have three. Cherish your moments.

> **One of the biggest drawbacks people see to this lifestyle,**
> **is leaving family behind.**
> **Out of sight**
> **does not have to mean**
> **out of mind.**
> **They will not forget you.**

Friends

I try to make my high school reunions, and always get together with a handful of classmates, when I return to Dowagiac High School stomping grounds in Michigan.

Linda Bassett and I graduated from Elkhart University together in 1955. We've cherished a close friendship through the years. She was widowed in 1993.

We enjoyed a six-week trip to Europe together in the fall of 1995. I had never been there, so everything was new and exciting for me. As much as I liked seeing new places, and doing different activities, I would not do it by tour again. We took two tours for three weeks, then went on our own. If there is ever another time, it will be by RV.

When I return to Michigan, I get together with other friends who have remained close. We meet at a restaurant after church on Sunday, or if I have more time, we share a campfire and a sing-a-long.

> **There is a point to telling you all this personal stuff. If you had <u>strong relationships</u> when you were housebound, that filmy thread of love will go with you, no matter where you roam. When you return, you reel them all in for hugs.**

Even more friends

The lifestyle attracts men who would give their eye teeth to live it, or perhaps they are living it, and are lonely.

After attempting several serious relationships, I find I am happier with the freedom to do whatever I want to do, and go where I want to go. By the same token, sometimes I would give my fortune (that isn't sacrificing too much) to share life with that special person.

There are days of frustration, like yesterday, when I threw out the fifth mouse I've caught this week, or this morning, when the sewer decided it needed my personal attention. If a male person had shown up on my door-step about 7:30 and said, "Will you marry me," I would have, without even asking his name!!!

Should I ever have another proposal, the first question should not be, "Is she marrying me for my money," but more likely, "Is she marrying me for my mechanical, problem-solving, computer, and secretarial abilities, or is it true love?" Hmmm.

Because of the nature of the following story, I have taken it out of con-text. I have no desire to hurt anyone.

I will get a lot of flack from woman about the following comments. They will think it smacks of being a rat fink. I know that whatever stories I hear, it is the point of view only, of the person with whom I am speaking. Even in ex-aggeration, there is usually some truth.

From other conversations I've had over the years, I've come to the con-clusion the *average* male, has more of a desire to travel and explore, than the *average* female.

I met a man. I'll call him Frank. Our meeting was quite by accident, and I didn't know he was married. I don't think he was concealing the fact; it just didn't come up, and given the situation, I assumed, mistakenly.

I finally asked if he was married. He said, "Legally, yes, technically, no." This man was well retired from a major company, but he was doing "scut" work to pay his way to spend the summer in Alaska.

All the guys I go out with treat me like a lady because I expect it, other-wise I wouldn't go out with them. A couple have had some pretty salty lan-guage, but even that softens when they see you inadvertently wince. This fellow was gentle spoken, not the least pushy in any way, and spoke of his grown family, and his wife, with pride and affection.

He didn't say anything against his wife except, "She won't go anywhere. She won't go to Florida because of the bugs. She won't come to Alaska be-cause of the bears. She wants to spend all her time with our children and grandchildren." He said they had each gone their own way for years.

He was quite shy. He didn't strike me as someone who would normally ask a woman out, since he was married, so his response to my comment at the end of the day, surprised me. I told him it was nice to meet someone with whom I shared so many common interests, as well as family and moral values. He said, "Yes, every since I met you, I have been trying to find a way around them."

However, after a day of exploring the countryside, and lots of conversation, I realized his attraction to me was the same as many other men. I am living their dreams. Because he was interested in living life, and at sixty-nine, still had major dreams twirling in his brain, I was attracted to him, as well. If he had been single, I might very well have found an excuse to stay in the area for a while.

I hugged him good-bye. He wished me safe travels, and while holding my hand said, "I will remember our day together...always."

I felt really sad that there was a lady out there in the world somewhere, who had a permanent hold on this man, but she didn't appreciate him enough to practice the art of compromise. Major flack!

> **Spouses, be kind to each other,**
> **learn to compromise.**
> **Don't take each other for granted.**
> **In the snap of the fickle finger of fate,**
> **you could be (and will be)**
> **alone,**
> **and then it is too late.**

Church Family

If you had an active church affiliation when you were landbound, there is no reason to give that up. I tend to look for a Presbyterian Church, but I have been welcomed into Mennonite, Catholic, Anglican, United Methodist, Seventh Day Adventist, Unity, and Lutheran Churches in Mexico, Canada, Alaska, Hawaii, and the "lower 48."

You learn a lot. One minister said, "If you cross a praying mantis with a termite, you get a bug that says grace before he eats your house." A sign declared, "Work for the Lord, the benefits are terrific!"

I love the Children's Sermons. They are simple and more understandable. One minister gave each child a peanut. He told them to shake it, to feel the vibration. He said, "This is the way it is with God. We can't see him but we can feel him moving in our lives, and if we listen, we can hear him inside." Another minister showed the children an embossing tool. He said, "From the moment we came to be, even though we can't see it, we are imprinted by God."

Don't you love the sounds in church, Bible pages rustling, whirring summer fans, clunking winter registers, bells chiming at another church, or rain hitting the stained-glass windows. You can see I pay great attention.

It's great when the babies are baptized. You never know what will happen. One baby had her feet going like windmills. She explored the minister's face with her tiny fingers, when he put his hands on her head. She never let out a peep. In Grand Forks, North Dakota, the minister said, "Baptism is a good way to get Presbyterians in the front seat."

At a church in Davenport, Iowa, the choir was almost bigger than the congregation. They sang, "*When I Survey the Wondrous Cross*." It started soft as a feather, and built up to a rumble that made the floors tremble. Bell choirs, including ours back home, have a beautiful sound, or is that heavenly? One church organist was 93 years young.

Ministers get pretty creative. One compared "*Dixie on my Mind*" by Hank Williams Jr., to "*Egypt on my Mind*" by the Israelites. The story of the Prodigal Son became a complaint letter to Dear Abby about 30 AD. It was signed: "Indignant in Israel." I've stood in Friendship Circles, where everyone in the congregation, spread around the outside of the church interior, and held hands, giving affirmation of faith and singing the benediction.

I sang in a choir in Livingston, Texas, at Christmastime one year. In Yarnell, Arizona, the new church hours hadn't been circulated, so I arrived an hour early. They were starting choir practice, and invited me to join them and sing for the service. I did. I miss singing the "amen" at the end of the hymns. Who made the decision to drop it?

You get the picture. No matter what size the choir or building; no matter what denominational name graces the church front; no matter whether they dunk, dip, or sprinkle; no matter whether it is real wine or grape juice; we are all the family of Christ.

One of the most poignant sermons I have heard is, "Ours are the eyes through which Christ sees the world; He has no hands but ours, with which to heal or offer health and food; no feet but ours, to go to those in need; no ears but ours, to hear the burdened heart; no lips but ours, with which to speak or sing a word of love.

After my husband died, the Thursday night choir practice and Sunday morning practice and service, were my social life and my salvation. I really wouldn't have survived, without the hugs and warmth of my fellow choir members, and friends from church. No matter where or how far I roam, when I return, I go to the First Presbyterian Church on Fourth Street, and color it home.

I will have the very special privilege of flying back to Niles to my own church very soon. Our beloved choir director of forty years, Walter Ginter, is retiring. All present and former choir members are invited to sing on Sunday morning. We all love him so much (and his wife, Sally) that I expect the walls to bulge.

And the last but not the least relationship, animals

He is tall for his species, darkly handsome, soft to the touch, and wiggles all over. His scientific name is "Dogus Unconditional Lovicus." He is wonderful and his owners love him. He and his rolling doghouse are parked next to me. I love him, too, especially if his chain doesn't reach into my space. I totally appreciate him if he only barks for a good reason, doesn't jump all over me, and is generally well behaved. His sister, the cat, only bothers me when she has been allowed out sans any control, jumps onto my roof, and screeches at another cat.

No, I don't hate animals. I grew up with dogs, and my kids grew up with guinea pigs, rabbits, dogs, cats, and goldfish. I choose not to have furry traveling companions because I am selfish. Animals take time and TLC. I have often shared time with people who have to return early, to walk, let out, or feed something. I wouldn't want to leave animals behind without company or relief, for the many hours I choose to be gone. I want to follow my own non-schedule.

I received a lot of flack about the chapter I wrote on animals in *Freedom Unlimited, The Fun and Facts of Fulltime RVing*. I didn't pull any punches about disliking dogs who barked and whined, hour after hour, when their owners left them behind. For that matter, sometimes the owners are inside the RV! My thoughts haven't changed a bit.

Many, many RVers take their animals with them. They are great company. Most RVers keep their animals under control, pick up after them, and make sure they don't disturb anyone. **If you are in this category, you are not the problem**. You can skip this part of the chapter on animals.

For the owner of the dog who is five-foot-six on his hind feet and currently looking down into the baby blues of this five-foot-two silver gypsy, **you should read this chapter**. Don't tell me, "He wouldn't hurt a flea." In case you hadn't noticed, I'm not a flea. And I'll clean my own ears, thank you.

A letter from a reader, confirms how I feel, "My husband and I RV six to eight months a year, and to say we love it, would be an understatement. The only real problem I have found, is unleashed dogs. They **absolutely terrify me** when they come bounding up to me. I never know whether they are friend or foe."

I followed Joanne Lyon, a Volunteer Wilderness Ranger at Snowmass-Maroon Bells Wilderness, on a hike to American Lake. I say "followed" because there was no way I could keep up with her. It is her job to check the trails, answer questions, police wilderness campsites, and carry dog leashes for those who insist their animals will never leave their heels. It is against wilderness policy to have dogs unleashed.

Two hikers stopped her, and complained about a dog running loose, so we had already had a complaint before it, and its owners arrived. Joanne advised them that dogs were to be leashed on the trails. You would not believe the flack they gave this volunteer. She firmly stood up to them, and they did leash their dog. We ran into them again later in the parking lot. They made nasty remarks about her all the while they were getting ready to leave. If I had been her, I would have called in the troops. She had the power to call a ranger and have them arrested.

**So please, when you have a "Dogus Unconditional Lovicus,"
or any other pet traveling with you,
pick up after it, and
don't let it disturb other people.**

A reader wrote about his first RVing experience. He rented an RV. To make it a true test of what his life would be like on the road, he took his sidekick. "Simone is a barn cat who has become my pal and part of my life," he explained. To make a long story short, a very noisy propane furnace frightened Simone, and the first time an opening presented itself, she lit out for parts unknown. Despite a diligent search, Simone was gone and lost forever, lost forever, like Clementine.

Be sure your pet is properly licensed and inoculated. If your vet's name and address is on the inoculation tag, you stand a better chance of getting it back, if it runs away, or is stolen. You can also get a pet ID tag with your name and address on it.

In this marvelous electronic age, you can also have a small microchip implanted under your animal's skin, with identifying information, that may help your pet find its way back to you.

I have always thought that if I ever did succumb to the charms of an animal, it would be a cat. In my mind, they would be easier to travel with, but that is personal preference. This would require a litter box. Some people keep litterboxes in the bathtub.

The neatest idea I ever heard though, was to make an opening from the RV, to inside one of the outside holds, and put the litter box in the outside hold. This way the cat could go in and out at will, and the outside door could be opened to clean the litter box. It gives the cat privacy, and there would be no odor.

Someone else had built a removable box to attach to the window (could be anywhere) in the overhead bed. When they were parked, the cat could be safely outside in the sunshine. People come up with such great ideas.

Keep in mind, that you will need to have places for food and water bowls. Considering I stumble over my own two feet, and am constantly bruised, I don't think I would fare well with extras on the floor.

If you are staying in private campgrounds, you might check with them, or your directory, to see what their restrictions are for animals. A few campgrounds do not allow pets, others put them in sites next to other animal owners, and a few require refundable deposits when you register.

The Leavenworth, Washington, forest fires were close enough that Janet and Bill were advised to vacate the premises. We packed their car and the Sprinter with their treasures. Rebecca was concerned for the silver-haired, blue-eyed (just like Grandma Sharlene) Siamese cat, Sarah. It was Rebecca's duty to keep the cat calm on her first motorhome ride.

All the way to a friend's ranch, out of fire danger, Rebecca repeated her Mom's reassurances, to Sarah, word for word. Disoriented Sarah, soon decided motorhome life wasn't half bad. In her excitement, she lost triple her usual amount of fur. Soon, the motorhome, Sarah, and Grandma Sharlene were all silver-haired.

That night Rebecca bathed in Grandma's tiny bathtub, and had her first lesson in conserving water (she'll make a great boondocker). When she was emulsified and wrapped safely in Grandma's arms, we discussed the fire, and the safety of all Rebecca's loved ones. Sarah curled up at our feet and listened too, at least she "pawsed" to reflect.

With that thought, we'll "pawse" for a trip to the litter box, and then head into Tween Chapter #4 about a town you've probably never heard of but that's part of the fun.

Granddaughter, Rebecca, baking cookies at Grandma's house.

Marble, Colorado

This is another story about getting off the main roads. This little town has special significance you'll recognize.

Marble has more than its fair share of hunks, but it doesn't have manicured lawns or precise buildings. A couple of Victorian houses have survived from another era. Cabins are big, little, old, fixer-uppers, fallen downers. Trucks are as numerous as the cabins, old, new, fallin' apart, kept for parts.

But to those hunks. The Yule River that runs through the town and is known, on occasion, to flood the town, has giant hunks of marble piled along its banks. Great blocks of marble also line the road leading into the town, throughout the town, and in the Meri-Daes RV park. The owner of the campground said, "I'll bet you've never used a marble dump station before." Marble delineates everything in Marble, Colorado, sidewalks, driveways, flower gardens, and parking spots.

What connection does that have with you? The marble taken from these mountains has been used to build public buildings throughout our country. You are more apt to recognize having seen or touched, or been touched by, the Lincoln Memorial, the Washington Monument, and the Tomb of the Unknown Soldier in Washington, D. C. Marble from Marble was used in all of them.

Perhaps you never thought about whence the marble for our public buildings came. I didn't either. It's a tiny town, winter population seventy-five, summer population ninety-five. Marble is off the beaten path, with fewer visitors than resort havens like Aspen or Vail. There isn't a whole lot to do there compared to those places either. Perhaps that's why it appealed to me. It reminds me a bit of Thornton Wilder's "Our Town."

The volunteer fire house sits on the corner by the stop sign where nobody seems to stop. They sell hunks of marble for a donation. A "Be honest" sign admonishes the donor to be somewhat realistic in their donation.

Kitty corner, beyond the stop sign, is Marble's front porch. It belongs to the Marble General Store, elevation 9,560. Most Americans have forgotten how much life passes by when you sit on a front porch. It's a friendly town. Everybody waves whether they know you or not. The paved road, such as it is, ends at the edge of town. The stirred up dust reminded me of walking country roads when I was a kid. Your teeth get gritty.

It was Saturday of Labor Day weekend. A parade of cars and trucks drove down the street. Old Glory flew alongside the Colorado flag. A bulletin board displayed community interests. A lawn mower plugged along in the distance although I hadn't seen any lawns. People stood on the porch eating ice cream cones.

A couple sitting on the long bench drinking pop, at the other end of the porch, were from Washington, D. C. I advised them on things they shouldn't miss, and felt like an old-timer sitting there shooting the breeze. Laughter bounded out the door as David Jones exchanged stories with visitors from all over the country.

Jones, and his wife, Meridith, have owned the store for nineteen years. They sell everything from marble ear rings to marble post cards and heart-carved marble plaques until Labor Day, then close until Memorial Day. They also own the Meri-Daes RV park across the street where that famous marble RV dump resided. The Jones' raised four children in Marble.

As we talked, a lady fed a popsicle to a dog. His tail-wagging, he gently took small bites, then licked the stick as she held it. Everyday life in Marble. I mentioned how relaxing it was to sit there on the porch watching the world go by. David said, "That's just Marble."

The Jones' live in Denver in the winter, but drive to Marble occasionally. The road is kept open for the school bus. "We all come up for Thanksgiving, cut our tree, decorate it and the rest of the house and then close everything up. When we come back for the holiday, we open the door and it's instant Christmas." Jones was a school principal at one time. In his oversized overalls and friendly folksy manner, you'd never guess it.

We talked about local roads. David said, "They're maintained by Mother Nature and she doesn't do much to improve them."

On Sunday morning the church bells ring, calling to a small but devout flock. A different guest minister comes each week. The tiny room was full. The rafters rang with song and prayer; and afterward, everyone gathered in the gazebo under the trees for coffee, juice, treats, and fellowship.

In the afternoon, a brother and sister parked their bikes along the gravel road and went fishing in the Yule River. They waded to the gravel spit in the middle, and fished until drawing mud pictures took their fancy. They dropped that activity for a water fight. They went home with mud up to their armpits, and a wonderful summer day to cherish when they are old enough to appreciate the memory. That kind of carefree day should be bottled for every kid in the world to enjoy at least once in a lifetime.

Sitting on the Yule River Bridge was almost as good a people-watching place, as the porch at the general store. The clouds moved so fast they made me dizzy

The bridge supports a bright orange caution sign you can't miss, "Travel at your own risk. Speed limit 10 mph." It leads to the marble quarry, a steep, narrow gravel road, one where you quickly develop an attitude of constant prayer. Beyond the parking lot at the locked mine gate, the path winds along the rushing Yule River. A railing on the bridge over the ravine was a little iffy.

Arrows pointed a path through a jumbled array of marble that had cascaded from the mine above. The switchback path paralleled a fence signed with, "Danger, do not climb on rocks. This is an active dump site." Of course you needn't heed the signs. At the very least, if something shifted, your friends would be comforted to know you had a headstone of the most magnificent marble...lots of it.

Great weathered canvas curtains were gathered to the sides of the mine like the entrance to a grand stage. I looked into the "maw" of Marble Mountain. It was awesome. An enormous marble room had stairsteps leading to various levels. Through the barbed wire intruder barrier, I saw ledges and dynamite markings where the blocks had reluctantly come off the wall. It is cut in twenty-ton blocks, trucked to Glenwood Springs, and shipped to a mill.

Sans workers in the still-operating mine, there were no sounds save the hollow, eeriness of the slight wind stirring the giant ragged curtains. Silence in a marble world.

Outside, I climbed the chunks of stark white marble and surveyed the valley below me. I thought about having touched the cold marble of Lincoln's tomb, and the Tomb of the Unknown Soldier in Washington D. C. and now being here, where it was produced. Impressive. The sun was making its way over the mountain, bringing the heat of the day with it. It was time to drive back down before visitors wanted to share that narrow road.

"Danger!" signs warned of avalanche activity. Raw new springtime avalanche paths, had shorn timber like matchsticks, and strewn it down the mountainside. The, "10 MPH," well, going up I couldn't, going down I wouldn't. The aspen groves were beginning to look a lot like autumn. Industrious beavers swam in their ponds; marmots posed on the rocks.

I dropped in at the Crystal River Way Station Restaurant, intending to have a cup of coffee. The minute I was inside, I knew I was hooked. A porch with a latticed roof, overlooking a valley, beckoned me to an outside table.

The menu informed me, "Our objective is to provide a relaxing, friendly atmosphere to nourish the spirit as well as feed the body." John, the cook, had aspirations of becoming a great chef. Everyone should follow their dreams, I can vouch for that, and if breakfast was any indication of his talents, he'd make it. Two eggs, home-fried potatoes, toast, and a bottomless cup of coffee, plus a pleasant smile and conversation for $3.75. John asked if I enjoyed my breakfast. I said, "I'd hire you in a minute."

Mailboxes lined the front of the Beaver Lake Lodge and the bait shop. The only phone in town was on the porch. Souvenirs are available at Sneeze Weeds Store. The Raspberry Ridge Bed & Breakfast, caters to folks not lucky enough to have their home on wheels, like me. The Lost Trail Studio and Gallery, had working artists in residence. Unique businesses are finding their way to this inland town.

Marble's attractions included four-wheel-drive-jeep tours to Crystal City and Lead King Basin. The driver, tall and lanky Bob Cook, was multi-talented. Before building his own cabin half way up the quarry road, he built his own boat and sailed all over the world. Now he teaches Tai Chi and Kung Fu six nights a week, and is a four-year veteran driving these "Oil Pan Paranoia" roads.

Several times when I offered to get out to walk, he said, "This is the good part." He proved to be right. The four-wheeled vehicle, with its six-ply, heavy-duty truck tires, climbed huge boulders and steep, narrow inclines and of course plowed unconcernedly through streams and gullies.

I asked if he ever got scared and he said, "No, but sometimes I have to pay attention." That helped my confidence. I clutched my Power Bar, my water and my sparse lunch, on what seemed at times like a deep sea voyage with eight and ten-foot waves. Sometimes only the sky was in view; sometimes I saw only ground. Occasionally, Bob leaned out the door to watch the placement of his wheels, and make sure we didn't slide over the edge. Wise decision.

Asters, daisies, fireweed, and red skyrockets carpeted the meadows. Old snow stuck in the bowls and clefts of the mountains. The highlight of the Lead King Basin was a picnic under a magnificent blue sky with white billowy clouds next to a roaring waterfall.

The excitement of the second tour, was stopping at Crystal Mill, one of earliest mills built on the Crystal River. I had seen pictures of it for years, but never knew where it was. Bob's area stories, both historical and recent, plus his driving expertise on unbelievable and seemingly non-existent roads, completed a great adventure at Marble, Colorado.

That's about it, folks. If you want a really neat adventure, you'll have to leave the Interstate to get it. And if you want fancy, don't go to Marble. If it ever gets that way, don't tell me about it. God Bless.

Crystal Mill, Colorado

SAFETY AND COMFORT

ALWAYS BE AWARE OF YOUR SURROUNDINGS

⇒ Never display your money in public. You never know who is watching.
⇒ If you want to sleep with the window open, wedge a bar in the track, and leave the opening small. Sleep with your head at the opposite end.
⇒ If you use an ATM machine, either find one that is inside a business, be exceptionally aware of your surroundings, or last but not least, be sure it is in a well-lit area. Recently people were arrested for reading PIN numbers with binoculars, a block away from the bank.
⇒ If you aren't happy about where you are leaving your rig, and you have no choice, leave a light on, play a radio talk show, or leave most of the drapes closed.
⇒ Lock your RV when you are filling with gasoline.
⇒ Park with your RV door toward the business you are going into.
⇒ Do not leave anything of any value, where it can be seen from the window of your car, or RV.
⇒ If you don't have a deadbolt on your RV, put one on.
⇒ Shut off all propane (water heater, ceramic heater, stove, refrigerator, etc.) before you go into a station to fill with gasoline or propane
⇒ Keep flares, and a small fire extinguisher, where they can be easily reached somewhere outside of the RV.

This story relates to being aware of your surroundings. I was parked with friends, Jan and Hoagy Carmichael, near Buckeye, Arizona, for a couple of weeks. They were in the middle of the desert, property-sitting for another couple, while they worked on their bus conversion. Another couple was visiting, also.

We all went walking after dinner, but one fellow decided to return to his RV early, and took a shortcut through the brush. He suddenly came bounding back out of those weeds. We looked up and saw an enormous rattlesnake, curled and ready to strike, with his head high in the air. Neither the guy nor the snake, were happy campers. He threw a rock at the snake, and the snake wiggled and writhed away, in an indignant huff.

The fellow was all right, but a little shook up. I had never seen a rattle-snake in all the time I've lived and traveled in Mexico, in the south, or southwest, except once, on the highway. It certainly made the rest of us very aware of where we were walking after that.

Basic First Aid stuff for your medicine chest

Chances are, you already have these items to transfer from your house into your RV. It is a good idea to have the basics.

♥ Adhesive bandages
♥ Gauze bandages rolls
♥ Epinephrine auto injector (Prescription for anyone who has a severe, allergy to stings)
♥ Antiseptic cream
♥ Adhesive tape

If you are making a First Aid kit for your tow vehicle, add

♥ Scissors
♥ Safety Pins
♥ Latex gloves
♥ Cleansing wipes and alcohol swabs
♥ Blanket
♥ Double-bed-size sheet for slings, bandages, transporting
♥ Chemical cold packs
♥ Change for pay phone

Personal Safety

Before I went on the road full time, my children requested I do two things, take a course in self-protection and CPR. I also took a first aid course. I have reinforced those a couple of times since.

Make a call to your local (before you leave) American Heart Association, or the American Red Cross, to find out where they are giving free CPR classes. Make sure your spouse goes, too. You can save each other! Some-times campgrounds have someone come in to teach classes (even after you're on the road).

I do not have one, and haven't tried the CPR Prompt Rescue & Practice Aid, manufactured by County Line Ltd., but I have read about it, and it makes sense to me. It walks you through life-saving techniques for twelve different kinds of emergencies. It operates on batteries, and provides up to twenty-two hours of talking time. It costs $99.95. (Resources)

Shell Oil Company puts out a small booklet, "On-the-Road First Aid." It should be in everybody's glove compartment. They put out a series of *Shell Answer Books* including:

Guard against attack in and around your car
How to get more miles per gallon
How to be a smarter driver
How to drive safely in bad weather (Resources)

Identification

Put your name, address, and phone number; information about any special physical problems; pertinent medical history; allergies; blood type; current medications (and dosages); doctor's name and phone number; and name and address of two people to contact in case of an emergency (spouse, and another), on a card. Put this information where it can be easily found, in the glove compartment, a purse, or wallet.

Put the name, address, and phone number of the current campground your "home" is in, on a sticky note (easily changed). Stick it to the dashboard of your tow car, when you leave it to go hiking, exploring, or shopping. As full-timers, our mail-forwarding addresses would leave anyone clueless.

SKPs encourage putting this information in a small plastic container labeled, *Vial of Life*. Tape it underneath the top shelf in the RV refrigerator. A corresponding sticker, with the same name, should be stuck to the outside of the refrigerator door. When emergency personnel see it, they know to look in the refrigerator for further information.

Something that all SKP parks do when you register, is ask for an emergency phone number of someone they can reach, if a camper has a problem. As a single, I especially appreciate it. You have to realize that SKP parks are more "personal" than the average camping place, but it would be a good idea for all parks to ask for that emergency phone number.

Driving Safety

∇ Keep your speed down, for your safety (and everyone else's) -- Speed increases your fuel consumption at the rate of 2% for every mile per hour over 55.

∇ During heavy traffic times, let the land-bound have at it. Stop for a leisurely coffee break, read a book, have a conversation, wash your windshield, or find a campground for the night. Others will be happy you aren't in front of them, and you may avoid a case of apoplexy.

∇ Run with good tires, good alignment, and good tire pressure.

∇ Leave an extra distance between your RV and trucks.

∇ Don't cut in front of trucks.

∇ When you are entering a freeway, be aware of what is happening to that vehicle coming up on your left. Maybe he can't go into the other lane because of someone on his left.

∇ If someone is entering the freeway ahead of you, get in the other lane if possible, or slow down and flash your lights to signal they can go in front of you.

∇ Be aware of blind spots for trucks.

∇ Be aware of buses and trucks swinging to the left to make right turns.

∇ Flash your lights to let truckers, motorhomers, and others, know that they are past you far enough, to safely pull in ahead of you.

∇ When truckers (or anyone) are kind enough to flash their lights to signal you, flash your lights as a thank you, when you are safely back in your lane.

∇ **Don't tailgate.**

Be a courteous driver

When I am driving down mountains or steep hills, I use second gear (or first) to slow the Sprinter. If I still have to use my brakes, and they get hot, I go into a pullout to let them cool down. I also use second (rarely, first) gear to help the Sprinter up, when we're climbing. Keep alert to the signs warning truckers what is ahead. Consider yourself a truck, and follow their rules for staying in the slow lane, when your RV's energy drags.

What do you do in bad weather?

I have a weather radio that is helpful in letting me in on what is going on, in the area where I'm traveling; unless, I can't hear anything because of the weather! If I'm on a main highway where truckers travel, I turn on my CB, and listen to the truckers. While I'm learning what is happening to the weather, I also learn new words to use the next time I am replacing a sewer valve. Think of everything as an advancement.

A battery-operated weather radio is available at Radio Shack for $29.99. If you set the storm alert, the radio begins broadcasting on its own when bad weather approaches.

Listen to the weather forecasts. A **watch** means that severe weather is "**possible**." A **warning means, "It's here**." Avoid bad weather if possible. If you can't, then get off the road. I once drove kitty-cornered across Oklahoma and Kansas, not realizing they were experiencing tornadoes all around me. Like I said, the good Lord looks out after those of us that are dumber'n rocks.

If you hit a heavy rain, find a safe place and get off the road, preferably in a protected spot. If you have no choice but to keep driving, travel at a slower speed. This doesn't mean crawl, but a reasonable speed, so nobody plows into the back of you. If they're going 50 mph, and you slow to 20 mph, and the visibility is low, there's going to be a problem.

It takes one second for every ten foot of vehicle to stop.
If you are going over 40 mph,
add an additional second.
Bad weather requires even greater spacing.

Pick a sign post. Watch the back bumper of the vehicle ahead of you. When it passes the post, count two seconds (one-one-thousand, two-one-thousand). If your bumper passes the sign post before you finish counting, you are too close.

Road signs warn you, in areas where you are likely to encounter wind gusts or crosswinds, but the wind doesn't always read the signs (just like animals). On a windy day, they'll hit ya' right out of the blue. Driving out from an underpass, coming out of a canyon, or any time the highway is no longer protected by something, watch for wind gusts. Semis and buses sometimes cause major turbulence when they go around you. Slow down. If that doesn't help, take a break.

Remember that big lakes and high bridges, are wide open for the wind to come zooming in.

In the wide open country west of the Mississippi, it might seem like the wind is never going to stop, but it is usually calmer in the early morning and early evening. If it doesn't let up, take it easy, stop often. That, too, shall pass.

Just looking at the sky, should put you on the alert to bad weather. If you are in tornado country, keep your ears glued to that radio. In fact, why don't you get off the road, before a problem develops. If you're too late for that, and you see that twister a comin', find shelter for yourselves. That could mean a brick wall, a ditch, or some other low place **outside of your RV**. I've heard tornadoes sound just like a freight train.

I remember one coming over the farm when I was a kid. We were eating stewed tomatoes for lunch. Funny what you remember. The tornado touched down across the creek, and laid a tree down, nice as you please, right there while we watched. We didn't hear it coming, and it disappeared almost before we knew it. If it had hit on our side of the creek, I wouldn't be writing this.

I was on the outskirts of Hurricane Hugo, near Watertown, New York. The hurricane had died down some by the time it got that far north, but Watertown was a mess when I drove through it the next morning. Hurricanes give more warning. Sometimes you can get out before they get to where you are.

Wind, in itself, is bad enough, especially with the broad side of an RV as a target, but you may also find yourself in a sandstorm. Our family once camped in Joshua Tree National Monument. It was windy and sandy, but we were from the Midwest, we didn't know what we were getting into. When we got to the main highway, we turned east.

The California State Police were keeping traffic from driving into, what we had just driven out of. We drove in from the middle. The sand can do a real number on your vehicle, just one quick sandpaper job. We shook sand out of everything but we had no bad effects.

If there is flooding, don't enter a gully or low spot. Never attempt to drive through water on the road. The highway may have given way underneath the water, and the water may be deeper than it looks.

Flooding can happen anywhere. In desert country, signs are posted warning people not to drive through dry washes, riverbeds, or gullies, with water in them. Don't park your RV in them, even when they are dry. It could be beautiful weather where you are, but up in the mountains, miles away, it could be pouring rain. Water is funneled through low points in the desert. Many people have drowned, miscalculating flash floods.

If flooding is coming, and you have no way to avoid it, scramble for high country. If this means leaving your vehicle, do it. We think we are so strong and safe in our RVs. That may be true most of the time, but neither we, nor our RVs, are a match for the forces of nature.

As full-time RVers, you probably can avoid this one, but not always. Most of us follow the sun, but I recall I was following the sun the time I was caught in one whale of a blizzard for two days going through Amarillo, Texas. If possible, get off the road when it appears there will be an accumulation, not just anywhere, but in a town, service station, or mall, and stay put.

If you are caught in a blizzard, and you are immobilized, stay in your RV and wait. If you are using a forced air propane furnace, only use it if you absolutely have to. It will run your batteries down in a hurry. If you have a generator, and you have enough gasoline, use it when you want to run the furnace. Make sure the exhaust pipes are clear of snow. Lucky for you, at least in an RV, you usually have food to last for a while.

I have driven in my share of snow and icy conditions. The Sprinter holds well to the road, but I know, once it starts sliding, it will go where it wants to. Don't chew on the bumper of the guy ahead of you. It's going to take you a lot longer to stop. For one thing, you don't want to be forced into slamming on your brakes, or you will lose it for sure. Make your stops easy ones, steer into a slide, and get off the road if possible. We're full-timers, remember. Find a place to hole up for a while. Let the land-bound have at it while you read a book, eat popcorn, or sleep.

For that matter, I don't find it all that comfortable driving in the extreme heat. I like to park during the heat of a scorching day, and drive in the evening and early morning. I know there are a few RVers around who don't like to get up in the morning, but it's a great time to watch the world wake up.

If you are in an earthquake, stop driving, avoid buildings, overpasses and utility wires. Stay put until the shaking stops, then avoid bridges, and elevated structures.

When I went back to Michigan a few years ago, I parked in my former neighbor's yard. In the night, we got one of those wild, electrical storms Michigan gets once in a while. With the rubber tires, I was probably as safe as I could be anywhere. I was next to some trees, but not high ones, that would have fallen on me. I did, however, get out of the upper bunk over the driver's seat, and sleep (well, maybe not much) on the couch.

One of the first things I do, is pull the electric plugs. All I need is a burned out computer. If you have an antenna up, put it down. This is one time you have permission to be as small, and as low, as you can be.

All this brings to mind, that you might be out in your tow vehicle when the weather gets bad. Make sure you have proper supplies with you. Whenever I take off, I have a blanket (I throw it over the "stuff" I keep in my mobile garage). I also keep a very small, lightweight package that has a silver "space" blanket in it, tucked in the car somewhere. A gallon of water is good to have on hand, for a thirsting you, or a thirsting vehicle. A shovel lives underneath that blanket, and when I remember to replace it, I also have matches and fire starter.

It all goes back to the Girl Scouts.

Be Aware
Be Alert
Be Prepared

Lights

I wipe them off frequently in bad weather. I wipe them off when I walk around the rig to check things out.

In Minnesota, I had driven off I-90 to visit a former Girl Scout. During the evening, it began to rain. When I left it was dark, and the rain had become a deluge. The pavement was new. It hadn't yet been painted with the yellow line in the middle, or the white line along the edge. The pavement was new enough that the shoulders were packed for parking on. That was when Murphy's law reared its ugly head, and one of my headlights went out. I don't remember how many miles it was to the freeway, but it seemed like forever.

I knew there was a rest area just on to the freeway. I reached that and stopped for the night. I carry spare lights, but between road, weather, and nighttime conditions, I couldn't have changed it then anyway.

Guns

Many people ask me if I am afraid to travel alone. No, I'm not, but I do try to use my head about where I go, stop, and stay. If I boondock going across country, I try to park where there are other RVers or trucks. This hasn't always worked out. When I am completely alone, either along the highway or in the forest or mountains, I keep a lower profile than usual, until I am familiar with the area.

The next question is always, "Do you carry a gun?" No, for many reasons. First of all, I don't know enough about guns. I would probably shoot myself in the foot, and then I couldn't even run away.

If you are going to carry a gun, make sure it is legal, and be sure you know how to use it correctly. If you use it, be prepared to suffer the consequences. The laws have a way of backfiring, even when you are protecting yourself, or loves ones. Before you know it, you are behind bars, instead of the criminal who started the whole problem.

When I first started RVing, a friend offered to help me choose a gun, do whatever was necessary to make it legal, and teach me how to use it. Before he would tackle that project, he said he wanted one thing, "Promise me that if you ever point it at someone, you will shoot to kill." I thought about that and realized I couldn't answer honestly whether I would or not. I believe that if my life was threatened, I would have no problem shooting to kill. I would more likely injure them, and that is more dangerous.

The other reason I don't carry a gun, is that I travel in Mexico, and if they catch you with a gun, you may never see the light of day again. We'll discuss guns in the Mexico/Canada chapter.

The one factor in the favor of the RVer, is that unless someone has been watching a rig for a long time, no-one knows how many are inside. They don't know if you have a weapon, a dog, tiger, or attack rabbit.

Those bent on mayhem, like "<u>easy</u>" targets. Even if it's an illusion, make it seem like it would be a problem if they had the audacity to even touch your rolling palace.

Keeping a low profile

When I need to use the phone, and there is a single vehicle and/or person nearby, I have talked to this mythical person inside as I am closing the door, perhaps even opening it again and saying, "What?"

I can't stress strongly enough, that this applies to couples, as well as singles. Couples are nearly as vulnerable as singles. Many ploys are used to make RVs seem less desirable to break into. Some singles carry a blown up figure in the navigator's seat, a hat on the dash, a dog's dish outside, or rig up a recording with a dog barking.

I'm not so sure it matters in a formal campground, but it isn't a good idea to put out the cutsey little signs with your names on it. Someone could call out your name. Thinking you know them, you might open the door. Always look through the window first, before opening the door to anyone. At night, turn on the outside light. If you are not in a campground, turn the inside lights off and the outside light on, before you open a curtain to look. You can see them but they can't see you.

It would be pretty difficult for someone to get inside your RV undetected, with you inside (even if you have a forty footer). Read ads in the back of camping magazines, or in camping merchandise magazines, you'll get scads of ideas for burglar alarms.

Even when I am in a formal campground, which is relatively safe, I lock doors. It has become such a habit. It is a good idea to keep doors and windows locked, especially outside of a campground. Since my rig has reached senior citizen status, the door sometimes flies open when I am on the move, another good reason to lock it

If I am not in a designated campground, I park so I can move forward. I keep a key in the ignition, ready for flight. A vehicle could park in front of me, but I could do a lot of damage to it, before it stopped me, and I would.

I went to a writer's conference in downtown Muncie, Indiana, and parked in a big parking lot belonging to the hotel. Everything was fine until Friday night. I was awakened at I a.m. by police cars with sirens blasting, people screaming obscenities, and everybody running around. I moved to a closer parking lot. I didn't get much sleep with strange activity going on the rest of the night.

Don't ask for trouble by parking on a city street in a broken down part of town. Having told you that story, I'll say,

Avoid High-Crime Areas.

Singles should carry two folding chairs to put outside, rather than just one. The extra one comes in handy for visiting RVers anyway. When you are boondocking, it is a good idea to keep your gear, including chairs, put away or locked up. Our family once had a bike stolen from the very middle of ten Girl Scout tents in a circle, right in front of our tent. It is easy to steal away with small, or rolling items, under cover of darkness.

I have heard of a couple who were startled in the middle of a hot summer night, by a screen being cut. They were able to get the window shut before anything happened. If I need to have windows open, I put wooden dowels in the window track, so it is blocked to open only a few inches.

It is amazing how RVers look out for each other. I was parked at my Coast to Coast park, Emerald Cove, near Parker, Arizona. Some days I get up early, and work on the computer, not turning on lights, or opening drapes, until as late as 10 a.m. One morning, a knock came on the door. It was the kind gentleman from next door. He and his wife had not seen me all morning and wanted to make sure I was all right. People are good.

No matter what safety measures you follow, no one can promise you will be <u>completely safe</u> in the full-time RVing lifestyle. No one can promise you'll be <u>completely safe anywhere</u>. Always be aware of your personal safety, then the safety of your vehicle. Cut your vulnerability, but at the same time, don't be boxed in by fear. Don't let the criminals and crazies of this world, put you in a little box. If you do, they win! The other thing is, don't break the law yourself.

When I "take off," I put everything where it belongs. I bungy strap equipment, shut cupboards securely, and generally make sure that nothing will fall on the floor, or fly through the air. I have gotten more cavalier with how I "secure" my belongings through the years. I really hate to put projects completely away, until I am through with them.

Then I read about a collision someone had with their RV, and it really brought me up short. No one was hurt in the accident; but, she talked about items being thrown around the RV. Doors flew open, mirrors came off the wall, and everything became a dangerous, fast-moving missile, searching for a target. Obviously, we can't prevent some things from flying around, but it made me think more seriously about storing everything possible where it belongs, before I roll on down the highway.

Reduce the risk
put it away or fasten it down

Fire Safety

The Sprinter came with a small fire extinguisher housed in a cave in the wall, next to the outside door. I replaced it with a big one that rides behind the driver's seat. From time to time, I change its position from upright to flat and back again, to keep the powder from compacting.

Check your extinguishers. Do the gauges read full? Are the dates current? If not, take it to a refill center. If they'll let you, discharge it yourself. That way you'll learn how to handle it.

Think about all the emergency possibilities, fire, overturning, being hit by another vehicle, flooding. Where are the emergency exits? Vent? Window? Can you get through them? Where are the fire extinguishers? Make a "plan of escape," whether you are traveling alone, or as a couple, and more especially, if you have children with you. In panic, people often do the wrong thing.

This is especially important: If you discover a fire, scream. In the tight quarters of the campground, your neighbors might be in as much danger as you are. Bang on their door or the side of their RV.

Being often in different campgrounds, take the time in each place, to know where the phone is located, and how to explain to emergency people, where you are. Do the other people in your RV know how to use the CB? Cell phone? Call 911? Is everyone familiar with the Stop, Drop, and Roll rule? (Stay where you are, cross your arms across your chest, drop to the floor (or ground), and roll over and over slowly, to put out the flames.) What would you do if the RV next to you had a fire?

When I was traveling on the Blue Ridge Parkway in Virginia, a few years ago, an embankment was on fire. People were slapping at it with towels. It wasn't working. One person called the fire department with my CB, and others used my fire extinguishers to put it out. You never know when you can provide help, even if the emergency doesn't involve you or your RV.

Last fall, I came in soaking wet from a rainy beach walk. I quickly lit the stove, plopped the teakettle on it, and stepped into the bedroom to peel off my wet clothes. I smelled something awful. I opened the curtain and smoke was rolling. Fire was flaming all around the teakettle. I shut off the propane burner, and doused the kettle in the sink. When I had picked up the teakettle, the pad beneath it had stuck to it.

The problem was limited to the stench, the loss of a rubber pad, and a blackened kettle bottom. It is so easy to create an emergency. Keep baking soda within reach for fires in the kitchen.

Safety is important in any kitchen; but, in an RV kitchen, where space is extremely limited, it is really necessary. Keep cooking pan handles turned over the counter. Be careful not to catch a sleeve (nightgowns and robes) in the flame.

My extinguisher is a KIDDE A-B-C, multi-purpose, dry chemical type. It is for all common classes of fires, wood, paper, cloth, flammable liquid, and electrical. It is guaranteed against pressure loss for six years. The easily-read instructions, are printed on the side. A hose is included with instructions to aim at the base of the fire, and "Stand back eight feet." That might be a little difficult depending on where it is, but then they are talking house, not RV. It has an all-metal head and valve.

It's a good thing I'm writing this book. I'm ashamed to say, I hadn't really **looked** at mine for a long time. I re-read the instructions, and checked to see if the arrow still pointed to the green light. It did.

Don't neglect fire extinguishers, they are important.

When you are in a campsite, use a Y connector at your water supply. Connect your clean drinking hose to the RV. Have another hose fastened to the other side of the connector to use in an emergency, either yours or a neighbor's, or for other needs.

I mentioned facetiously about the guys out rubbing and polishing their RVs just to keep busy, but it is more important than that. If you take the time to check all your batteries, hoses, tires, fuel lines, and keep your rig clean, and free of grease, you are less likely to have a fire, at least from those sources.

When your RV is hot from driving a long time, be careful where you park. If dry weeds come in contact with your hot exhaust pipe, they could get hot enough to start a fire. Also be careful of using your generator in this situation.

Never re-enter a burning RV (or anything else).
Don't let anyone else go in either.

Campfires

If you like campfires like I do, there are rules to follow there, too. If campgrounds allow firepits, it will already be established. In boondocking areas, look around. Has a firepit already been set up? If so, use it. If not (and it is permissible), dig a small pit away from trees or bushes, and surround the pit with rocks.

Clear an area a safe distance around the pit, and scrap away litter or natural debris. Keep a bucket of water, and a shovel nearby. Keep your wood stacked away from the fire, and upwind from it. Throw your match into the fire. **Never, never, never leave a fire unattended**. When you are through, put out the fire, and make the firepit disappear before you leave.

It amazes me how often people retire for the night, or drive away, and leave fires burning. You never know when an ill wind will blow into something. **PUT IT OUT!**

Propane

If you smell Gas:
Δ   Extinguish all open flames, pilot lights, and smoking materials
Δ   Do not touch electrical switches
Δ   Shut off gas supply valve or connection
Δ   Open doors, windows, vents
Δ   Go away from the RV until odor clears
Δ   Have the system checked, and problems corrected, before using it again

Propane Sniffer

Have a propane sniffer installed. Mount it low (propane is heavier than air). It will go off if you have a propane leak. It sometimes goes off with gasoline and carbon monoxide fumes, too.

I had one installed when the Sprinter was new. Unfortunately, it went off while I was driving through downtown Seattle, during rush hour traffic. I had no place to get off without getting deeper in traffic trouble. I listened to it squeal for an entire hour, until I could get out of town and off the Interstate. It was set off by traffic fumes.

Unattached vertical DOT cylinders from truck campers, trailers, and fifth wheels, are easily filled. Motorhomes have a horizontal permanent tank. Watch attendants when they fill your tank. A few times I have had to tell them how to do it. Now that's scary! I have had the tank filled in places where I wondered if the attendant, the RV, and I would all soon be on the way to meet our Maker. I go to a propane company, if possible. In the boonies, sometimes you have no choice.

Never let them fill the tank more than 80% full. A faulty automatic shut-off valve was removed from the Sprinter last year. It wouldn't allow the tank to be filled. It shut off at a half gallon. It took four repairmen in different parts of the country, to finally tell me what was wrong. I was told that the valve couldn't be repaired, and the entire tank would have to be replaced. They said it was very expensive, and not necessary. They said when the safety liquid-level valve on the propane hose, shoots escaping liquid, the tank is filled at 80%.

Don't let anyone smoke while they are filling your RV. I actually had a fellow do this once. I told him to put it out. He did, but he said everybody was "paranoid," and that propane wasn't all that dangerous. In my opinion, his life expectancy was zero to zip.

Carbon Monoxide Detector

Have your RV and generator exhaust system checked regularly. Carbon monoxide is odorless and deadly. **You cannot smell it**. Make sure nothing is blocking the exhaust pipe when you use the generator. If you begin to feel "funny" while it is running, shut it off immediately, and get fresh air. Don't take a chance. Have the system checked and repaired, before using it again. Symptoms are:

- Dizziness
- Headache
- Weakness
- Sleepiness
- Muscular twitching
- Inability to think coherently
- Vomiting

Shut your windows and the door, on the side your generator is running, so the fumes don't come in. Be careful parking next to a semi with their engine running. I've had them pull in next to me in a rest area, in the night, and had their exhaust come right in my windows or vent. Fortunately, diesels make enough noise, it always woke me up.

Smoke Alarms

Smoke alarms can be a pain in the gluteus maximum because they tend to go off whenever something is cooked, baked, or burned (often, in my case). They are inexpensive, yet priceless, if they save your life. Test the batteries once a month, and replace them at least once a year.

Tires

Tires are important. If they decide to throw in the towel while you're going down the highway at 55 mph, you could be in trouble. A tire alarm lets you know when a tire has met its demise. If a single tire on your RV bites the dust, it won't take you long to know it. If it's on your tag, or a dual tire, it might take too long for you to realize what has happened. Either situation is a fire waiting to happen. Alarms are expensive but considering the alternative, a good safety device to have on the RV and the tag. (Resources)

I have been fortunate. Although I have found blue smoke coming from a flat I didn't know about, I usually catch flats by "tunking" the tires, and doing a "walk-a-bout" around both vehicles, almost every time I stop.

Usually when I get new tires, I replace them all at once. In Whitehorse, Yukon Territory, last summer, I was advised that two of the tires were still in very good shape, and could be put on the front. I bought four Michelins, instead of six. I had all new ones installed in December of 1992. Considering their rough wear, they are lasting very well.

When you get "new" tires, check to see that they really are new. Read the last three numbers of the DOT number on the sidewall of your tire. The first two numbers are the calendar week of the year they were made. The third number is the last digit of the year they were manufactured. According to the 382 on my front tires, they were manufactured in the 38th week of 1992. I was lucky. Sometimes when you buy "new" tires, they are much older than the date you actually purchase them.

We talked about levelers in Chapter 5. This is very important, as is making sure your RV is in proper alignment. Check out your springs and make sure your air bags are filled if you have them.

Often when people are parked for any length of time, they cover their tires with burlap, cardboard, plywood, or commercial covers. The sun, especially in the sunbelt, is extremely strong, and will do a number on your rubber tires. Keep your dashboard covered against sun damage, as well.

Animal Alert warning signals

A set of Animal Alert warning signals live on both the RV and the car. I have seen a lot of deer, elk, buffalo, sheep, caribou, moose, bear, ocelot, and large spiders on the edge of the road. Either these gadgets work, or it just wasn't their turn to walk in front of the Sprinter or the Little Lynx.

Getting Goosed

Hazards come in all forms. Janet and Bill and Rebecca were visiting me at a Coast to Coast park near Orick, California. Every time we left the Sprinter, this goose couple were on the road. The male would strut my direction, hissing, and then really come after me. I kept him at bay with a foot or my purse. He was an ornery cuss, but I didn't let him push me around. (I am woman!) I came back to the motorhome from somewhere and the kids were all excited because the goose had knocked on the door. Yeah right. I didn't just fall off the turnip truck. They've played too many tricks on Mom.

The day after they left, I was working on my computer. In the middle of great frustration at something it wouldn't do, I heard a knock on the door. I looked out the window and the goose pair were outside my door. The female was knocking by biting the door. They were looking for a handout. I kid you not. I was forced to believe.

Bugs

A couple of years ago, I picked up a colony of ants while I was parked in my brother, Leo's, woodsy, back-forty campground. I took them all the way to Colorado. Ant traps and poisons weren't effective. They either avoided it or enjoyed it. On the advice of friends, I sprinkled Comet around the wheels. This sort of worked. It didn't keep them out, but they cleaned the sink as they tromped through it.

I tried the red pepper flakes idea to keep ants away. That didn't work either, and their "God bless yous" kept me awake all night. They finally packed up and left. I was leaving the mountains and they didn't want to go with me.

I recently read that spraying with WD-40, or sprinkling Borax around the tires, discourages ants. I've stored that knowledge in my memory bank for later use (Now if I could just remember where my memory bank is). I've only had one or two bouts with ants.

One of my remedies to keep ants out (before they get in) is to put petroleum jelly around the hoses and light cord, to keep them from crawling up that nice long round path into the RV. The last time I did it, I forgot it. When I started rolling the hose, I got caught in it. That only proves the method works, I'm an aunt. After all, petroleum jelly doesn't have a brain, it doesn't know the difference between ant and aunt...oh, forget it. You have to remember to wipe it off.

Mice are the problem. As soon as I'm parked, they put out a newsletter and call everyone to a family reunion in Minshall's Hotel Wheels. I have used so much foam in the front of the motorhome, I hardly have room for my feet to maneuver the footpedals. One of these days.

Being outside, and in out-of-the-way places so much, I am very aware of safety. A few friends and relatives wouldn't agree with that, but what do they know. All RVers who follow the sun and like hiking, swimming or just *being* in the outdoors, should prepare themselves by having good information on how to survive whatever lives there. I highly recommend Sawyer's "A Practical Guide to Outdoor Protection." It really gave me insight into overly friendly bugs that sting, bite, burrow, or would otherwise make my life a living heck.

It is a comprehensive guide covering bites and stings; sun, wind and cold exposure; and poison from ivy, oak, or sumac leaves. It gives the backgrounds of each creature or plant, their location, how to prevent exposure, and what to do if you are exposed. It describes spiders and what they will or will not do. Each subject has a likeness drawn. If you see a blank space, it is probably a "no-see-um" picture. They are extremely difficult to draw because nobody sees them, and they don't sit still for very long.

These seventy pages get right down to the nitty-gritty, with prevention sections listing the dos and don'ts. A loose-leaf binder makes it easy to keep the book open to a particular page -- handy, if you are consulting it while fighting a Portuguese man-of-war or wrestling with 747-sized mosquitoes.

The book advises on choosing repellents and how they work. It tells how to select a sun block, and the type needed for different altitudes and latitudes.

I was concerned with ticks and Lyme disease. The book states, "The blood test designed to diagnose Lyme disease is not 100% effective. If you suspect Lyme, be persistent in seeking medical advice."

After hiking through tall grass along the shoreline in Redwoods National Park, I found a tick had burrowed his way into my life. I put clear nail polish on the tick. He backed out, then suffocated. I removed it with tick pliers and put him in a plastic bag. The nail polish perfectly preserved him. Of course, if I had read the book, I would have known I shouldn't have used nail polish or Vaseline.

You're also not supposed to dislodge them like we did as kids. We lit matches to their backsides to make them back out. I wonder if my brothers were really trying to get rid of my ticks. Hmmm.

The National Park Rangers suggested I see a doctor. He examined the tick and me with equal interest which doesn't say much for my scintillating personality as compared to a dead tick. He declared I would probably live. He prescribed Doxycycline, which broken down, didn't sound so good and the mile-long side effects included, in capital letters, IF YOU PLAN ON BECOMING PREGNANT.... On the positive side, if it didn't give me a severe skin reaction to the sun, diarrhea, nausea, vomiting, or an upset stomach, I might experience loss of appetite. The latter in itself might have been worth getting ticked.

When I finally reached my own doctor, I had a blood test and Lyme disease was not found. After three years, however, the red spot where the tick burrowed in, is still quite prominent.

The following are a few tips, but get a brochure or booklet, with full particulars on ticks, and other nasty beasties, before you spend much time outside your RV. (Resources)

* First you might try to avoid tick areas during tick season. Stay on paths or roads. Most of the time, you get ticks by walking through weeds or vegetation. According to what I read, they do not fall from trees (and usually not from the sky). You may find them in your hair because they crawl upward.

* Light colors and long sleeves are best to wear so that you can see these tiny, dark creatures. Wear your shirt tucked in and your pants into your socks. Cover all exposed skin if possible. This gets to be a survival problem in itself during 90 degree heat.

* Apply lotion repellent to exposed skin and spray repellent to clothing. I won't advise any particular kind or the amount of Deet because this

seems to change from time to time. Be aware that safe amounts are different for children.

* Do frequent tick checks. If you have a tick buddy (as in you can check each other), you are ahead of the game and besides it could be fun (depending on the buddy, of course).

* Immediately remove ticks. Grasp the tick firmly and as close to the skin as possible, using Tick Pliers™, tweezers, or thumb and forefinger (using tissue or rubber gloves).

Mosquitoes

Mosquitoes and I don't get along awfully well. I keep repellent on hand. Everybody is different but you'll probably need it from time to time. Some of these hints came from the National Park Service:

- Don't wear perfume or other scented products.
- Don't sweat, the chemicals on your skin calls to bugs
- Do not drink alcohol. Flushing skin with blood and sweetening its odor attracts bugs.
- Do not breathe. The carbon dioxide you exhale will draw insects from miles away.
- Eat a clove of garlic every day for a week before and during your vacation. (That will keep the bugs and humans away!)
- This might work, too. Take a chlorine-bleach bath with one capful per tub to keep insects away for 24 hours. (They are less likely to find you in the bathtub anyway.)
- Other unusual products: Put toothpaste on insect bites and stings to stop the itch. A product called *After-Bite* is great for bug bites.
- Wear light colors or pastels. Insects are attracted to bright, patterned or dark clothing.
- In grassy, brushy or wooded areas, wear tightly woven fabric.
- Tuck your pant legs in your socks and your long-sleeved shirt into your pants.
- Wear a hat.
- Check yourself for ticks after every outing. (It's more fun if you check each other.)
- Only female mosquitoes draw blood so if you see one wearing a skirt, smack her before she gets you.

If you are still bugged, go on to the next chapter about attitude.

ATTITUDE, LATITUDE, AND GRATITUDE

Attitude

Okay, you've made up your mind. You want to be a full-time RVer. You've bought your RV. It's time to pack.

> **The first thing you should always pack is a sense of humor.**
> **If there are two or more of you,**
> **pack your senses of humor.**
> **Next,**
> **Pack your common sense.**
> **Next,**
> **Pack the rest of your senses.**
> **Next,**
> **Pack your dollars and cents.**
> **And now that I have put my two-cents worth in...**

I have a tendency to get upset about things when they happen. Sooner or later, I look at them as fodder for stories, then I can see the humor. Be prepared. Be open minded.

We've already talked about getting along in the confines of an RV, in an earlier chapter. The good thing about RVing, is that if you follow the sun, you will be outside more. Even though you are married (or not), nothing is carved anywhere, that says you must do every single activity together. It is nice if you each get involved in a different activity, once in a while, or pursue your own hobby interests.

Be honest with each other. If you wake up on the wrong side of the bed, tell your mate you are having a bad day. Sometimes just bringing that out in the open, makes you feel better. We aren't mind readers, although after living together for many years, we think our mates should know exactly how we feel. Tain't so. Have some honest communication.

Laughing

Did you know that laughing is one of the most important stay-healthy exercises? It is also a really wonderful thing to listen to (if it isn't too long and loud). I love to hear a little kid get tickled about something. They laugh from the tips of their souls and toes. We need to do that once in a while, too. It gives you such a good feeling to have a really good belly laugh, one of those where you have a hard time stopping, the kind that brings tears.

According to an article in <u>USA Weekend</u>, June 1, 1997, a laugh a day, might even keep the doctor away. Laughter has great healing possibilities. If it is that potent, think what at least one good laugh a day, will do for you. You're already healthy. Maybe it will help you stay that way. We never know how we affect other people. Maybe your laughter will bring joy into someone else's life. Isn't it great? Maybe you'll start a domino effect!

Speaking of domino effect, have you ever noticed how quickly smiles are passed on if you start one. Let's not forget hugs either. I love hugs. That's what I like about being a SKP. We are a huggin' bunch. Some people don't like that close contact, so I try to respect that, but hugs give me a warm, fuzzy feeling. If the hug-giver happens to be 5' 10", blue-eyed, silver-haired, and single, that's even better!

Just think what the world would be like if we each passed just those three things on to two other people every day, a laugh, a smile, and a hug. What wonders we would behold.

One more thing about attitude--I recently wrote an article about turning sixty. The exercises I put in the article might help us all.

Get out of bed, march into the bathroom, and look in the mirror (perhaps, one other activity first. At our ages, let's be practical). It might also be wise to comb your hair first (or put it on). I tend to look a little frightening at first light, like a silver witch caught in a wind tunnel. Look in the mirror and grin (put your teeth in first--you don't want to scare yourself to death before the exercise).

There now, look deep into your eyes (put your glasses on first--I have to take mine off to see anything up close). Don't scream, just say with great passion, **"I love you."** I mean, if you don't love yourself, who's going to, besides God, and he loves us all regardless. Doesn't that feel good? No, well tough turkeys, babycakes, maybe you can try it again after you've had your coffee (I absolutely refuse to let the grumps in this life get me down).

We full-time RVers are a privileged bunch. We should wake up every day with an enormous grin on our faces. Yes, we're getting older every day, but what a great way to do it. I guess it boils down to enjoying whatever age you are, and living life to the fullest each day. Remember, we may not like advancing birthdays, but one good thing about them, they force you to get up in the morning, 'cause you ain't dead yet.

Latitude

Webster says latitude is, "The extent or distance from side to side; WIDTH." My latitude is stretching.

Nutrition is a good subject to tell RVers about, considering it concerns everyone. Since the FDA stamped my Sprinter hood with "McMinshall's fast foods and/or cooking habits may be injurious to your health," I'm not too confident. Actually, the CIA got involved when it was reported the food in my refrigerator had been there long enough to start fourteen cultures, thirty-two colonies, and three new countries.

Nutrition is important. I know this. Keeping our weight down is important. I know this. There should be a way to combine the two, without so much suffering. If we can put a man on the moon, why can't we make dieting and good nutrition, an easier combination?

Chocoholism is overwhelmingly present in our world. Why hasn't some enterprising, brilliant scientist, found a way to present vegetables disguised as chocolate? Throw out the cherries. Make chocolate-covered brussel sprouts. They're even the right shape. They make huckleberry fudge, for Pete's sake. Why not string bean spumoni? Parsnip preserves? Cauliflower cake? Chick-pea pie?

Why is breakfast my favorite meal? Because guilt and visions of my sainted mother, do not make me order vegetables!

Instead of asking questions nobody can answer, I am chastised by all the magazine articles on weight and nutrition, to adjust my mental attitude. Think thin. Eat in moderation. Exercise and focus on living a healthier lifestyle. Right! All good points, along with a hundred others I've read, and tried, through the years.

It all works to a degree. I start the day with oatmeal for lowering my cholesterol; non-fat, low-sodium, vegetable soups for lunch with baked, no cholesterol crackers, and a diet, caffeine-free soda, for a snack in the late afternoon. That leaves evening.

I'm convinced dieting, or eating balanced meals, would be easier, no, make that possible, if I threw out the TV. I'm tired in the evening. I've slaved all day in front of a hot computer (Do I hear violins?). I like to forget myself in a good movie. Movies have commercials. Commercials are about food. By the time the evening is over, I've eaten everything that doesn't run away (even if I have to create it -- that's desperation), and the pizza man is knocking on the RV door.

With living in a motorhome, especially alone, everything takes on a different light. I talk to myself a lot. I talk to my surroundings a lot. The refrigerator has taken on a personality. He has become my friend. His tone is seductive. When he says, "Hey, baby, come on over for a snack," I don't want to hurt his feelings.

They say you should maintain a stable weight. I do. I weigh as much as a horse. I've even started using "Mane 'n Tail" shampoo (I'm not kidding, I love it). The articles all say success depends on your focus. They say, "Focus on talking rather than eating." That's fine, unless you're talking to your refrigerator.

A friend of mine refuses to eat any of the diet foods. He claims it tastes like cardboard. So? I like cardboard. It beats the usual taste of my cooking. (I haven't cooked for him yet!)

My daughter joined a national dieting chain. I thought if I followed her menu portions, I could lose a few unwanted pounds. She poured her pre-measured cereal into my bowl. Good gravy! It barely covered the bottom. Cereal is my staple. I love cereal. I eat it for main meals, Sunday dinner, and holiday feasts. My bowl is one of those fourteen-inch-in-diameter soup bowls with six-inch sides, and I fill that hummer to the brim. But then again, now I know what the problem is.

"They" have come up with so many slogans through the years, one being, "You are what you eat." Have you ever thought about life as a collard green? That's enough to scare you to death. Death does make one thinner. I do eat a lot of bananas. Does that mean I'm "potassified" or I have appeal? Sorry.

Let's get serious

Take care of your health. At our ages (any time after twenty), our bodies are beginning to break down. Eating properly, and getting exercise, makes a definite difference in how long nature takes to bring us to our knees. Good health also means we can pursue the things we really like to do, like RVing.

Eat foods with the lowest fat and calorie content
Cut back on between-meal snacks
Drink eight glasses of water a day
Eat lots of fruits and vegetables
Exercise regularly

(And don't make friends with your refrigerator)

Exercise

Watching people is a revelation. I've done this myself but usually not. They drive around and around and around, looking for a parking space immediately on top of whatever establishment they are seeking, rather than park three blocks away and walk. On the way back to the RV park, they exercise at the local gym.

A NordicTrack Sequoia, a ski-type exercise machine, lives on the pedestal, that used to hold the couch. I use it faithfully (for a month at a time). Something always manages to distract me from my appointed skiing, like wild flowers growing or dust accumulating. Actually, I do quite well with it, if I use it while I'm watching TV. That way I concentrate on the program, and not my sobbing cellulite

My preferred exercise is walking, with an occasional sprint from telephone pole to telephone pole. Fortunately, I walk on the wild side.

There are seldom amenities like telephone poles.

Walking really is great exercise, and I do prefer it to any other kind. If you have a bike, stationary, or otherwise, use it. Some of the campgrounds (more like resorts) have extensive exercise rooms, and some have swimming pools. Do something to get daily exercise, even if it isn't any more than twiddling your thumbs.

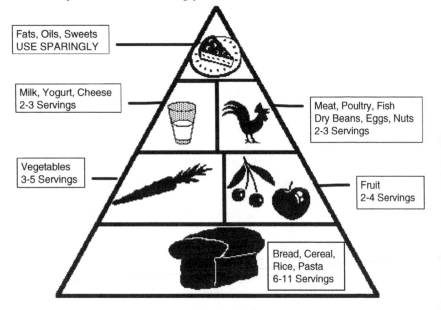

Fats, Oils, Sweets
USE SPARINGLY

Milk, Yogurt, Cheese
2-3 Servings

Meat, Poultry, Fish
Dry Beans, Eggs, Nuts
2-3 Servings

Vegetables
3-5 Servings

Fruit
2-4 Servings

Bread, Cereal,
Rice, Pasta
6-11 Servings

Gratitude

We need to enjoy the world around us. Most of us do, in a way, but we tend to skim over things. We don't really **think** about what's around us. Stop for a minute, **really listen**, and **really look** at that flower, or bird, or scene. These are the things I have been grateful for over a lifetime.

**Aspen,
Colorado**

If you have heard
A cricket...
The taunt of a mockingbird...
The whirring of hummingbird wings...
The belly laugh of a child...
A rushing mountain stream...
A crackling fire...
The rumble of thunder in springtime
Gentle rain on the roof that washes the flowers, the trees, the grass...
A symphony of birds at dawn...
Church bells on a Sunday morning...
"I love you;"

If you have seen
The dogwood in bloom...
A foal wobbling near its mother...
The deep purple and bright yellow of a pansy face...
The moon at two a.m....
Old gnarled hands clasping a communion cup...
Heavenly heat flashes against a storm-darkened sky...
A mountain stream carving its way through a landscape of ice and snow...
The silhouette of a desert cactus against the setting sun...
A star-studded sky;

If you have savored the taste of
Sweet icy watermelon heart...
Gooey chocolate chip cookies...
The first strawberry of the season...
Butter on hot homemade bread...
A ripe tomato picked from the vine and eaten in the patch...
The taste of nothingness when a snowflake melts on your tongue...
Cold water when you thirst...
A kiss;

If you have sniffed the fragrance of
Lilacs in June...
Pine in the north country...
New mown hay...
Pure mountain air...
A roasting turkey...
Fresh ground coffee...
Cinnamon...
Autumn;

If you have felt
The coolness of fall...

The crispness of winter...
The warmth of summer...
The freshness of spring...
Warm sand between your toes...
A baby nibbling on your cheek..
A wiggling puppy...
A hand holding yours....
Joy at the birth of a baby...
Gentleness;

If you are enjoying
A friendship...
Sharing life with your mate...
Loving, caring, sharing...
Remembering...
The gratefulness of Thanksgiving...
The anticipation of Christmas...
The promise of Easter...
The pride of the Fourth of July...
Being needed...
Being wanted,

Then you should be grateful, my friends, very grateful.

**International Peace
Garden between
Canada
and the
United States,
celebrating the
world's longest
undefended border**

Fudge a little
on your RV Vacation

Michigan holds a special place in my heart because I was born in southwestern Michigan. I raised my kids, and still have brothers, in-laws, nieces, nephews, and friends there. We saw a great deal of our own state before we ventured to parts unknown. One of our favorite places to visit was Mackinaw Island. Read on, McDuff.

It was called Michilimackinac or "great turtle" by the Indians who believed the island was formed by supernatural forces. Because of its strategic position on the new frontier, ownership bounced back and forth between France, England, and the United States from the early 1700s through the French and Indian Wars, the American Revolution, and the War of 1812. In the mid-1800s, it began to develop as a resort area. By the mid 1900s, tourists were enveloped in chocolate and peanut butter fudge. We call this three-by-five mile limestone rock, Mackinac Island, Michigan.

My favorite transportation to the island is Shepler's Mackinac Island Ferry, a twenty minute hydroplane ride from Mackinaw City. Other choices are hydrojet, twin-hull catamaran, or ferry boat.

Pushing through the wild waves of the Straits of Mackinac gives us a fish-eye view of the five-mile-long "Mighty Mac" bridge connecting Michigan's Upper and Lower Peninsulas. The Mackinac Bridge is one of the world's longest suspension bridges and great fun to walk Labor Day weekend with thousands of other walkers, the only time foot passengers are allowed on the bridge.

Shortly, the magnificent Grand Hotel comes into view, the 660' porch with its bright red geraniums and gleaming white pillars, grins like an ecstatic Cheshire cat sitting on a cliff. A bit to the right we see the prominent snowy white walls of Fort Mackinac.

We are soon stepping into the early morning shadows of the nineteenth century. Since only emergency vehicles are permitted, transportation is by wagon, horseback, buggy, bike, or good old-fashioned feet. A few of the roughly two thousand Mackinac Island employees scurry about their jobs. Horses pulling supply wagons plod along, nodding to each other with a "Yup, it's anuther day all right." Prime concerns are avoiding collision courses with bikes piled high with teetering luggage, and sidestepping the velvet softness dropped by the equine population. Although diligent, the workers who do clean-up are always "behind" in their jobs.

Main Street is lined with restaurants and shops touting the famous Mackinac Bridge or Mackinac Island Fudge. The American flag waves from the porch of the mellow yellow Windermere Hotel. Main Street establishments greet the day, each having a more magnificent view, or more history, than the last one. Overnights on Mackinac Island are magical. A half-finished fiction story lurks in my files, a product of staying at Stone Cliff, a turn-of-the-century mansion on the top of the island. Jessica Fletcher would love it.

The Visitor Center has exhibits and slide presentations. Eighty percent of the island's 2,200 acres is Mackinac Island State Park, Michigan's first state park.

I sat in front with Larry, a driver for the Mackinac Island Carriage Tour who introduced me to his horses, Darryl, and The Other Horse, Darryl. I knew from experience the humor would go down hill from there. Drivers are a good source of history, but their jokes are ghastly. Another driver once told me, "With three inches or less of top soil, corpses can't be buried in the cemetery, they are screwed into the rock."

I'll elaborate on a few of the twenty stops. Dr. William Beaumont and a wounded French Canadian made medical history here in 1822. The patient's gunshot wound in the stomach never healed. Through the opening, Dr. Beaumont observed and documented for the first time in history, the workings of the human digestive system. The Beaumont Memorial building houses the army physician's tools and dioramas.

At the Michilimackinac County Courthouse, a man was convicted of

Mackinac Island,
Michigan

murder for killing someone in the act of destroying a building on his property. The Michigan Supreme Court freed the man because, "A man's house is his castle" and he was allowed to protect it by forceful means. Ah, would that it were still so today.

The grand Grand Hotel, with 319 guest rooms and space for you and 499 of your closest friends for dinner, was built in 1887. A strict dress code is required after six p.m. so don't try to get in with depressed jeans like mine. One can walk the grounds or rock in one of the many rocking chairs lining the famous porch for a fee, even if you are not a guest.

The hotel gardens are also grand. Larry said, "It takes eight gardeners and $200,000 a year to keep them up. The pool was built for an Esther Williams movie in the 1940s, but it was too cold for her, so the scene was filmed in Florida with palm trees in the background." "*Somewhere in Time*" was also filmed there in 1979, starring Christopher Reeve.

Another lovely hotel, The Island House, claims the title of the oldest operating hotel. It was built in 1852.

The drivers provided comic relief. As an oncoming carriage approached, ours stopped. The driver looked at Larry and said, "Grey Poupon?"

Approximately six hundred horses live on the island in the summer. Larry said, "The animals are worked five or six hours, then have 12 hours off. Three vets care for the animals but only one doctor is available for the million human visitors." He added, "Of course the horses are unionized, they're Teamsters."

The tour stops at Arch Rock, where the legend lives of the Indian maiden, She-Who-Walks in the Mist, and the post cemetery where thirty unknown American soldiers are buried. The Governor's Mansion can be toured certain days of the week. The last stop is Fort Mackinac which overlooks the busy streets of the town. Costumed interpreters explain daily life. Rifle-firing and other dramatic re-enactments of fort life in the 1880s takes place on the parade ground.

Bikes can be rented if you have the good "scents" to arrive during the Lilac Festival the second week of June, and take my favorite bike ride around the perimeter of the island. It is an easy nine miles of shoreline scenery fragranced by the lilacs plummeting down the cliffsides. Hiking and biking trails of a more strenuous nature go into the island's interior.

After being inspired by how John Jacob Astor became America's first millionaire, visiting the Missionary Bark Chapel, and all that hiking, biking, buggying and getting stuffed with history, exhaustion set in. It was time to buy a chili dog and Pepsi, crash on the fort lawn, and watch the rest of the visitors scurry until time to catch the return ferry. Of course I didn't have much appetite after all that silky smooth sinful fudge.

That's about it, a great day in the fresh air on beautiful, historic Mackinac Island. You might want to catch a slower ferry on your return trip to the mainland. ZZZ*zzzm*.

HOBBIES, HOLIDAYS, AND FAIR FESTIVITIES

Once we've talked about Photography and Computers, the rest of the chapter is festivals and fairs. They are all across the country, and delightful to visit. These stories are from Alaska, Washington, California, Arizona, Colorado, Michigan, Ohio, and West Virginia. Welcome to the exciting world of RVing!

Photography

Photography is a natural for the full-time lifestyle. You'll be seeing fascinating country, places, and people.

I am often asked what kind of cameras I use. I have an Olympus Infinity SuperZoom 330. I use it mostly for inside shots because it has an automatic flash. Most of my shots are outside, with the Minolta Maxxum 5000. I have had it since 1987. All the photos in this book and on the back, were taken with the Minolta. I took prints in the beginning, but switched almost exclusively to slides in 1992.

I use 100 ASA Kodak or Fuji film. If you are really into photography, read the instructions on the boxes, and get specific speeds, for specific needs. You can call a Kodak 800 number for any questions you might have. (Resources)

Cameras have changed drastically in the last couple of years. A point-and-shoot camera will give you some terrific photography, if you know a little about composition.

Please be sensitive with your picture taking.

I ran into a fellow in Mexico a few years ago, who claimed to be a professional, which I didn't think was a good excuse. He shoved his camera in the face of his subjects (without permission), and made traffic stop, so he could get that perfect shot (I would have run over him).

My favorite shots are reflections and clouds, and people close-ups. When I was in North Dakota, I had the privilege of taking college graduation pictures for University of North Dakota student friends, who couldn't afford them otherwise.

We went to a local park, and I photographed them lying on the ground with their hands under their chins, hats on their heads, and big grins. Others were shot while they were leaning against rocks or trees. They were relaxed in fun clothes, and I got some great photos. I often have my granddaughter play model for me. We both have fun.

The only time I was ever able to get decent shots of my youngest daughter, was when I could get her in a Cheryl Tiegs mood. Otherwise, every shot of her growing up, either had her eyes crossed, or her tongue sticking out. Thankfully, she's changed.

Keep plenty of film and batteries with you (in the refrigerator or freezer). The most frustrating situation, is discovering you don't have any film, or you are finally in a position to make that perfect shot, and your battery looks you in the eye and says, "Pfhht!"

I carried many rolls of film when I headed for Alaska. I didn't intend to take many, because I had taken so many slides in 1992. Yeah, right. I made a lot of trips into new territory, and used up what I had. I had an awful time getting slide film up there. I was always in the wrong place, a small village or town, where people don't ask for slide film. I headed for Inuvik with print film, and I wasn't happy. I really regret not having slides for some of the road shots. Oh well.

If you want a picture of you and your RV, set up the RV the way you want it (watching the background). You should be about halfway between the camera and the RV. That way you get a full shot of the RV, and you aren't lost in it. It makes a great Christmas card.

A few pointers

- Take your telephoto lens. This will allow you good animal (or scenery) shots without getting too close.
- Frame photos with trees, branches, flowers, and people.
- Flash photos do not work for distances.
- Include people or rocks or trees, etc., for perspective.
- Tripod is nice to steady the camera for low-light shots.
- In your foreground, capture sand, footprints, a brick wall, tree limb.
- Use foreground as an arrow pointing to your main subject.
- Take a couple disposable panoramic cameras.
- Slow down, take your time, really look at the composition.
- Whatever doesn't belong in that photo, will be the most noticeable object in it. (I had a great shot of a couple by their RV until I had it developed. His hand was resting on her shoulder, but the photo looked like she had a growth coming out of her neck).
- Take vertical as well as horizontal shots.
- Make certain any water lines in ocean or lake shots, are perfectly horizontal.

- Watch for those shadows. Get the sun right on your subject or wait until the sun goes under. (I took a picture of all my kids near a waterfall. It should have been great. They looked like they were wearing eyeshadow--half way down their faces.

Computer

A computer is another natural for the lifestyle. It can be used as a toy to wile away a lot of hours learning it. Use it for writing a journal of your travels, playing games, or for starting a new hobby or vocation you can do on the road.

In my office, I have a Gateway 2000 desktop 486 computer, and a Texas Instrument microLaser Pro 600 printer. I also have a Gateway 2000 Handbook 486 computer, that I use away from the RV. I use it whenever I have to fly somewhere to give seminars, or visit family.

My preference is working on the desktop. Both computers have Windows. I have spreadsheets to keep track of vehicle maintenance, gas, mileage, and costs. A Quicken program has been a terrific way to record all cash or credit card transactions, with cumulative reports showing me whether or not I will eat next week.

Don't tell anybody, but word processing capabilities is a terrific way to keep up with correspondence. I write specific paragraphs that I know would interest my family or whomever, then each new letter is drafted in and around, those paragraphs. It takes me much less time to write a letter, and yet each letter is personal, in that everything else in the letter, is in reference to the person I am answering.

Other people with computers use this method, too. I expect to get caught this way, sometime. I won't give you her name, because I don't want to embarrass this good friend. This winter I received a letter directed to me, all the way down to the middle, where she made a specific comment to "Mom." Gotcha! Technology is wonderful.

Every year I see letters to advice columnists about the hated Christmas letter. Tough turkeys! I love getting Christmas mail and what I "hate" is getting a card signed, "Joe" or "Cindy." To begin with, I might know four people named Joe or Cindy. They need to put their last names on the card...or...write me a Xeroxed Christmas letter so I can connect with who they are. I care enough about people to want to know what they are doing.

I write a Christmas letter. If people don't want to read it, it is their prerogative to ignore it, and merely look at the edging and know it is a Christmas greeting. In the meantime, keep those Xeroxed letters coming!

As you travel across country, find out what is happening locally. It is great fun to run across a local brand of entertainment.

If you're an antique car buff, or even a young car buff, you wouldn't want to miss the

Auburn-Cord-Duesenburg Festival

Auburn, Indiana

This festival held every Labor Day weekend, is considered the "World's Greatest Classic Car Show." It is the home town of my friend, Linda Bassett. As widows and former classmates, we "did the town" together.

The festival offers much more than just cars. They have golf tournaments, historic tours, quilt shows, volkswalks, antique shows, swap meets, and a huge craft show. It was the cars that held my curiosity.

They have a great "Parade of Classics." Approximately 250 sleek and shining Auburns, Cords, and Duesenbergs glided proudly through the streets on Saturday, oohed and aahed over by an estimated 100,000 drooling visitors from all over the world.

If you wanted to drool over them individually, you could visit the A-C-D Museum. Considering my interest in any car is that it have wheels, an engine, a place to sit and it gets me where I want to go, the museum was a fascinating place.

It is in the original showplace where the cars were sold. The bottom floor main area is all Cords, Auburns and Duesenbergs. The back rooms and upstairs, have a mixture of restored autos, horseless carriages of the 1890s, modern sports cars, and a 1922 Ford half-track snow conversion mean machine.

The Duesenbergs are associated with the rich and famous -- Clark Gable, Greta Garbo, John Paul Getty, and Howard Hughes. You know, your everyday neighbor types.

You tend to gravitate to your interests, so who would have thought I'd make it to the Annual International Collector Car Auction. Dean Kruse began his collector car auction industry at the festival in 1971, and is going strong.

There were two selling arenas back to back in the same building, with huge turntables displaying the cars, RVs and trucks. Auctioneers did their tongue-twisting while workers took bids from the audience.

Nearly 5,000 cars were auctioned over the long weekend, including a 1928 LaSalle Phaeton and a 1913 Rolls Royce London Edinburgh Tourere, once used by the Prince of Wales. Not to be outdone by royalty, a 1975 Lincoln continental Mark IV was presented. It was purchased new by Elvis Presley.

Linda started to point something out to me, then stopped herself. She said, "Don't even scratch your head in here or you'll own a Classic." I was fascinated by it all, but kept my hands firmly planted under my gluteus maximus. The stress of it all brought hunger.

Food was abundant. One-and-a-half inch-thick porch chops titillated the tastebuds, but we settled on something masquerading as sticks of fish. Fortunately we split it. It turned out to be an enormous onion, opened, dipped, and deep fried. They called it a "blooming onion." It was good, but a half plate of pure grease makes you crave homemade ice cream to soothe your linings. Thanks to the Amish booth, we found that, too.

Although full-time RVers take an oath not to "collect," it is great fun to look in an Arts and Crafts Show. You never know, you may be able to squeeze just one more crafty do-dad into a niche.

RVs were part and parcel of this craft sale. RVers rolled out the awnings and indoor-outdoor carpeting, and were in business with all the comforts of home.

You could start your day with a hearty pancake breakfast, then proceed to a Hoosier Steak Fry later in the day. Wouldn't it be fun to attend the A-C-D Museum Gala Ball on Saturday night? Ah well.

I started to wave good-bye to Linda, then remembered a Duesenberg is too big to tow (just in case the auctioneer was watching), and I already have the Little Lynx, Bless His Heart.

A number of theme villages have sprung up over the last few years. This one has been around for a while. My oldest daughter and her family have lived there for the last few years, so it is more than just a favorite place for me. I think you'd like it.

A Village for <u>All Seasons</u>
Leavenworth, WA

It was my privilege to travel in Europe for six weeks for the first time during 1995. Germany's Bavaria, was every bit as beautiful as I imagined, with snow-covered mountains, picturesque chalets, and shopkeepers dressed in lederhosen and dirndls. Fortunately, your credit cards don't have to cough and gasp in shock to experience the same things I did. All you have to do is visit Leavenworth. It's right in the middle of the state of Washington.

Speaking without reservation (and that is the only thing you can do without reservation in Leavenworth), the Cascade Mountain Range that nestles this Bavarian Village of 2,000, is every bit as spectacular as anything I saw in Europe.

You can easily get into the Bavarian mood by watching Bob Johnson, the owner of the Enzian Motor Inn, balancing on the fourth floor railing and playing his twelve-foot alpenhorn. He plays at 8:15 and 9:15 a.m. every day of the year.

There are undoubtedly more festivals in Leavenworth in a year, than in the entire state of Bavaria. The fun begins in January with the Bavarian Ice Fest, highlighting a fireworks display and the "Great Leavenworth Smooshing Race." This cross-country ski race consists of four people on each pair of skis, with interesting results. Have you ever considered the probabilities of putting a committee on skis and having them agree on anything so they can move forward? The Fest also includes sleigh rides and a sled-dog pulling competition. The local Kiwanis Club freezes small change in colored water and has an Ice Cube Free-for-all for children.

Springtime brings the Maifest and warm weather. Everybody gets involved. The Amberleaf Theatre presents plays, the Lion's Club has pancake breakfasts, the Chumstick Grange has a bazaar, and the bandstand in the park is filled with musicians, dancers, choirs, handbell ringers or bands.

During June, July, and August, concerts, summer theatre, and just plain dancing under the stars, brings joy. I mean, who can keep their toes from tapping to an accordion playing *The Beer Barrel Polka*. These days everybody is into doing *The Chicken Dance*.

It's fun to walk through the shops or just stroll through the quaint, spotless streets. Beware walking under any of hundreds of flower baskets during early morning watering time, or you'll receive a free shower. It takes a heap o' watering to keep all the barrels and pots of flowers hydrated.

Beautifully hand-painted alpine murals, decorative signs and trim, grace the nooks and crannies of the buildings. Every hour the clock chimes from the Village Pharmacy, and figures parade around the glockenspiel on the Tannenbaum Building.

Foreign tongues intermingle with the familiar during festival times, with singing and laughter and shouts to friends. It's the same in any country. Happy sounds mix well with street music fresh mountain air.

If the annual Fasching, the children's Kinderfest, the Wenatchee River Salmon Festival, the Craft Shows, or the Gala Holiday Food Faire festivities don't float your boat, you might try Der Quacken Floaten Duck Race. This is surely considered the last great duck race of the century. The win-by-a-bill can earn you as much as $1,000.

Specialty shops and restaurants line the streets. The shopkeepers are friendly and helpful. The Hat Shop is a fun place. Every hat you ever wanted to own but were afraid to appear in public wearing, is there. Mirrors encourage trying and buying them all. In Die Musik Box, they actually suggest you wind the keys and listen (my favorite shop). You could stroll through Art in the Park spring, summer and fall.

There are so many things to see every season in Leavenworth that it makes sense to contact the Chamber of Commerce for their listing. Don't forget to make reservations well in advance of any festival time. Do be careful where you park. The Gingerbread Factory has a sign in its parking lot, "Violators will be baked!" I love it.

Autumn is synonymous with swiping colorful branches from unsuspecting trees, and sticking them into flower barrels, for the Washington State Autumn Leaf Festival. The last vestiges of multicolored petunias and bright red geraniums, surround the branches. Orange and red and yellow leaves rattle in the cooler September and October breezes.

Leavenworth is picturesque at all times. With two to three feet of snow sparkling in the sun, or under the old-fashioned street lights, it is especially so. The snow is usually removed from the streets and parking areas, well before most people are into their first cup of wake-up coffee.

Winter follows fall with the most favorite festival of all, The Christmas Lighting. Picture a magnificent live greeting card. Leavenworth is decorated in evergreen ropes and velvet ribbons. Familiar carols float through the frigid mountain air, along with the fragrance of chestnuts roasting on an open fire. Children slide down the hill on sleds. Sleigh bells jingle when shop doors open and it's entirely possible, you'll meet Scrooge walking the bricks. Mr. and Mrs. Santa Claus make an appearance, and Jack Frost always nips a few noses.

Prayers are given and the crowd sings *Silent Night*. Suddenly the audience is silenced in common awe, as the lights are lit in unison. It is a little like being transported into the gingerbread village of your imagination where every tree and every building is outlined with tiny lights. Everyone cheers. The Christmas season begins.

Leavenworth is a village for all seasons, but if you want an extra touch of magic, visit at Christmas.

I love summer festivals and fairs. This one was a winner.

Bob Evans Festival
Gallipolis, Ohio

Joyful voices singing Gospel music, were intertwined with dulcimer playing, the clang of championship horseshoes hitting the target, and the chugging of various sizes and types of antique stream engines. It was a smashing October day in the hill country between Rio Grande and Gallipolis, Ohio, a hefty stone's throw from the Ohio River. I wandered the Bob Evans (of "Down on the Farm" fame) Farm Festival.

Tantalizing aromas pulled me along by the nose. One of the first with good olfactory news was the Bob Evans sausage. Even the price was reasonable. Apple cider was squeezed fresh that very moment.

All that doesn't even touch the sausage and gravy, bean soup and cornbread, apple dumplings and ice cream, homemade pie, and a whole tent full of cheese. Forgive my drooling on this column. Are you hungry yet? This was definitely the day to leave the diet at home with the cottage cheese and tuna fish.

For once, I wasn't the only one going in circles. At the Sorghum Mill, a horse was going around and around, grinding sorghum stalks. It was boiled into a thick goo. I tasted a bit of it on a cracker. It wasn't bad. It wasn't good, either, but it wasn't bad. Corneal grinding and corn shelling were shaping up at the Gristmill Barn.

If you wanted busy, you found it. Activities abounded for the three days and they were geared to all ages. Horse-pulled wagon rides were free. Minus the wagon, children rode horseback for fifty cents.

Clogging and milking and storytelling. It was all around. If you were in full voice, hog calling might have been your challenge. I learned a high-pitched "Suie, suie" down on our farm, but some of those calls, I couldn't believe.

A Chicken Scratch Contest was offered along with an Egg Toss. The Apple Paring was appealing, but you haven't lived until you've been part of a Cow Chip Throwing Competition.

On the hillside near the pond, spectators cheered a woman and man competing in log rolling. She won two times out of three. Wouldn't you know, he claimed, "I had the fast end of the log."

When you want an expert, find someone who has been around a while. One fellow was 77 years young and hailed as the champion woodchopper. He chipped out places in the tree trunk for the ends of two boards to be fitted into, then stood on them to lop off the tree with an ax. He did it in record time.

"Canoe jousting" was the old-timers' way of settling logging disputes. Two people battled against each other while standing in their canoes. Assistant paddlers behind them attempted to keep the canoes upright. Combatants tried to knock each other down with jousting poles. It didn't take long before one of them went swimming.

A lazy curl of smoke rose from the pipe of the man who was working with the velocity saw. He made little wooden cutouts to give away to children, like me. His bandaged fingers suggested a story that rippled my goosebumps.

While the animals prayed for someone with warm and steady hands, shearers with sharp shears shamelessly sheared the sheepish sheep and shared their shapeless and woolly wool. Soapmaking, basketweaving and other traditional crafts and exhibits, were spaced throughout the grounds, along with demonstrations of early American know how.

All ages, from the tiniest babies to elderly Grandmas and Grandpas, toe-tapped to country, bluegrass or jazz, or wandered through the booths.

Crafts were the "for real" kind you only find at country fairs. The absence of "Made in Taiwan or Japan" was duly noted.

Among other gems were signs for every occasion: "Teenagers are hormones with feet."

Hand-painted pumpkins antique photography, quilts and pottery, among others, were there for admiring and buying. The artisans were friendly and willing to explain their particular art form.

Clouds formed and leaked a few drops of liquid sunshine. Umbrellas popped and newspapers unfurled, but the fun continued.

On the Homestead Stage, the musicians talked about "bantars and git-joes." They sang one song especially for RVers: "You're always gone but you're always home, living in a mobile home." He called it "Ramblin Fever Down in our Bones" by the Rarely Herd.

In the middle of all this was "The Homestead." It was built in 1820 by Nehemiah Wood, from brick made on the farm. The homestead was once a stagecoach stop and inn, and is now on the national Register of Historic Places. In 1953, it was bought by Bob and Jewell Evans. It was their family home for seventeen years, now used for a multipurpose building during farm events.

For campers staying the three days, they have water, restrooms but no electricity or showers. A free-Old Fashioned Hoe-down" was scheduled for Friday and Saturday night. No reservations are necessary.

It is a great experience and happens every year the first part of October.

Full-time RVing sometimes brings about creative thinking, especially where family is concerned.

Let me tell you about our family reunion that took us deep into the old west, at least for a day. Even if you don't do this activity for the same purpose, it is great fun and a terrific outing for kids or grandkids, that they'll never forget.

Cowpokes and Cowpunchers

Starry Pines Bed and Breakfast was more than we were expecting. With our taking three rooms, we were the only guests. The two couples had king-size beds and shared a bathroom and shower area. Rebecca and I (The important ones) had an apartment that we used as a gathering place at the end of the day.

An enormous cathedral-ceiling living room with fireplace and TV was available to us, but we didn't use it much. We spent a lot of time out on the deck overlooking the rushing Snowmass Creek. The guys and Rebecca, discovered it had fish in it to be caught. You know where they spent a lot of time.

The hot tub on the side deck saw a lot of use and every morning, Shelly, the owner, fixed yummy breakfasts including hot biscuits, hot breads, and hot chocolate for Rebecca. She said most people sleep in and she has to tell them she will not serve after 9 a.m. We had her up by 6:30. We packed a lot in our days.

Bona fide papers exist that say we are now all entitled to the special "Rights and Honors due to Cowpokes and Cowpunchers." We have "The honor and privilege of telling tall tales, tossing cow chips, hog-tying dogies," and all other wonderful and exciting western activities that city slickers only dream about. All this because we were "Rocky Mountain Cattle Moo-vers" for a day near Carbondale, Colorado.

With our red bandannas and straw hats in place, we mounted horses according to our abilities. "Abilities" was synonymous with "know-how, prowess, technical skill, and agility." Sitting atop a thirty-hands-high mount named Iguana, I immediately sensed we didn't see eye to eye. It wasn't until he actually moved, that I recalled my six months working on the Bar-M Dude Ranch in NE Oregon.

The wranglers had snickered at my insufficient knowledge of equine anatomy to know which end of the horse was which. The association with the horse went downhill from there. The relationship with the wranglers, only improved to the point they quit laughing, when I was within hearing distant. It isn't my fault my aptitude is highest in mechanics(!).

Sometimes you just do what you gotta do. I squared my shoulders, sat tall in the saddle, and was transformed into Jill Wayne, rider of the purple sage, conqueror of the Rocky Mountains, and horsewoman extraordinaire. Iguana was philosophical about the whole thing, but a language barrier surfaced. When I concentrated on the perfect photo shot and whispered "Whoa" in his ear, he took off after a wayward longhorn like a bat out of a hot place.

Nevertheless, I stubbornly refused to grasp the saddle horn, in my usual desperate claw-like grip. I guided the horse with one hand on the reigns, and with the other, maneuvered the camera.

I expected a farce. It wasn't. It was great fun. We had the freedom to "Head 'em up, move 'em out" according to our whim. I tried to forget those cows and horses had made the trip hundreds of times, knew every nook and cranny, and if I took off my bifocals, I might find they were wind-up toys.

The youngest of the riders was about ten. I reckon I was the only grandma ridin' herd through Colorado bluebells, columbine, orange paintbrush, shooting stars, scrub oaks, twisted juniper trees and pinion pine. Four-footed wranglers, natural cow punchers, nipped at the heels of cattle stragglers.

Three hours of horseback riding and the danger of my legs dropping off, coincided with our arrival in a lovely meadow for what they called a Chuckwagon "lunch." If that was lunch, dinner would have subjected us to belly blow-out. A singing cowgirl sizzled steak, crisped chicken, and roasted corn on a long grill.

The guitar player encouraged us to sing along. He played everything from *Sweet Georgia Brown* to *Country Roads,* and threw in a few songs he wrote himself. The *de de du du dums* we threw in between words we didn't know, mixed with the shouts of successful ropers of stationary steers and the clanging of horseshoes.

While the horses whinnied in the wild flowers and cattle grazed, I chatted with the wranglers. They told me about the "Wild Cow Milking Contest." "We roped and mugged the cow in record time only to discover she was dry" and once one of them "Roped a steer but forgot to let go of her. Flew straight off the horse."

The most hectic time with visitors is when everyone is getting "horsed up." "About half of them feel they are experienced. They are the biggest problems and usually cause the most accidents." I didn't worry about them labeling me "experienced."

The opportunity was given to ride horseback on the return trip as well, but we all opted to ride with Rebecca and Janet in the hay wagon. You see different sights from the back of a wagon. It bounces a lot but it doesn't have a mind of its own. Our driver was a Kenny Rogers look-alike. He was once a bull rider but he broke ribs and collar bones and enough other miscellaneous 2000 body parts that, "I finally smartened up."

The ranch also offers rodeo events, a teepee village for overnighters, and other activities from June through September. During the busiest part of the season, the number of visitors averages 35 but occasionally there are as many as 65 or 70. Paul said, "One lady was celebrating her 50th birthday and invited 101 of her closest friends."

And me, my cup runneth over. As I rode along the ridge, looking at Mt. Sopris, with its 12,953 snow-covered feet, I had an incredible feeling of happiness. Not only were all my healthy children right there in my sights, I was that "cowgirl" that I wanted to be from the days when I sat wide-eyed in the local theatre in Dowagiac, Michigan, on a Saturday morning, watching Dale Evans and Roy Rogers make cowboy history. *'Yip-ei-o...yip-ei-a..*

If you're heading south for the winter, a great November festival is in Death Valley, California.

The '49ers (Death Valley Days)

Death Valley is a quiet, lovely place. When I drove in from the north side through the twisting, turning, snake-like road, it was early morning, and nary another vehicle was in sight as I passed Scotty's Castle. I came back to Scotty's Castle the next evening. The park rangers and their characterizations of 1930s, came alive during an evening history tour.

Archeologists believe primitive man lived here 10,000 years ago on the shores of a huge prehistoric lake. When the waters evaporated leaving the great salt flats, Indians referred to this place as "Tomesha" or "Ground Fire" for the relentless summer heat sometimes reaching 134 degrees. But as merciless as the summer heat is, so are the winters cold and unforgiving. Legend has it that as 1849 settlers fought their way out of the clutches of this land of extraordinary beauty and uncommon desolation, one turned around and said, "Good-bye, Death Valley," thus giving it a name.

A wagon train of gold seekers and settlers left Salt Lake City, Utah, in September of 1849, under the leadership of Captain Jefferson Hunt. He had successfully, the year before, led the first group ever, to Los Angeles from Salt Lake City. Human nature being what it is, someone else had a shorter, better, but untried route through the rugged Panamint mountains.

Following that lead, the Bennett-Arcane party crossed the salt flats and camped at what is now known as Bennett's Well. With supplies fast dwindling, scouts hiked 250 miles across snow-covered mountains to find a feasible route and provisions. Four weeks later they rescued the remaining half-starved families, and continued to Los Angeles.

In 1949, thousands of people gathered in Death Valley to honor the pioneers of 1849. They visited Bad Water, 279.6 feet below sea level and The Devil's Cornfield, in the shadow of the Funeral Mountains. They were awestruck by the beauty in the Artist's Palette and Dante's View. They re-enacted historical events. It was decided to continue the pilgrimage, and call it the Annual Death Valley Encampment.

The entire colorful history of the valley, intertwines with the Encampment's commemoration of the '49ers including the "Borax Era." In the 1880s the famous Twenty-mule teams trekked the 165 mile "Death Valley Road to Mojave," hauling 46,000 pounds of borax to the railroad.

It encompasses tales of silver and gold and riches in another medium. National Park Service Ranger, Stan Jones, plucked away at his guitar around a Death Valley campfire, until he created the haunting ballad, "Ghost Riders in the Sky."

Pre-encampment is almost as much fun as the real thing. The evenings were blessed with impromptu groups "jamming" on the grounds. The Encampment brought hundreds of lawn-chair-carrying visitors to hear fiddler's, tall tales, and sing-a-longs, as well as concerts by professionals.

If you craved four minutes of fame, you signed up for the "Coyote Howl," an informal talent show. If you tired of one entertainment, you took your chair and found another. If tripping to the light fantastic tickled your fancy, each evening offered square and round dancing under the stars.

Jeep tours and shutterbug seminars were available or if you were bent on proving your prowess, you joined the "Old Prospector's Race." This involved setting up camp, lighting a fire, and frying an egg. If developing your own claim was your bag, a seminar on how to pack a mule to carry your supplies was in order.

If you signed up ahead of time, you might qualify to drive or ride a wagon train for one hundred miles over five days. If you didn't want the animals to have all the fun, you signed up for a two-day, twenty-five mile hike from Lemoigne Canyon to Stove Pipe Wells.

Less strenuous activities were admiring working artists at the Invitational Western Art Show, or relaxing on the Visitor Center patio, while real range-ridin' cowboys told trail tales, or recited cowboy poetry. Golf and horseshoe tournaments and gold panning, were options as well.

National and International visitors became acquainted in hungry lines awaiting sausage, scrambled eggs, and biscuits and gravy at the Hootenanny Hoe-down Breakfast.

Saturday night we listened to a concert in the key of "G-Whiz" while we wrapped in blankets against the chill. "Those pioneers had one advantage over modern travel, they always knew where their luggage was." A stiff breeze carried just enough sand to give us grit in our teeth, and a brief moment of what the pioneers faced on a daily basis. We listened and clapped and wanted more, until "The Star Spangled Banner" signaled us to stand, and reluctantly, leave.

The Sunday Morning Hymn Sing was an opportunity for inspirational mini-sermons. The sing-a-long ended with *God Bless America."* Apropos. With hugs to old cronies and warm good-byes to new friends, participants and visitors, gathered belongings "until next year."

Just in case you make it to the "far" North country some time, this is a little on

The Alaska State Fair

The Alaska State Fair at Palmer, was celebrating its Diamond Jubilee the last week of August, and the first week of September. It was compact, with lots of activities and booths. Animals were different than at the Van Buren County Fair back in Michigan, llamas, alpacas, musk ox, and reindeer, among others.

The fair is in the heart of the Matanuska Valley, famous for its oversized vegetables. Cabbages weighed in at more than eighty pounds. A Diamond Jubilee Giant Cabbage Weigh-off offered prizes of $4,000.

We ate everything that wasn't nailed down, deep-fried halibut, ice cream in home-made cones, cheezy popcorn, pizza, elephant ears, and anything else we could get. There was plenty of variety. Talk about junk, but that's what an evening at the fair is all about.

I love being caught up in fair excitement. Various stages had people performing with guitars or fiddles, or both. A big name I didn't recognize was drawing a crowd to a grassy embankment for the evening's entertainment.

Activities were varied through the two weeks, stock car and pig racing, a lumberjack show, and a mud bog. The Guess Who came (I guessed and I still didn't know who). Alaska wasn't too far away to attract the rave of Nashville, LeAnn Rimes. Events included woodsplitting, ax-throwing, cross-cut and bow sawing and other activities most of us rarely see.

It was a perfect evening at the fair.

I happened to be in southern Indiana during early December one year.

Christmas letters

In the town of Santa Claus, Indiana, Holiday World and Toyland exist, and streets are named Jolly, Three Kings, and Chimes, but I was interested in the post office. Postal employees had hand-stamped 23,000 pieces of Christmas mail that day alone, but they handle upwards of 500,000 pieces of Christmas mail throughout the year. They have a pre-printed Christmas letter sent out by volunteers, to answer children who write to Santa Claus. There were 200 on that day and it was before noon very early in December.

Another taste of Indiana Christmas

I was convinced Santa's magic dust had reduced me to elf size in Nashville, Indiana, the "Village of 100,000 Lights." Lights outlined everything and holiday music played in the background. It was as though I were walking through a gingerbread village on someone's hall table.

The Pine Box Theatre in Nashville was originally an old funeral home. It was a big "undertaking," but the new owners did it up in fine style and provided an "Old Fashioned Christmas," that included a Christmas sing along.

A few years ago I was in the Arizona desert and attended a "Cowboy Poet's Christmas."

A Cowboy Poet's Christmas Gathering

We sit in the fairly large room next to the art gallery. Conversation stops. We listen, enchanted as male and female riders sing and play their songs, recite their poetry and tell their stories. We are at the Annual Cowboy Poet's Christmas Gathering at the Desert Caballeros Western Museum in Wickenburg, Arizona. They aren't dressed in fancy. They are working people in Saturday night jeans and well-worn cowboy boots. Hands are toughened and callused from real "cowboyin'."

Some of the songs are without accompaniment, the way they would be sung in the saddle. A musical instrument isn't needed; the music comes from the soul.

Humor helps a cowboy who forgets his lines, "I left all my brains and memory in my other hat."

One sings of the ultimate gift of love, "There's nothing like nothing for

Christmas, when I know it's comin' from you." One tells of "Cutting a Christmas tree with a pocket knife. Never roped a calf half as rough as that Christmas tree."

Weathered wranglers recite, and we soon forget they are perched on a stool in front of us. They use no notes. They speak from the heart. The words come from the very depths of their souls, and we feel their joy and loneliness and spirituality.

The words of these down-to-earth Cowboy Poets, transport us to a mountain meadow in the high desert where a campfire is crackling. The smell of fresh coffee elicits a yearning for a hot swallow, to ward off the brisk night air cooling our exposed side, as we turn front to back to capture the warmth of the fire.

The poets take us deeper into the purple sage where the coyotes howl, and the forlorn sound echoes across the ages. "Winter creeps along the mesa" and the fierce winds blow. We pull our sheepskin-lined coats tightly against our bodies, and huddle closer to the fire.

In our imaginations, we are up where "*The Cowboy Shepherd of the Range*" is in charge and a "*Line Camp Christmas Letter*" is being written to the folks back home. In the dim firelight, a stubby pencil gripped by a cold unsteady hand, scrawls this message on a lonely Christmas Eve, "Those critters sure are driftin'...Merry Christmas to you all."

A cold Michigan Christmas

Wandering has taken me back to my home-stomping grounds in Michigan for Christmas, only once since I went on the road. I really looked forward to being in my own church, and volunteered to be in the "living Nativity."

It was so cold, the sheep were looking for wool coats to wear over their wool coats, and only a few hardy souls showed up each half hour to help. I played a wiseman and an angel, (not at the same time). Never has an angel been so well padded.

Many full-timers drive, or fly home for the holidays, or sometimes stay where "home" is until after Christmas, then head south for warmth and old friends (the ones they've made since they started full-timing).

The following outing turned out to be a real stroke of luck. When you can combine history and holidays, the fun is even greater, as in...

A Historic Christmas in Shepherdstown

We had traveled many miles. We arrived at the inn. There was room.

Margaret Perry, our gracious hostess, gave us a tour of the historic Thomas Shepherd Inn, and settled us in our rooms. The "we" included my daughter and son-in-law, Tracey and Tom. The Sprinter stayed behind, flirting outrageously with another RV the entire Thanksgiving weekend. Our plans were to visit the Antietam National Battlefield at nearby Sharpsburg, MD. With pure luck riding on our bumper, our destination town was celebrating its annual "*A Historic Christmas in Shepherdstown, W. V.*"

Mufflers, mittens, and multiple mantles in and around our person, we trooped down the steep hill into the crisp autumn night to assuage our rumbling tummies.

Chestnuts roasted on an open fire at the corner. I discovered I didn't like roasted chestnuts, after all these years of singing about them. The fire, built on a portable surface, called to us as Jack Frost nipped our noses. We joined the merry group of revelers warming their backsides, frontsides, and sidesides, and sang joyous carols into the frigid air.

A "twist" in Charles Dickens tales of Oliver, were young "Pocket-Puts." Rather than encourage pickpockets, Mrs. Hi-Penny and her scruffy scholars of the night, smuggled goodies *into* the pockets of unaware visitors.

The only thing stolen in Shepherdstown that evening was dessert. Finger-licking treats were offered at several businesses but being smarter than average bears, we selected Ye Olde Sweet Shoppe Bakery. They were featured in Bon Appetit and Gourmet magazines. We weren't surprised, after tasting their "Honest to Goodness Old World German Stollen." They almost guarantee this fantastic delicacy will take you "half way between ordinary ecstacy and the Heavenly kind." I'm a believer.

Town criers informed us of coming events. A mixture of street peddlers, strolling carolers, and townspeople costumed in the flavor of Dickens, roamed through the crowd. Suddenly, everyone was silenced in common awe. The enormous Christmas tree lit up and church bells rang. Santa arrived in front of McMurran Hall to the cheers of all the little children, and all the big people whose hearts were that of children, at least for one night.

Tired and cold, but happy, we trudged back up German Street hill to the Inn. Visions of a hot bath to thaw my 2000 body parts, were dancing in my head.

Between the French and Indian War, the Revolutionary War, and the Civil War, this town has undergone numerous changes. The town of Mecklenburg, Virginia, came into existence twenty-eight years after Thomas Shepherd obtained a 222 acre land grant in 1734. In 1798, it was renamed "Shepherd's Town" and in 1820, to the present "Shepherdstown." The transitions weren't over. The last change was after the Civil war. Shepherdstown became part of a new state. Since 1868, it has been known as West Virginia's oldest community.

Saturday and Sunday mornings before a home-cooked breakfast at a B & B are delightful. Both days we lounged by the fire, read the morning papers, and became acquainted with interesting guests of varying backgrounds and occupations.

We didn't throw any silver dollars across the Potomac River; but we did hike up to the overlook. We admired the monument to one of the town's creative sons, James Rumsey, "Inventor of the world's first steamboat." I admit I always gave credit to Robert Fulton but perhaps he just had a better publicist. Our wanderings also took us to see a model of Rumsey's steamboat at the Rumsey Museum.

The little house is called just that, Little House, and when I saw it, I wanted to wrinkle my nose and bring my granddaughter, Rebecca, across the miles from Washington State to see it. The Little House is a block building, big enough for adults to stand in hunched over, but movement was limited. I flattened against the stairs to see the upstairs bedrooms and bathroom. A kitchen and living room were downstairs. All furniture, light fixtures, and utensils were geared to little people. It was decorated for the season both in and out ,and a delightful place to take children.

We had lunch in The Old Pharmacy Cafe and Soda Fountain, and felt we had walked into a set from "It's a Wonderful Life." That "Step back in time" was what we experienced whether we were inside the Opera House, the Entler Hotel, or walking the streets.

"The Gift," a "moving" play in song and verse, was held at the Thomas Shepherd Inn where we stayed. Churches gave musical concerts and served refreshments. The two weekends of the festival are packed with activities. The big event is the Charity Ball given by the Rotary Club the second Friday night of the celebration, in the Shepherdstown Fire Hall.

If all of this action isn't enough, hiking the Chesapeake and Ohio Canal's towpath beside the Potomac River or walking the nearby Civil War National Battlefields of Harper's Ferry and Antietam, are alternatives.

As for me, I had a great time, but I had to get back to the Sprinter. I heard rumors he was getting hitched. Merry Christmas to all of you wherever you are, from the Silver Gypsy, wherever I am. God Bless.

I haven't hit nearly as many fairs, festivals, and special holiday celebrations as I would like to, but I intend to remedy that. In the next chapter, I'll show you how you can be with "extended" family, if you're not going to be with your own immediate family.

Street scene, Leavenworth, Washington, a Bavarian Village

YOU'RE AN ESCAPEE?...
FROM WHAT?

Campgrounds, Directories, RV Organizations, and Volunteering

I have really enjoyed my membership in Escapees, Inc. for a lot of years, and a lot of reasons. Most of us who are SKPs, have the emblem of a house in a wagon, on our RVs. If I see that emblem, I'm almost sure I've found a friend. Recently, I was attending church in Peshastin, Washington. An RVing couple who were guests, were introduced as full-timers. Afterward when I was talking with them, I asked where their base was. She said Livingston, Texas. I immediately asked if they were SKPs. They were, and I collected my hugs.

You'll see a lot of Texas license plates and Texas addresses. Most of them are Escapees, or SKPs.

Even though the membership is probably close to 50,000 people by now, it is the warmest RV organization I have ever belonged to. It doesn't mean people run up to you and hug you, if you don't want to participate, but often, a hug results from meeting other SKPs. I like that. There isn't enough warmth between people any more. We seem to be afraid of closeness. Now, on to other thoughts.

While I enjoy staying in formal campgrounds sometimes, I really prefer **primitive** camping with my generator, solar panels, inverter, computer, printer, VCR, TV, air conditioner, and microwave. Well, somebody's got to do it.

National

On April 30, 1997, new or increased fees, were instituted in nearly a hundred National Park Service Parks, Historic Sites, and Monuments. The U. S. Fish and Wildlife Service and Bureau of Land Management, also increased their fees in some areas. This is all part of a three-year Recreational Fee Demonstration Program, to raise funds for maintenance and capital improvements on public lands.

Keep in mind that many of the government parks are now run by concessionaires, and they take reservations months in advance. Some campsites are usually left open on a first-come-first-served basis. For specific in-season or holiday times, or if you need full hook-ups, reserve well in advance.

I prefer national forest campgrounds, or boondocking, depending on where I am. Many state park fees have bounced right out of my league. The highest fee parks are usually in seasonal tourist areas, that I wouldn't choose to visit anyhow. I belong to Coast to Coast and some of their sites are outrageously close. Others are nicely arranged with green barriers between. I usually don't go to private campgrounds because of the expense, and I don't use enough of their facilities to warrant $20/night (or more).

Usually, magnificent scenes in the boonies, outweigh the times I need or want the amenities. Needing or wanting the social part of campground life, makes a different, too. I enjoy company sometimes, but I am not a card or game player. Many people love the camaraderie that builds in a campground situation. I have made many friends that way also.

If you choose to park overnight in a rest area, leave the key in ignition and the RV headed out for quick get-a-way. Unless there are a lot of people around, use your own facilities instead of going inside. Don't advertise whether you are alone or a couple. We are all vulnerable. Park where there are other RVs or trucks.

My rules for boondocking outside designated camping areas:
>If it is posted, don't stay
>Don't block anything
>Don't knowingly park on private property (without permission)
>Be unobtrusive
>>Don't dump anything
>>Don't leave any kind of mess
>>Leave it better than you found it
>If it is a public area (Wal-Mart, grocery store, gas station, etc.) don't stay more than one night. Don't tear down your rig to do mechanical work. Ask permission. Buy something.
>Get there after 7 p.m.
>Close your drapes before it is dark enough people can see in
>Leave early in the a.m.
>Keep a quiet, low profile

Directories

It makes good sense to have an RV campground directory in your RV, especially, if you need or desire shore power every night. They list private campgrounds, state parks, rules, discounts, tourist attractions, maps, RV service centers, dump stations, and LP gas locations, among other helpful things. They have ratings for facilities, restrooms & visual appeal. They often give availability of sites for big rigs, or whether you will share hookups. The months and hours of operation are given also. The cost is from $10 to $20.

If you are a member of Good Sam, 10% discounts are offered at some parks. You must remember to ask about discounts. They are usually advertised, but registration people don't often remind you about them, when you are signing in.

The 1997 Trailer Life Directory offers a 45% Good Sam member discount for the directory.

KOA (Kampgrounds of America) has a free Road Atlas, Camping Guide and Directory for over 500 private campgrounds, in the United States, Canada, and a few in Mexico. They offer a two-year KOA Value Kard for $10. This allows you a 10% discount on daily registration fees at all KOA Kampgrounds, plus express check-in since they already have the information. Directories are available at any KOA.

The S*M*A*R*T (Special Military Active Retired Travel Club) Directory of sites and facilities, is available from the club, and at military commissaries. This is low-cost (or free) camping on approximately two-hundred military bases for active, retired, and reserve military, and defense employees. Daily and weekly camping rates are lower than nearby public or private campgrounds. These "Fam-Camps," national and international, are often in picturesque spots, and convenient to attractions.

The Escapee Club offers a variety of facilities for their $50 annual dues. Rental spaces for a night, or a season, are open on a space-available basis (and some have leased lots for sale) at eleven SKP co-op campgrounds. In addition, five Rainbow Parks have rental campsites and/or deeded lots. All parks offer inexpensive, but limited boondocking. They are located in the southeast, south, southwest, west, and northwest. A member Discount Directory lists a 15 - 50% discount at hundreds of commercial parks. This same directory lists overnight parking spots at the homes of fellow SKPs.

I anticipate receiving the deed to a 50 X 70' lot at a SKP Rainbow Park between Wickenburg and Congress, Arizona, by the time I return there in late fall of 1997. It already has a 10 X 12' shed on it, and will have a cement patio pad. I paid $8,000 for it several years ago and the value has gone up.

If you are a member of the Elks, you have the privilege of staying in their accommodations. Some Elks Clubs have more elaborate camping facilities, but most of them are parking-lot-type overnighting, sometimes with electric.

Membership Campgrounds

There are at least two membership campgrounds, Coast to Coast and Thousand Trails. They are similar in that they provide less costly RV parking for a week, or two weeks at a time. Less costly, once the initial price is paid, that is. I paid $3,800 for my membership through Colorado River Adventures, in 1988. They have four parks in Arizona and California. I seldom visit them because they are not in my path. If I do, I usually go to Emerald Cove, near Parker, Arizona, because they offer phone service in my rig. As a full-timer, I have gotten my money back.

Different types of memberships at various prices, are offered in Coast to Coast and Thousand Trails. Second hand memberships are for sale in the

RV magazine ads, but buyer beware. Make sure you are getting what you want.

I believe you can stay in Thousand Trails parks for two weeks at a time, with a week out. Coast to Coast allows two weeks in your home park, and one week out, before returning. You can do that indefinitely in your home park. They also have a program during the less busy season, where you can pay for the "out" week, and stay on your site.

You are allowed to stay in the approximately 500 other Coast to Coast parks around the country for one week in, thirty days out, then one more week. You can do that once a year, in that specific park. You can do that same thing in the other 499 parks.

They have other types of memberships as well. Coast to Coast is offering "Welcome Coupons" for $7.78 a night (at 228 luxury Coast to Coast resorts) to allow non-members to find out what the system is all about. That is a good deal. It lets you visit, talk with other people, and make up your mind without pressure. Keep in mind, the ad says "luxury." Parks around the country come in all stages of good, bad, indifferent, and "luxury." The luxury parks really are just that. When you get in those you'd like to stay forever. In all fairness, C to C is trying to weed out the problem areas.

In the beginning, these membership parks used really high pressure sales people. If you decided not to buy in, you were really treated badly. I did not buy in at the place that treated me that way, and I got a better deal at a later time, in a better park. I don't know what their sales tactics are now, but don't be pressured into buying anything. Check with other owners, look into the background and finances of the places you are interested in. Look over their rules before buying.

To find out if you have a need to belong to a membership campground, wait for six months or a year after you go on the road full time. It would be helpful to have access to one of their books, to check this out. Maybe a friend has an old one. Do you find the campgrounds are in your path or nearby? Are they inconvenient to reach? Do you find yourself choosing recreational or state parks, because you like the woods or the seashore better? Do you need or want full amenities every night? All these are things to consider.

Someone at a rally said you should travel for a year, and if you weren't without a campsite at any time, and didn't feel you had overspent for campgrounds, then you probably didn't need membership campgrounds. We go right back to choices.

With the cost of private and public campgrounds going up, the $4 a night will become more and more attractive to those who want full hookups.

I wish more campgrounds, private, public, membership, or organizational, would offer campsite phone service (with on-line service -- I don't want much!). I am willing to pay for the privilege. This is an unpaid political announcement.

Volunteer Organizations

SOWERS
(Servants on Wheels Ever Ready)

This volunteer group of RVers travel around the country, working at least a month at a time, on church construction or renovating children's homes. They are usually given a parking space and full hook-ups, by whoever is hosting the project. It's a matter of taking your skills and talents on the road, and putting them to good use while you see the country and make new friends.

RV Habitat Gypsies
A division of Habitat for Humanity International

The one summer I was free to work with RV Habitat Gypsies, I was not able to make connections. It is one of many organizations who need volunteers.

RV Habitat Gypsies work in partnership with new owners, in building and renovating decent, affordable housing. Their philosophy is "A hand up, not a hand out." Makes sense to me.

Mercy Ships

Since 1993, I have carried an article on "Mercy Ships." When I checked the #800 number (Resources), it was still current. This is the maritime arm of Youth with a Mission, international, interdenominational ministry. They are open to people of all ages and need a variety of skills and talents "to make a difference in the world." The mission of Mercy Ships is to deliver medical care and disease relief to countries throughout the world.

You can serve on a short-term basis of two weeks to three months or get into terms of a year and more. You pay for training and pay your way monthly in this non-profit Christian relief agency. The Mercy Ships have taken medical care, relief aid, and long-term sustainable change to the places they have visited since 1978.

I can only tell you about what I've read. It sounds exciting.

Education, Service, and Fun combined

I've often run into Elderhostel groups, and some close friends are also active with them. They offer opportunities to do service through several organizations. They are active nationally, as well as internationally, and intergenerationally (Whoa! That's a mouthful). Their activities might include being a part of a musical performing group or digging at an archeological find. You might find yourself doing research or writing short stories. The programs are varied and interesting.

If you're going to be staying in one place for a while, check out that class that you've always wanted to take at the local university.

Didn't you always want to learn to paint--or get back to it?

I've always wanted to play the guitar. One of these days I'm going to find time for it. Have you always wanted to play an instrument? What is the matter with learning now?

Try a new hobby.

Magazines

There are two national magazines you can get off the rack in the local store, Motorhome and Trailer Life. TL Enterprises puts out an updated RV Buyers Guide every year. It gives photos, floorplans, and specifications of all the latest RVs on the market.

The regional RV magazines are sometimes offered free at campgrounds, but they are also sold by subscription. They are filled with information about campgrounds, special activities, and places to visit in their part of the country. They each have technical writers who answer questions you send in, or write on specific problems facing RVers. And of course, they have articles like this columnist writes. As you might have guessed, my columns are low-tech, high adventure.

A quarterly magazine I highly recommend, is Loren Eyrich's Two-Lane Roads. It covers just about anything that might be of interest east of the Mississippi, and occasionally, west of the Mississippi. Eyrich travels around the country in his RV, then stops to put out his magazine. Well, kids say the darndest things -- and this editor kid does too. He has fun with his magazine and you will too. (Resources)

Life On Wheels Conference

Life on Wheels Conferences are being offered around the country, as extension classes from the University of Idaho. So far they are scheduled in Idaho, Pennsylvania, Nevada, Texas, and Oregon, with plans to continue spreading classes around the country. This is the brainchild of Gaylord Maxwell. He has pulled in instructors with expertise in all areas of RVing.

I had the privilege of flying back from Alaska last summer, to be an instructor, and have been invited back this year, and also will be in Pennsylvania and Nevada. Classes focus on the educational, rather than the social, although several events are planned. It is a great learning experience. (Resources)

RV Organizations

I have never been much of a joiner, but when I first went on the road, I joined every organization. As time went on, I had reasons to stay in some, and drop others. The following will give you a scoop on what the national meetings are like, as well as give you insight into what each organization offers.

National Meetings

People join RV organizations for various reasons, usually for camaraderie with those of similar interests, but it might also be for message and mail-forwarding services, or even a break on insurance and towing rates. Regardless, they all have local, state, and national meetings known as Samborees,

Escapades, rallies, conventions, or whatever.

RVers who have never attended one, ask, "But what do they *do* at these things? I only go to big group activities when they are in my path or if I'm giving a seminar; however, when I have gone, I have never failed to have a great time. Smaller, more localized meetings or rallies are more intimate, sit-around-the-campfire type, but any kind of meeting, local or national, offers a fresh view of almost everything. This is a national meeting composite.

The mountains are hazy in the early morning sun or gulls dip and dive over ocean waves or maple trees provide shade in the midwest or palm trees tremble in the desert. Flags flap in the breeze of a new day.

Volunteers, mostly on foot, others in golf carts, guide RVs of all sizes and shapes to parking spots just big enough to fit with the awning extended. Tags are unhooked and parked. Treat these volunteers with great courtesy. They were here at 5 a.m.

After settling in and registering, an opening ceremony includes raising the flag by representatives of the Marine Corps and hundreds of voices singing our National Anthem.

The next day at 6:30 a.m., lively music mixes with the laughter of early birds deep in chit-chat sessions with new-found friends. "Are you fulltim-

Stuart, Florida

ers?" "Where are you from?" Joyous hugging reunions be-tween old friends accompany the hot coffee. "Where have you been?" "Did you ever make it to...?" This is discovery time. It really is a small world.

Delicious barbecue aromas follow brisk walkers, slow walkers, a few with canes or wheelchairs, or braver ones on in-line skates, to seminars. Instructors begin, "There are no dumb questions except the ones that you haven't asked."

Seminars range from learning crafts or driving, to fixing your refrigerator or diesel engine. Each person has his or her own need or interest and there are plenty of seminars from which to choose. Couples break up and attend different seminars to compare notes later. Everyone wants to learn something new or unique to better their RVing years. Some attend classes for the inside story of what full-timing is all about or how to manage alone. They want suggestions on how to get rid of accumulated "stuff." They want reassurance they won't be forgotten if they go on the road.

Neon lights on mobile kiosks advertise hot coffee, fresh pastries and other irresistible cholesterol makers. Enormous red, white, and blue umbrellas shade picnic tables, providing comfort for reading the material picked up at the last seminar. Mobile telephones provide access to elderly parents, grandchildren, or neighbors who are watching the house.

Yellow shuttles, strangely reminiscent of ye olde school buses, deposit passengers with sore feet and tired backs at their parking spaces. They gather them up for activities or for walking through commercial exhibits.

"Doing lunch" consists of going "home" to the RV or trying fry bread, hot dogs and hamburgers, or some of that previously mentioned barbecue, with non-fat frozen yogurt for dessert. In the afternoon, more seminars beckon, or maybe a visit through new RVs displayed in the parking lot. At designated areas and times, guitar players or singers or magicians perform for your pleasure before the next seminar or instead of, if you've absorbed enough knowledge for one day.

A lively alternative to seminars is learning to line dance. A tall, slender fellow in high-heeled cowboy boots and a western hat leads potential line dancers to the *Cowboy Boogie*. "Left behind left, right behind right." Somehow his fluid movement is much more graceful than theirs. They hang in there. By the time he is through with them, only a few are doing left behind right, right behind left and OOPS, "What do I do with this leftover foot."

A little round dancing brings out, "Guys what are you doing while she's turning? No, not admiring the view." Clouds form above two couples who are squaring off and considering divorce their only answer.

By four or five o'clock, friends gather for happy hour outside of a rig or a "chapter" from a certain state or locality has a planning session for going out to dinner.

Raucous cheering accompanies the winners of a myriad of prizes as the evening's assorted entertainment begins in the auditorium. If the gathering is big enough, large screens show the activities or speakers on stage for those sitting in the higher altitudes.

Music ranges from Gospel to the *Twelfth Street Rag* to the *Can Can* and songs from *Leroy Brown* to *Elvira*. A haunting flute melody might take you back to an ancient time. You might hear sage advice from a hundred years ago about prospecting through gold country, "If you stumble on a rock, don't cuss it, cash it." Explicit directions follow instructions for drum making, "If you make a drum by spreading animal skins over a board, it is best to take the animal out of it first."

The entertainment might be The Eagle Dance by a local Indian family or Folkloric dancers twirling in colorful skirts. It might be the Knife Dance or a Mexican Hat Dance, anything to set the hands to clapping and feet to tapping.

A ventriloquist tells about a fool-proof way to avoid sky jacking, "You get into a plane and sing the Iraqi National Anthem. If anybody stands up, get out."

On the last night, a shiny silver ball whirls its magical lights onto couples dancing to *Kansas City* or *Begin the Begin.* They dance in red-fringed cowboy boots, sandals, loafers, tennies, and silver dancing shoes. Mostly, they dance in light-hearted joy.

Doughnuts and coffee are a traditional send off on the last morning. Laughter abounds with bear hugs and good-byes, "Until we meet again."

If you haven't gone to a national meeting, I urge you to go. Please don't hide in your RV. Nothing will happen. You have to meet these experiences half way or they won't bring you any pleasure. The best way to participate is to volunteer. I guarantee you will meet a lot of really interesting people and you will make more new friends than you'll know what to do with.

Volunteering through your RV organization

You can join the leagues of volunteers as a full-time RVer. Opportunities are many. The RV organizations sponsor different projects. Good Sam sponsors "Dogs for the Deaf." FMCA has "Round Up for Homeless Families" and "Round Up for Literacy" campaigns.

Singles

Many singles would not enjoy this lifestyle as much as I do, if they had to do everything alone. It isn't necessary to be alone. There are many people traveling solo, and a number of singles organizations. The following will give you an idea of what is out there for those who want to, or are, traveling single.

"Singles" are individual enough to handle being alone, independent enough to take care of inevitable problems, free to be themselves, and take advantage of whatever adventure crosses their path.

Although there are concerns among those who haven't tried it yet, traveling alone does not have to be "lonely." You are usually only as alone as you want to be.

There are as many singles organizations, as couple-oriented organizations. Singles International is a chapter of FMCA. Thousand Trails/Naco organize their single members according to region. BOF (Birds of a Feather) Singles are a part of Escapees. LoWs are Loners on Wheels and LoAs are Loners of America. WIN (Wandering Individuals Network) was organized for RVers born after 1927, and "RVing Women," is exclusively for women.

The various singles RVing groups share common ground. Each club has a newsletter with addresses, hobbies and interests of their membership, RV tips, upcoming activities and invitations to park at member homes. Their rallies and campouts usually include educational sessions on anything from solar energy Vs generators to fire safety to medical emergencies.

The purpose of the singles organizations is to provide camaraderie for people from all walks of life. One of the benefits is getting warm hugs from each other.

The members are diverse in personality and age with some groups emphasizing adventure more than others. The clubs give members a chance to meet others who have like interests, fishing, hiking, skiing, dancing, etc. It gives them a chance to form caravan groups for going to Mexico or Alaska or wherever. Singles often join several groups for the variety of people and interests.

"The Slabs" in southeast California is a popular place to spend the holiday season. This is a former military base where deserted cement foundations provide a solid base to "boondock" in the desert. The world's largest flea market and gem show calls singles to Quartzsite, Arizona, in January and February. Coyote Howls in Why, Arizona, is also a favorite winter place, along with Texas and Florida. Singles scatter to the four winds in the hot summer with northern chapters hosting more of the rallies.

RVing Women has a Resident Resort Park in Apache Junction, Arizona. SKP singles have access to Escapees Rainbow and Co-op parks in the south, west and northwest. Lozark Park at Ellsinore, MO, is billed as "The only singles campground in the country" and welcomes singles with or without a group affiliation.

Any time of the year you are apt to find singles on BLM (Bureau of Land Management) land; state, regional, county, national forest, or Corps of Engineers parks, sometimes working for a season as a volunteer host. Some singles take advantage of belonging to Coast to Coast and/or Thousand Trails membership parks.

Activities are endless and range from horseshoes to tubing a river to y-jumping. Any style dancing is a major form of entertainment with a Sadie Hawkins Day Dance or a "Singles Stomp" or an old-fashioned "hoe-down." They go to Blue Grass Festivals and join impromptu or planned-in-advance caravans that may take them to the Mardi Gras, the Biggest Halloween Party on Earth, or the beaches of Baja, Mexico.

For all of you "Wannabee" single RVers, you don't have to go it alone unless you choose to. You can join the singles organizations, and still be a free and independent single.

Other

One of the really terrific benefits to being a full-time RVer, is that it gives you "chunks" of time, to do wonderful things you never had time for before. I have taken advantage of this time, by living on a beach in Mexico, volunteering for the United States Forest Service, being a "Kitchen Girl" at the Bar-M Dude Ranch in Oregon, a guinea pig for a government study in North Dakota (while I wrote *RVing North America*), and house-sitting in Washington.

Maps and information!

I am usually lost somewhere. That is how I've seen a great deal of North America. Carry good reference material with you. Mostly it won't matter if you get lost because you'll see a few surprises, and occasionally have an adventure, you weren't counting on. Don't do it by boondocking in downtown big city USA. Big cities have a great deal to offer, but that is also where the greater danger is. Take tours in bigger cities or go in with really good information and directions. Wandering in the wee hours in a big city, is not always a good choice.

If you are going to Canada and Alaska, the best information and map will come with the Milepost magazine. No, you shouldn't consider going without it. Use it in conjunction with my latest book (other than this one), *RVing Alaska! (and Canada.)*. I also recommend their other publication, i.e., Northwest Milepost.

I suggest you get the trucker's Atlas with the laminated pages that won't tear. As a full-timer, you will use it a lot. I like individual large maps of each area I'm traveling in. An Atlas isn't as detailed as I like, but they are great for quick perusal, and the big picture.

If you hike, bike, or explore beyond the main highways, I recommend getting the Atlas and Gazetteer for specific states. These are detailed topographical maps with side roads and trails. I haven't always found these to be entirely accurate or updated, but they are better than a regular map for specifics.

If you belong to the American Automobile Association, they have Tour-Books with detailed information on every State, Canada, and Mexico. For the size of their book, they have a tremendous amount of information. The Automobile Club of Southern California, specifically, has an excellent information book on Baja.

Send for maps and information. You'll be inundated with material and good maps. They will let you in on festivals, holiday celebrations, and whatever is unique in their area, and the dates. Trip routing is available from your RV organizations, FMCA, Escapees, Good Sam, Coast to Coast, etc. Computer buffs do keyword searches and find tons of information on the internet. (Resources)

I highlight my route on the map. If I'm going through a city, I write down the turns and landmarks on paper, and tape it to the dash. It only takes a glance to know where I'm going. I still get lost but I do it with style.

If you're going to order anything, have it sent directly to someone's address (children, friends). It won't come through your mail-forwarding that way. That can get expensive. It will keep your mail-forwarding address from being put on a list. "Stuff" will come from every direction after your name is sold to a thousand lists. After you have collected your information and run, your friends and family can dispose of the junk mail for the next ten years.

Visit all the information booths in each new state or territory. Ask for maps, often they are kept behind the desk.

Information centers are great places to meet other RVers and exchange road conditions, and possibility information. Take it all in, add a grain of salt, mix it with your own knowledge and desires, then toss out what you don't need, and go from there.

Keep your material organized. Keep it handy. I've never done this in my life, but it's a **great idea**.

Talk about Information Highway, if you have access to a computer, you can find out about any place, how to get there, what to do, and how to do it. Computer information is to the point of real detail these days. A friend of mine pin-pointed the house I was house-sitting in this winter. It's scary to realize technology has taken us to individual houses. At the same time, if used wisely, it is a great boon to people who want to know where they are -- I'm not sure it won't take the adventure away.

Mapping programs are available on CD-ROM, and as close as your credit card number. I'll list some addresses in Resources.

Where can I go?

You are limited only by your imagination (and the clearance of your vehicle!). I never dreamed this Midwestern Presbyterian Widow would drive 200 miles north of the Arctic Circle, or 1,000 miles south of the Tropic of Cancer.

It was wonderful when people finally realized they didn't have to stay in one spot. Wheels were put under boxes filled with conveniences, and comforts, engines were added, or hitches attached, and we were able to take our homes on the road. Not to be outdone, campgrounds have taken to the road too, or more succinctly, to the waterways.

In 1990, it was my privilege to be on the maiden voyage of a barge campground on wheels, a "cruising campground, if you will. We went from New Orleans, Louisiana, along the Intercoastal Waterway, up the Atchafalaya River, into the Mighty Mississippi River, and back to New Orleans. It was a ten-day, 450-mile loop trip. Three custom-built barges were hooked together, with a carrying capacity for 42 RVs. It was a full-hookup 800' campground.

We made stops along the way, that included going through Ante-bellum mansions, touring ships, "callin' up the alligators," and taking part in a mini-mardigras. We spent several days in New Orleans. Of course, this included Bourbon Street and the French Quarter, with lots of honky-tonk and jazz. It was a great trip and a lot of caravan companies offer this. (Resources)

Life beyond RVing

I absolutely love Bed and Breakfast places. I see such interesting-looking ones as I cross country. What, you say, I am a rat fink for giving up my RV. Well, it isn't any different than when you lived in your land-bound house full time. Once in a while, it is fun to do something different.

What I had in mind to tell you about, and these things can all be done in conjunction with RVing, is renting a firetower (or volunteering in one) or a lighthouse. (Resources)

What can I do?

You are limited only by your imagination (and the clearance of your credit card!). I never dreamed this Midwestern Presbyterian Widow would canoe ten miles beyond the Arctic Circle or ride horseback through the waves of the Pacific Ocean, 1,000 miles south of the Tropic of Cancer.

Yes, I've done all those things and more, but not everyone has the spirit of adventure that I have.

> **You can have a great time full-timing and never leave the forty-eight continental United States. There is so much to see and do. You couldn't possibly see it all in one lifetime.**

Perhaps you are oriented more to traveling from point A to point B, and staying for six months at either end. Many people do that. The lifestyle still gives you more variety to your life, than hiding behind the snowdrifts of Maine, Michigan, Wisconsin, Washington, or wherever. The desert warmth in winter, and mountain coolness in summer, is yours.

General Store, Shuswap Lake, Sicamous, British Columbia, Canada

People often ask me, "What do you do with your time?" I don't have a problem with that. My days are filled with writing, traveling, and doing things I can write about. I am not retired; I am still working.

A lot of people go into full-time RVing after retirement. That's great, and they think it is great, and their kids think it is great. You won't be traveling every minute. Were you a workaholic? Have you always had a workshop, or filled your time with tinkering, sewing, quilting, making things? If you have, then you may not find complete enjoyment from traveling. Some people can. Right now, I'd love to forget I ever saw a computer, but that's because I'm in the middle of two books.

Take along whatever it takes to keep you, and your mate busy and happy. Don't go off into the hinterlands with nothing to do. Those who are bored to tears, will either start their happy hours earlier and earlier, or they will soon give up the lifestyle, and move back into a workshop or sewing room.

You may be perfectly happy "just sitting" for a while, or forever, but a lot of couples and individuals, are much happier, if they are doing "a little something." They like to volunteer for a few hours a week, sometimes in exchange for a place to park.

I do notice one thing as a single. I have a hard time keeping up with everything, mainly because I spend a lot of time in front of the computer. The husbands are always out washing, buffing, and shining everything to a mirror-like surface. I would hate for one of these guys to see my generator compartment. It's great. Cleanliness really is important to rigs that are subjected to constant dirt and dust.

Full-timing can be what you want it to be.
Don't put it off.
Make it happen.

For those of you who like to boondock beside a mountain stream, or park beside a cactus out in the desert, or somewhere else where the air is fresh, and life feels good because you are free, it may not last.

The National Association of RV Parks and Campgrounds is aggressively seeking government ruling outlawing our freedom to park overnight in rest areas, or other places not specifically set aside for what they call, RV "camping." The organization uses the justification that it is "unsafe" for us to park anywhere but in a specified campground. I'm sure that includes their wanting us to park only in the "safe" campgrounds that belong to ARVC.

I have boondocked, and used public, private, and membership campgrounds, probably even some belonging to this organization, without ever having heard of them before. They are stepping on my toes. I don't want their protection. I will use my own judgment where I park. As long as I follow my rules for boondocking, and the laws of this country, I am probably as safe as parking on the ARVC doorstep.

I very much resent their wanting to "coerce" me into a formal campground. If they want my business, let them woo me. If campgrounds provided overnight "parking," sans amenities, in convenient, non-crowded, level, grassy, scenic spots, for a reasonable price, I would be willing to pay to park -- nah -- I want to pay for parking whenever and wherever, because it is my choice.

It would be interesting to see ten years into a future of always having to be in a campground. Will the prices have soared? Will they, indeed, have room for all of us, without packing us in like sardines? (Food for thought maybe, but the whole situation smells fishy to me.)

BORDERS AND BARRIERS

Shared border rules, Canada or Mexico

Keep vehicle registrations, birth certificates, and pet inoculation records, in a plastic zip-up bag in your glove compartment. Have them handy for border guards, should they ask for them.

Check to see what fruits or vegetables you can take over the border before buying. They took potatoes at the Canadian border, and eggs at the US border coming out of Mexico. Go figure.

Don't take anyone else's word for the rules (even mine). Get current brochures and information. Be informed. You are the one who is ultimately responsible.

If you have an unhappy experience, or you feel you have been unfairly or unkindly treated, report it.

I've crossed into Canada and Mexico and back, nearly twenty times into Mexico, and probably thirty or more times into Canada, and I've never had a **real** problem.

MEXICO

All of Baja is a duty-free zone

Although you can enter Baja at several points, not all of them are open 24 hours. Mexican regulations are always subject to change. Check border opening times and regulations.

TOURIST CARDS:
Proof of US citizenship (Passport or original birth certificate)

If your stay is no longer than 72 hours, you don't need a tourist card. If you will be staying longer, get one. It is a good idea to carry proof of citizenship with you, regardless.

A single entry card is valid up to 180 days.

I found it quite simple to cross into Baja in 1996, with barely a nod from the officials. I didn't have to go inside, get a permit or anything. It is always best to check the current **(that day)** rules and regulations in case they have changed. (Resources)

<u>VEHICLE PERMITS:</u>

Car permits are not required in Baja California (unless you'll be crossing by ferry to the mainland) You must have with you:

Original current registration or notarized bill of sale and vehicle title for each vehicle.

Mission , Loreto, Baja, Sur, Mexico

A free bilingual booklet, Traveling to Mexico by Car, gives detailed information about car permits. (Resources)

If you are traveling into Mexico by yourself and pulling a car. One person cannot take more than one vehicle into Mexico.

Mainland Mexico

<u>TOURIST CARD:</u>
You must obtain a Tourist Card from the border crossing immigration office or a Mexico Consulate office. This is good for up to 90 days. You will need:

A photo ID - Driver's license
Valid proof of citizenship (passport, original birth certificate, notarized affidavit of citizenship or voter registration card)

Going into Mainland Mexico, you must have:
Major credit card for paying U.S. $11 (Cash not accepted)*
Vehicle registration (one for each vehicle or boat trailer, etc.
Driver's license
Proof of US insurance
If your vehicle is leased, a notarized letter with permission
Proof of citizenship (Tourist Card)

With this information, you will be issued a sticker for your vehicle. It is valid for up to six months, and must be returned to the registration center when returning from Mexico.

*You must have a major credit card to pay a non-refundable $11. This is a fairly recent regulation, an attempt on their part to prevent theft, and smuggling of stolen cars into Mexico. You sign a paper promising to return your vehicle to the border. This registration center is about fifteen miles south of the border. Within fifteen miles of the border, and the 65 miles to Puerto Penasco, is a "free zone" where you need not register your car.

When I went to Puerto Penasco a couple of years ago, I wouldn't have known I crossed a border.

CUSTOMS:

When entering Mexico, you will be asked if you have anything to declare. If you are within limits of items allowed by law (below), you will press a button on a "random selection" device. The light will flash green if you are cleared to proceed uninterrupted. A red light will mean you are subject to a brief, informal baggage inspection.

You are allowed to take into Mexico: Personal clothing, luggage, and up to the following items (per person)
Three liters of alcohol or wine
400 cigarettes or two boxes of cigars
One movie camera and one regular camera
Gift items not to exceed $50 value.
$300 limit on items acquired from the border or "free zone"
Save your receipts for verification.

When re-entering the US:
Declare all agriculture products
Fruits, vegetables, and meats, fowl taken from the US to Mexico, may not be allowed to re-enter. (Check in advance with USDA Inspectors)
Items that cannot be brought into the US:
Firearms
Fresh fruits
Vegetables
Dangerous substances
Products made from endangered species

Is it safe to travel in Mexico?

The last time I traveled extensively in Mexico (other than Baja the month of January, 1996), was in 1986, 1987, and 1988-89 with shorter visits in later years, to San Carlos and Puerto Penasco. Puerto Penasco is a great place to get a taste of Mexico, only 66 miles below the border crossing at Lukeville, Arizona (You go through Organ Pipe Cactus National Monument south of Ajo).

On my first trip into Mexico (Baja), I followed good friends, who had spent many years traveling Mexico. If you are the least bit apprehensive, either caravan with other RVers, or join a commercial caravan, for your first trip into Mexico.

In January of 1989, fellow travelers said I was crazy to take a relatively new motorhome into Mexico. I crossed the border at Brownsville, Texas, into Metamoros, Mexico, down through Cuidad Victoria, San Luis Potosi, San Miguel de Allende. Over almost three months of travel, I went as far south as Puebla, Cuernavaca, Acapulco, and then north to Nogales, Arizona. I went through fourteen drug checks by the Federales with no problem. The Seelvar-haired gringa, she ees no problema.

Except for nearly running out of gas on lonely Highway 200 along the coast, I had no major problems. I admit to having some nightmares several months after I returned, but there was no logical basis for them. I found the Mexican people, especially away from the tourist areas, to be kind, helpful,

Roadside Shrine, Baja, Sur, Mexico

and generous. Perhaps they were, "Taking care of the loco lady who travels by herself."

It was a tremendous adventure (Covered in book *RVing North America, Silver, Single, Solo*). I don't necessarily advise anyone else to do it, but I had no problems with the people, safety, language, fuel, food (except the food poisoning in Puerto Vallarta), or money. I felt safe enough to go to the town squares at night, where all the Mexican world comes alive after siesta time in the afternoon.

By the way, one of the campgrounds I'd really like to go back to is Sayulita Trailer Park, 40 kilometers north of Puerto Vallarta, on Route #200. Thies and Cristina Rohlfs, who run the park, are super people, and it has to be the cleanest park in Mexico. (Resources)

But that's enough of my adventures. On to the important stuff.

Firearms

Do not take firearms of any kind into Mexico! Some guns are permitted during hunting season with the proper documents. Don't take chances. **Leave the guns at home.**

Pets

Any pet must have a veterinarian's vaccination certificate for rabies, and an Official Interstate and International Health Certificate for Dogs and Cats. If the pet is out of the US for over thirty days, the owner must present the rabies certificate when returning to the US.

Returning to the US

Keep a record, with receipts (and serial numbers), of expensive items like binoculars and cameras. These can be registered at US Customs. This is to eliminate their thinking you bought them in Mexico.

Insurance

> **In the Republic of Mexico, a vehicle accident is considered a criminal offense as well as a civil matter.**
> **It is not a misdemeanor;**
> **it is a felony.**

Vehicle accidents in Mexico are subject to the laws of Mexico only. They have nothing to do with the laws of the United States. If you have an accident, you will be detained until you prove financial responsibility.

The coverage under your insurance's endorsement may not be recognized by the Mexican authorities; in fact, it will more than likely, not be. Don't take a chance.

> **Buy insurance from a <u>licensed</u> Mexican Insurance Company for your vehicles before you cross the border.**

Sanborn Mexican Insurance is available near the border in several places. They have a comprehensive travelogue of Mexico. It is free with the insurance policy. The rates given to me on 6/4/97, were $5.24 a day or $162.86 a year, for all of Mexico.

For Mexican auto insurance, you will need:
Proof of ownership
Vehicle ID number

> **ALL ACCIDENT CLAIMS MUST BE REPORTED IN MEXICO BEFORE LEAVING MEXICO.**

I drove the length of Baja during January last year. It was rather a spur-of-the-moment trip, so I didn't get my insurance ahead of time. I bought it at the border at Tecate, California.

I paid $122.90 in US Funds for thirty days. Depending on who you are buying it from, and how long you are staying, it is sometimes cheaper to buy it for a year.

Cash or Credit Cards in Mexico

The currency is in pesos, and it fluctuates. The $ sign denotes pesos. I exchange US money for Mexican pesos at a bank on the US side, near the border. Otherwise, I use my VISA for a cash advance in a Mexican bank in Mexican pesos. I get the exchange rate for that day. This sometimes requires standing in line a long time (only to find you are in the wrong line).

Money can be exchanged at Casas de cambio (currency exchange houses). They are usually open longer than the banks. **Watch the exchange rate**. In 1996, I found the Casas de cambio to have reasonable rates of exchange. Bank hours are generally 9 - 2:30 Monday through Friday

Baja had changed considerably since I had lived on the beach. In the bigger cities in the north and at Cabo San Lucas, where tourism is rampant, they were accepting credit cards for payment. Often in the past, they might be willing to accept them, except the machine was broken or Uncle Jose's niece, Maria, had a sprained wrist.

Roads

The roads in Baja California Norte (North), were really bad in January of 1996. Baja California Sur (South) roads were pretty good. Short stretches of pavement were new and very good. There is one major road through Baja with a loop from LaPaz, down past San Jose Del Cabo and Cabo San Lucas. Route #1 from the border to just beyond Ensenada, and between San Jose Del Cabo and Cabo San Lucas, are four-lane divided highways.

Most side roads were gravel or dirt. Roads leading into larger towns were paved. Mexico Highway #3 from Tecate to Ensenada, #1 from south of Ensenada, and #19 are paved, and narrow, with almost non-existent shoulders most of the way. I haven't driven Highway #3 from Ensenada, or Highway #5 from Mexicali, to San Felipe.

The road to Puerto Penasco, was under construction a couple of years ago.

Mainland Mexico has four-lane highways, and toll roads, down at least as far as Culiacan. Other four-lane and toll roads, are in various parts of the country, but mostly, roads are two-lane, sometimes narrow, with no shoulders. Sometimes they offer discount coupons for the toll roads but you have to ask for them. Tolls are expensive. You can sometimes avoid the toll roads by taking the old routes. It may take you through the cities but you weren't in a hurry were you? It is fascinating, and cheaper.

Don't turn on red, unless a sign says you may.

Distances are measured in kilometers.

Don't use your left turn signal on the highway. <u>A left signal on the open road is an invitation to the person behind you to pass.</u> If you must turn left, pull to the side, let traffic pass, then cross the road and turn.

Don't go into Mexico, anywhere, with the idea of hurrying. For one thing, you won't see it that way. For another, the roads, animals in them, and broken-down trucks, are a consideration on two-lane roads.

I haven't driven all the roads by a long shot, but on the roads I have driven, situations are sometimes, enough to get your heart started.

Mexico is a fascinating country. Slow down, smell the dust, and return the smile of its people.

"Angeles Verdes"

What could make you smile more than meeting an angel? Throughout Mexico, The "**Green Angels**" patrol the major highways. They are government sponsored helpers in green pickup trucks who provide free emergency assistance to those in need. They carry limited parts, and gasoline (You pay the cost). They have radios to call for help or to tow you. They are supposed to pass by any given area, at least twice a day. The bi-lingual drivers usually have some mechanical skills.

Since I am always lost, my contact with the Green Angels has been asking directions. Signage in Mexico is terrible. I get even more lost than usual down there.

I came into Acupulco from the east, trying to find the correct turn for a campground on the beach, north of Acapulco. I couldn't find the road, and I didn't want to wind up in downtown Acapulco with the motorhome. I showed one of the Green Angels the map, and told him which campground I wanted to find.

He graciously offered to escort me to my destination. We went right into the city. We found **a** campground, **a** very nice one, but **not** the one I was looking for. After he left, I drove out of town, and eventually found my way out of the city, and along the ocean to the campground.

I have always loved my forays into Mexico. One thing I have learned. The Mexican people are wonderful people. They willingly and graciously give you directions to anywhere you want to go. It isn't often the directions take you there.

Fuel

Refueling stations in Mexico are called Pemex stations. It is a good idea to keep your tank topped off. This is not the problem it was years ago, but you never know where and when it will be a problem. You might pass three stations in a row, that are either closed for the afternoon, the holiday, or permanently.

"Nova" is a low-lead (81 octane) gasoline. "Extra" is unleaded (87 octane) gasoline. Diesel is available throughout Mexico. Again, these may all be available, then again they may not. Top off whenever you can.

Once you have been south of the border a while, you will get more of a feel for how long you can go before filling. And sometimes you start driving like the natives. Scary!

Gasoline is sold by the liter, 3.78 liters to one gallon. There are no self-service stations, and it is customary to tip your attendant.

Language

Language is not generally a problem. I speak only "Wounded Spanglish" and I always get along fine. I pick up more of the language each time I go down. It is fun to learn at least the basic phrases, and they love you for trying. The best thing ever to take across the border, with you, is a smile. You can go mile after mile with a smile.

In the tourist areas, most business people speak English. In the outlying areas where I traveled, even if they don't know English, between my Spanglish, gestures and smiles, it wasn't hard to make myself understood.

Take a Spanish-English dictionary in case you get really stuck. Learn how to say thank you, "*gracias*," and please, "*por favor*." In case you aren't close enough to your RV if you get hit with Montezuma's Revenge, "Where is the bathroom, please," is a good question to know how to ask, "*¿Dónde está el baño, por favor?*"

At the same time you are learning a few special words and phrases, get a Mexico map with the traffic signs and symbols on it and learn the most common. *Alto* is stop. *Escuela* means school. *Despacio* indicates you should slow down. *Ganado* means slam on your brakes, because there are cattle crossing the road!

Water

Use bottled water, put disinfectant in your tank, and/or get your water where the caravans do.

I never had a problem with drinking water in a year of traveling in old Mexico and Baja. I was never sick until I ate some tainted food in a restaurant in Puerto Vallarta. I was so sick I thought I would die, and was afraid I wouldn't. A Mexican doctor gave me a shot, three prescriptions. My campground hosts (Sayulita) and other RVing people gave me terrific TLC. Again, that was the first time in a year of traveling in Mexico that I had medical problems.

As far as buying food from street vendors or on the beach, most people don't, but I have also not had a problem with that. One might consider that after eating my own food for so long, perhaps I have the proverbial "cast-iron" stomach. If you are uncomfortable with it, don't buy anything on the street.

Shopping

It was always fun shopping. If you were in a tourist area, you were expected to bargain. On the beach you are expected to bargain. I bought a blanket on the beach in Puerto Penasco. After I washed fourteen pounds of sand out of it, it is the softest, most delightful blanket I own. I paid about $12 for it.

In a regular grocery store, brand names from the US were *mucho caro* (expensive). I tended toward local brands. Pictures are usually on the labels so it wasn't a problem to know what you were buying. I didn't buy much meat unless it was a big enough town that had an inside, regular meat market with covered meat. I ate quite a bit of fish I knew was fresh, especially on the Baja beach.

Fresh vegetables and fruits were abundant everywhere (Don't try to take them back across the border.). I always washed them thoroughly (A good thing to do in the US, too!).

**Remember,
in Mexico,
the only consistency,
is its inconsistency
Enjoy Mexico for its own sake.**

CANADA

They ask different questions each time I cross the border. This time the border guard asked if I had firearms, fruit, plant materials, and what route I was taking north.

Be friendly, but don't get smart with them, or kid around. They have a job to do, and they usually do it without smiles or a hint of personality. We have to realize, as innocent as we might be of breaking the rules, they often deal with the seamier side of humanity. They need no excuses to go through everything you have with you. Don't give them a reason.

Answer their questions truthfully and politely, but don't volunteer information. If you are wearing those confounded reflective sunglasses, take them off. Let them see your eyes. They can tell a lot about you that way.

An interesting comment I read recently, "As we drive close to the custom house, I get a sick feeling in my stomach; even if we have nothing to declare." That was a Canadian approaching the US border. We probably all have a twinge, no matter how often we have crossed foreign borders.

Remember, Canada and the United States share the "world's longest undefended border." They are friends. If you have nothing to hide, it is **unlikely** you will be detained.

I have included some comments on Alaska in this section because many of you will be headed that way. I have also mentioned the Milepost Magazine. You wouldn't go to Alaska without it would you? If you are interested in comprehensive information about traveling through Canada to Alaska, read my other 1997 book, *RVing Alaska! (and Canada)*

GOING INTO CANADA

Passports are not required for United States Citizens to enter Canada, or return to US.

Proof of citizenship must be carried:
  Birth or baptismal certificate, with photo ID, such as driver's license.
  Proof of residence may be required.

Minors: In addition to above, must have notarized letter of consent by both
  parents or guardians.

You must cross the borders when they are open and some of them are not open twenty-four hours. Watch your timing. It is illegal to cross without going through customs.

Remember that purchases made and sold legally in one country, may be illegal in the other. Check out hand-crafted items such as ivory, seal products, feathers, whalebone, fur, etc. before buying them and trying to cross the border.

Credit Cards and Cash

Most bigger businesses throughout Canada and Alaska now accept major credit cards. The thing I appreciate about using credit cards, is that you get the rate of exchange, for the day you are making your purchase. You are not subject to a business giving you only 20% or 25% of a 30+% exchange rate.

Carry Canadian cash with you. Again, **most** places accept credit cards but some places are just plain too small. Exchange your money at a national bank as soon as you cross the border.

Carry US cash with you, too. Some of the smaller places in Alaska don't honor credit cards, and they certainly don't all have banks or ATM machines.

263 Pound Halibut, Homer, Alaska

MEDICINE: Properly identify any medicine containing narcotics or habit-forming drugs, and carry the prescription or doctor's statement, as proof that you are using them under a doctor's direction.

EXEMPTIONS: Keep your sales receipts.

United States: **If you have been in Canada 48 hours or more**, you may have $400 US duty-free exemption (Every 30 days). There are limitations on alcohol and tobacco.

Canada: You are allowed necessary personal effects, duty free. You may have, duty-free, certain amounts of alcoholic beverages and tobacco (40 Imperial ounces of alcoholic beverages, 24 (12 oz) containers of beer or ale, 200 cigarettes, 50 cigars or cigarillos, and 2.2 pounds of manufactured tobacco). You are allowed gas to a normal tank capacity of the vehicle. (Gas is sold by the litre: 1 US gallon = 3.78 litres.)

GIFTS:

Canada: Bona fide gifts may be imported by visitors, duty and tax-free, provided the value of each gift, does not exceed $60 (Canadian) and the gifts do not consist of tobacco products, alcoholic beverages or advertising material.

SPORTING GOODS AND EQUIPMENT:

Canada: Visitors may take the usual personal sporting goods and equipment, i.e., boats, motors, camping equipment, cameras, TVs, etc., into Canada by declaring them on entry.

In RVs, we have TVs, VCRs, computers, etc. It wouldn't hurt to list everything, especially large items such as boats, motors, golf equipment, etc., along with the approximate values, or have the receipts.

PETS:

Canadians: Dogs and cats, over the age of three months, need a health certificate signed by a licensed veterinarian that clearly describes the animal, and declares the animal has been vaccinated against rabies within the past 36 months.The animal must be healthy, under control, and on a leash at the time of entry.

Americans: Rabies vaccination certificate issued within the past six months.

SEAT BELTS:

Required for all passengers **in Alaska, Canadian Provinces, and Territories**. Child restraint laws vary according to age or weight.

FIREARMS:

Canada: **All firearms must be declared** when you enter Canada. **Transporting handguns through customs is prohibited.** If undeclared firearms are found, they will be seized, and possibly criminal charges filed. **This includes possible seizure of the vehicle in which they are carried.** In addition, **they will not allow mace, pepper spray, or stun guns**. If you have weapons of any kind, or have questions, send for the booklet through Revenue Canada. The Milepost has comprehensive information on border rules, and information is also available on the internet. (See Resources)

Dawson City, Yukon Territory. **George Black Ferry across Yukon River,** bound for Top of the World Highway, and Beautiful Downtown Chicken, Alaska.

PLANTS, FRUITS, VEGETABLES

Some fresh fruits and vegetables commonly grown in Canada may be taken away from you. Think twice before you stock up previous to crossing the border.

House plants (rolling houses, too), supposedly, do not need to be declared.

VEHICLES:

Registration is a must, or a contract, if it is rented. Non-Resident Inter-Provincial Motor Vehicle Liability Insurance Card from your insurance company. (It is proof of financial responsibility.)

Trip accident policy recommended

NEW LAW AS OF APRIL, 1997

The following information is straight off the presses and out of a letter from Claire B. Eraut, Executive Director of Vehicle Policy and Standards Department of the Province of British Columbia as of April, 1997.

"Until recently, towed motor vehicles had to be equipped with coordinated brakes and an emergency breakaway device if the weight of the towed vehicle exceeded 3,087 pounds. In the context of this Ministry's primary commitment to the safety of British Columbia roads, the Motor Vehicle Branch reviewed requirements in comparable jurisdictions across North America. It was subsequently determined that this regulation should be changed to more accurately reflect the safety requirements and travel conditions facing motorhomes that tow motor vehicles in this province.

> **"The British Columbia regulation change, which took effect on March 26, 1997, increases the weight threshold to 4,400 pounds for motor vehicles towed by motorhomes.**

"This means that coordinated brake control and an emergency breakaway device may only be required if the laden gross weight of the towed vehicle is 4,400 pounds or greater. However, the new regulation adds a requirement that any towed motor vehicle weighting 40% or more of the motorhome's gross vehicle weight rating must be equipped with coordinated brakes and an emergency breakaway device.

"In conjunction with the new 40% weight ratio, the higher weight threshold of 4,400 pounds for towed vehicles achieves an enhanced balance of safety and mobility objectives, while corresponding more closely with towed vehicle requirements in jurisdictions with similar highway travel conditions."

GST TAX:

This 7% Goods and Services Tax is applied to most items and services in Canada. Non-Canadians may apply for this GST rebate on some items. You qualify for the 7% tax refund if you are:

Not a resident of Canada;
Have your **original** receipts (Minimums and maximums apply)

The refund doesn't cover:
Restaurants/meals, tobacco products, transportation, alcoholic beverages, some services (entertainment, parking, shoe repair, etc.), auto repairs (but it does cover parts), food, camping, cruising, rentals, or fuel.

> **You can claim your refund at any participating Canadian duty free shop or get it by mail with the appropriate application. You need to get a brochure with all the details so you will know what is covered and what is not. Keep your receipts.**

FINAL NOTE CANADA AND MEXICO: If you are the least bit apprehensive about traveling with only one rig, get several people to caravan with, or join a commercial caravan. Commercial caravans take care of where and how to get insurance, and know all the rules.

Moments in Time

I've talked about awareness for safety's sake, for maintenance' sake, and for Pete's sake; but, for the fullest RV experience, you need to be aware of your surroundings for **your** sake, enjoyment.

With the excitement of retirement, and the newfound freedom of being on the road, try not to see the entire country in a weekend. Full-timers have a tendency to do this when they first take off. Take the time to **experience the moment**.

Don't compare apples to oranges. Touching a living glacier in Alaska is awe-inspiring, but not more so than watching the breeze blow through a field of corn in Iowa. They are different experiences, but they are both magnificent.

I have learned to savor "Moments in time." These moments happen without warning. It is the greatest thrill in the world when I recognize them.

I was exploring Whidbey Island, Washington, with a friend. We had walked through shops along the wharf in Coupeville. We stopped to sit on a weathered and worn bench that wrapped around a mini-garden. When he put his arm around my shoulder, it was natural to back up against him, taking his hand in mine.

The shop doors opened and closed. Feet clunked on the boardwalk. Happy chatter mixed with raucous seagull conversations, and crisp leaves danced a final dance. The fragrance of autumn mingled with the last flowers of summer. We sat there for several minutes in the warm sunshine, neither of us saying anything. Then I realized it was one of those "Moments in time."

You might ask, "What's the big deal." That's just the point. It wasn't a big deal; it was a little deal. Quite suddenly I was unusually aware of my surroundings, the sounds, the fragrances, the feelings.

Other times I have raised my head to take a deep breath of fresh air. The sky was suddenly bluer, the clouds whiter, the sounds keener, the fragrance sweeter, and I would get goosebumps and realize it was another "moment in time" to treasure.

When my oldest daughter, Janet, was a baby, barely old enough to sit up, her father held her up in front of him in one of his huge gentle hands. She giggled and laughed that laugh that sounds like it is coming from the tips of the toes. We were enthralled. I guess I've been collecting special moments all my life.

Several times during a ten-day trip to Florida with my two adult daughters, I "stepped out" to look at what was happening. Janet left to take a shower while Tracey and I stayed on the beach. The sun went down and as the temperature cooled, I wrapped my arms around her. We watched night sneak in as we talked, mother and daughter, special, and yes, a "moment in time."

Sometimes I haven't known whether the goosebumps were due to the temperature, or my awareness. In September of 1996, I boondocked on a gravel pullout along the Top of the World Highway in Yukon Territory, Canada. I awakened about 12:15 and looked out my window and there it was, the Aurora Borealis. I watched them shimmering and dancing for nearly an hour. It was frigid that night. That cold and that scene are forever etched in my mind. A week later, God dumped a foot of snow in that area.

I loved to go into the little village of Mulege when I lived on the beach in Baja. One day I left the mercado and strolled down a hill on a curved, dirt street. A small Mexican lad came up the street, rolling a hoop in the dirt. He looked up and smiled at this Gringa, and said, "¡hola!" (hello). I can still smell the dust and feel the heat of that hot afternoon. I'll never forget the little amigo with the big brown eyes and the beautiful smile on his face. For whatever reason, it became another "moment in time."

I think of these moments as being captured in a memory bubble.

Everyone is down once in a while. When I am feeling "Lower than a snake in a room full of rocking chairs," as Tennessee Ernie Ford used to say, I recall my "moments in time."

HEAD 'EM UP, MOVE 'EM OUT

Do you remember Gil Favor from the TV show, "Rawhide?" He always said, "Head 'em up, move 'em out." It was a long time ago, a TGIF with pizza, before they gave Friday nights a name. That's how I feel now that we've come through the book together. Stick with me a few more minutes.

> **Unless you have an excellent memory, make yourself "to-do" check lists for set-up and departure. Laminate them and keep them where you will use them. The list should be comprehensive and geared to whatever type of RV you are using.**

Do a "Walk-a-bout"

♥ Have you closed all cupboards?
♥ Have you stowed and secured everything inside for travel?
♥ Do you have all maps and information where you can reach them?
♥ Do you have some toll change within reach? (You're not really going on an Interstate today are you?)
♥ Do you need to write down any directions or information?
♥ Did you put away the lawn chairs, bikes, kayaks, etc.
♥ Did you check all your fluids--engine, transmission, windshield wiper, in both vehicles.
♥ Have you checked water in the batteries lately? (including house batteries if they are the kind to need it)
♥ Did you check for corrosion on the batteries?
♥ How's your air filter?
♥ Did you clean the windshield, reflectors, headlights, all other lights?
♥ Did you check tires on both vehicles?
♥ Did you put away your sewer hose?
♥ Did you replace the sewer cap?

- Did you replace the campground sewer cap?
- Are your sewer valves securely closed?
- Did you put your water hose away?
- Have you unplugged your electric and stowed it away?
- Is the tow bar correctly fastened to the tow?
- Did you hook up the safety chains?
- Did you release the emergency brake in the tow?
- Did you put the tow in neutral?
- Did you lock the tow door?
- Is the entire lighting system working, brights, brakes, turn signals?
- Is anything hanging on your ladder?
- Are your storage areas locked?
- Have you picked up everything?
- Is your antenna down?
- Is anything sitting on top of the car, or on the RV bumpers?
- What time is it? Are you taking off during high traffic time? Could you wait a bit if it is?
- Is your step in?
- Did you record your mileage?
- **Is your mate aboard?** (Not as silly a question as you might think.)

I haven't driven off with the electric cord plugged in at a campground, but years ago in Michigan, more than once the cord that was attached to the block heater of the car, was left plugged in. Finding the electric cord strung the full length of the driveway, was a dead giveaway to my husband that I forgot to unplug.

I have a friend where my kids live in Virginia. Sue was all excited about going with me in the motorhome for the day. I was thrilled to show her my lifestyle. The first thing I did was drive off the blocks with a thud, instead of backing off. It's hard to be nonchalant when you've rattled a friend's teeth, as well as your own. I was embarrassed but more than that, I was lucky I didn't hurt anything.

If you feel the following box is a bit harsh, maybe you have more than a one-track mind. Your attention to detail is especially important when you are hooking up. I've known fifth-wheel owners to pull out with the truck, and hear their trailer thud down onto the back of the pickup, a sickening sound.

Do not disturb anyone when they are in their routine of setting up, or getting ready to leave. Hopefully, no-one will disturb you either.

Hellos and good-byes are wonderful and by all means, greet new friends, or say your good-byes with hugs and promises to write, but do it <u>after they are set up</u>, or <u>before or after they start hooking up.</u>

I really do appreciate help but it disturbs my routine. I either have to decline help or be extra careful to see that everything is done.

Only recently a friend was helping me, and I didn't observe my routine as closely as I should have. I left behind my sewer cap. It was my own fault, and this time the replacement wasn't expensive, but I'd rather spend that money on something more entertaining than a sewer cap.

Several times I have left a campground, and felt "something" was wrong. I discovered I hadn't put the car in neutral, or didn't release the emergency brake, which means I was literally dragging it. Much of that type of forgetting, and major problems come calling.

By all means, ask to help if you think someone needs it. If they decline, take their word for it and back off, until they are done. Please don't stand around and watch. This bothers a lot of people, including me.

On set-up, since I don't have built-in levelers, it is helpful if someone guides me, while I drive up on blocks. I can do it myself, but it sometimes takes several tries. I seldom ask for help on this, but once in a great while, someone has offered. I accept with thanks.

On departure, there are two tasks a single needs help with after everything else is done, and that is when it is time to check the lights. This means several trips back and forth to be sure the turning lights, tail lights, and headlights, are all working properly. It is almost impossible to tell if the brake lights are working, without help. If someone is around, I ask for help, and I have never been refused.

Last minute thoughts

Listen to your vehicle. I can't stress that enough. When it changes sounds, find out why.

Document what it is doing. Does it happen all the time? Is it a ping? A knock? A gurgle? Does Mama sing soprano or does Daddy sing bass? If you know these things, it will be helpful in explaining to a mechanic. He's the one in the blue uniform who removed his white hat and scratches his head the minute you start talking, "You know, the whatchamachallit inside the doohickey..." He is one of the reasons you should be familiar with the parts of your vehicle and the terminology.

Read your owner's manual

I have never gotten a bigger kick out of anything, than diagnosing a problem with the help of the owner's manual, taking it to be fixed, and finding out I was right. It really is fun learning.

Keep a maintenance log with dates, mileage, and types of repairs. Record your gasoline usage and mileage. Don't neglect having your vehicles serviced regularly. The miles go quickly and before you realize it, you've driven 10,000 miles without an oil change.

I have gotten into the habit of doing a **"walk-a-bout,"** whenever I stop. It stretches my legs, and tells me if everything looks okay. Travel with your lights on. It may not help you see, but you can be more easily seen, and it is the law in some states and territories.

As nonchalant as I must seem in my writing, driving an RV can be dangerous and expensive, or it can be safe and enjoyable (and expensive). It's up to you.

Read everything you can get your hands on. If it doesn't make sense to you in the beginning, it will after you start RVing and connect the reading material together with the "real stuff." Never stop learning. If you do, pinch yourself, you may have passed on, and nobody noticed!

Now you are a Full-timing RVer. Some people will look at you with envy. Others will think you are crazier than a hoot owl. When you visit friends, they will ask you to stay in their house in a "real" bedroom. They haven't a clue what you paid to have a comfortable "real" bedroom in the cozy, rolling "Home Sweet Rolling Home" in their driveway.

Sometimes their view of you will be a real winner.

A gaunt looking fellow in questionable shirt, ragged shorts, and sandals filled with well-used feet, came to share a bridge rail where I was watching a summer day progress. He was a self-styled guru, therapist, and world traveler of many languages who had just returned from Russia.

After exchanging lifestyle stories, he said, "Nobody understands my not having a home. I'm glad to finally meet another "homeless" person." In the eyes of that beholder, I was homeless.

With that thought in mind, I will just say, the full-time RVing lifestyle can be the greatest fun you've ever had, but it's like anything else, it will be what you make it.

Use common sense
Keep your sense of humor
Take care of your health
Keep your RV and tag in excellent driving condition
Have at least a smidgen of faith in your fellow man
Have a whole lot of faith in the Man Upstairs

OK, you've checked everything out, you've pulled down the antennae and pulled up the step; your mate is aboard. Take your time today. It is the first day of the rest of your life. Enjoy whatever is, wherever you are. Don't zip across the country as you used to have to do when you were on vacation. Stop, enjoy, be kind to each other. Be flexible when things go wrong or something unforeseen changes your plans. Flexibility makes you more fun to be around.

Remember what I said about being flexible.

Do me one last favor, just before you climb into your seats for take-off, and for absolutely no reason at all, take your mate in your arms. Give him or her a big smooch. It's a great way to start the day. If you're a single, just reach up and grab the mental one I've sent you. (We singles have to stick together.)

Gosh, it's hard to let you go. It's like putting your kindergartner on the bus for the first time -

---

If you see a Sprinter motorhome
with
"Charlie" written under the driver's window,
give me a shout,
we'll go for a drink (Pepsi and milk).

OK Gil, let's get all these RVers going. May I say it just this once,

Head 'em up, Move 'em out!

(Have a great life full-timing!)

God Bless

Glossary

ATM	Automatic Teller Machine
Battery	A storage box for electrical power
Black water	Sewage from toilet (Usually has own tank)
BLM	Bureau of Land Management
Boondocking	Parking without amenities other than in a campground
Carbon Monoxide	Odorless, tasteless, colorless gas, and poisonous.
Chassis	The frame, suspension system, running gear, and steering (Class C also includes the cab)
CORE	Corps of Engineers
CPR	CardioPulmonary Resuscitation
CRS	Can't Remember Sugar
Deadbolt	A lock bolt moved by turning the knob or key without action of a spring.
Doghouse	Cover over the engine in motorhome
DOT	Department of Transportation
Dry camping	Without amenities
Dump Station	A specific location for dumping sewage
EMT	Emergency Medical Technician
FMCA	Family Motor Coach Association
Fresh water	Hopefully, your drinking water
Full hook-ups	Water, electric, and sewer at each campsite. Sometimes includes cable TV, rarely, telephones
Full-time RVer	Someone who lives in an RV all the time.
Golden Access Pass http://www.nps.gov/ pub_aff/fee.html	This is a free lifetime entrance pass for persons who are blind or permanently disabled. It is available to citizens or permanent residents of the United States, regardless of age.
Golden Age Pass http://www.nps.gov/ pub_aff/fee.html	This is a lifetime entrance pass for those 62 years or older. The Golden Age Passport has a one time processing charge of $10. You must purchase a Golden Age Passport in person.
Golden Eagle Pass http://www.nps.gov/ pub_aff/fee.html	An entrance pass to national parks, monuments, historic sites, recreation areas, and national wildlife refuges that charge an entrance fee. It costs $50 and is valid for one year from date of purchase. National Park Service, 1100 Ohio Drive, SW, Room 138 Washington, DC 20242, Attention: Golden Eagle Passport
Gray water	Used dish/bath/cleaning water (usually has own tank)
Ins: Bodily Injury and Property Damage:	Liability protects you if you injure someone else or damage someone else's property while operating your vehicle.
Ins: Collision	Protects against damage to your vehicle if in a collision with another car or object regardless of fault.
Ins: Comprehensive	Covers against theft; damage by hail, falling objects, or vandalism. May replace or restore vehicle to same condition.
Ins: Medical Payments	Pays medical expenses to you, your family, or occupants of your car, no matter who's at fault. Covers you and your family, if you are injured in another.
Ins: Personal Injury Protection	This is also called "No-Fault" and coverage varies from

	state to state. Pays medical costs related to bodily injury, loss of income, regardless of who causes the accident.
Ins: Uninsured/Under insured Motorist:	Covers you and your car occupants if injured by driver who is not insured or under-insured.
Inverter	Converts RV 12-volt DC electricity into 120-volt AC electricity (Takes stored electricity from batteries (supplied by solar panels, generator, or alternator) and converts it into 120 electricity)
NPS	National Park Service
"The outside"	This is how northern Canadians and Alaskans refer to the "Lower 48."
Parking pawl	Sliding bolt on a machine, adapted to fall into notches, to permit motion in only one direction
Pigtail	A short electrical cord with an end on it to make you compatible with the campground receptacle.
PIN	Personal Identification Number
psi	Power per square inch
RV, Rig	Recreational Vehicle
RVIA	Recreational Vehicle Industry Association (Sets RV industry's standards) If your RV carries the label, it should fit the standard.
S*M*A*R*T	Special Military Active Retired Travel Club
SKP	Escapees, Inc.
Tag axle	A non-powered rear axle
Tag or Tow	Vehicle being towed behind RV
TLC	Tender Loving Care
USFS	United States Forest Service
Vehicle Weight: GCVR	Gross Combined Vehicle Rating: (Weight of loaded motorhome plus weight of tow vehicle)
Vehicle Weight: Dry Weight	RV without fluids on board
Vehicle Weight: GAWR	Gross Axle Weight Rating. The maximum allowable weight per axle.
Vehicle Weight: GCWR (Fifth wheel or trailer)	Gross Combined Weight Rating: (Weight of pulling vehicle, trailer, cargo, passengers, and fluids.
Vehicle Weight: GCWR (Motorhome)	Gross Combined Weight Rating: (Fully-equipped RV, cargo, passengers, fluids, and weight of travel-ready tag.)
Vehicle Weight: GVWR	Gross Vehicle Weight Rating: (Maximum loaded weight of single vehicle specified by the manufacturer -- (Found on the Certificate of Origin.)
Vehicle Weight: UVW	Unloaded Vehicle Weight: (Maximum fluids necessary for traveling without cargo, passengers, or usual trappings.
Vehicle Weight: Wet Weight	Filled: water, Propane, fuel.
Vehicle Weight: Wheelbase to length Ratio	Wheelbase (inches from axle to axle) divided by overall length of MH (inches) = per cent ratio
Weight: One gallon of propane	4.25 pounds
Weight: One gallon of water	8.2 pounds

Resources

I do not necessarily recommend all these resources. They are to give you <u>ideas or starting points, to do your own research</u>.

Alaska Marine Highway
P. O. Box 703
Kodiak, AK 99615
1-800-526-6731
http://www.dot.state.ak.us/external/amhs/general/resinfo.html

Alaska Public Lands Information Centers
605 W. 4th St., Suite 105
Anchorage, Alaska 99501
907-271-2737 - http://www.nps.gov/aplic/

Baja Information
Automobile Club of Southern California
1-800-962-BAJA, ext. 383

Baja-Bound 1-888-YES-BAJA
http://www.bajabound.com

Battery Maintenance
Solargizer
PulseTech battery-related products
1-800-580-7554

Bug Book
Sawyer's *A Practical Guide to Outdoor Protection* 1-800-940-4464

Campground Directory
Anderson's Campground Directory
Drawer 467
Lewisburg, WV 24901
304-645-1897

Camping World Supercenter 1-800-353-0850

S*M*A*R*T Fam-Camp
Military Living Publications
PO Box: 2347
Falls Church, VA 22042-0347
703-237-0203

Trailer Life Campground/RV Park & Services
Directory
P. O. Box 10236
Des Moines, IA 50381-0236
1-800-765-4167, Ext. 305 - http://www.tl.com

Wheelers RV Resort & Campground Guide
(Also have a Jumbo Road Map Atlas)
1310 Jarvis Avenue
Elk Grove Village, IL 60007
1-800-323-8899

Canadian Customs
Excise & Taxation Information Service
613-993-0534

Coast to Coast Membership
Information line 1-800-538-8136

Cruising Campground
Mississippi River 1-800-256-6100

Custom Cards
D & M Holdings, LTD.
6918 Woodlands Way
Arlington, WA 98223-7402
360-435-0772 or 888-638-7576

Denali National Park and Preserve
Box 9
Denali Park, AK 99755
907 683-1266 or 1267
Denali reservations: 1-800-622-7275
http://www.alaska.net/~denst1/

Easy Slip RV sewer hose
Camco Manufacturing 1-800-334-2004

Emergency Transport
SkyMed International Inc. 1-800-475-9633

Explore Europe by RV
Color brochure and detailed itineraries
1-800-322-2127

Firearm Laws:
Division of State Troopers, Headquarters
5700 E. Tudor Rd., Dept. P
Anchorage, AK 99507
907-269-5511

GST Taxes
1-800-668-4748 (Canada)
1-902-432-5608 (US)

Fire Towers
How To Rent A Fire Lookout In The Pacific Northwest
Tom Foley, Tish Steinfeld
Wilderness Press
2440 Bancroft Way
Berkeley, CA 94704
800-443-7227

Free RV travel and tip video
1-888-GO-RVing

Guide book
The Milepost (Vernon Publications, Inc.)
Northwest Mileposts
1-800-746-4707
e-mail: books@alaskainfo.com
Website: www.alaskainfo.com

Lighthouses
http://www.maine.com/lights/others.htm

Lubri-gas or Lubri-diesel
1-800-252-6516

Maroon Bells
White River National Forest campgrounds:
National Recreation Reservation System:
1-800-280-2267
Private campground: Aspen-Basalt
Campground phone: (970) 927-3405

Members only comprehensive guide
American Automobile Association
1000 AAA Drive
Heathrow, FL 32746-5063

Automobile Club of Southern California
2601 S. Figueroa Street
Los Angeles, California 90007

Membership
The Good Sam Club
64 Iverness Drive East
PO Box 6894
Englewood, CO 80155-6894
1-800-234-3450

Family Motor Coach Association
8291 Clough Pike
Cincinnati, OH 45244-2796
1-800-543-3622
513-474-3622

Escapees RV Club
100 Rainbow Drive
Department JMI
Livingston, TX 77351
1-888-757-2582 (toll-free) OK As of May, 1997

Membership Park
Coast to Coast Welcome Coupon
PO Box 6892
Englewood, CO 80155-6892
1-800-368-5721

Membership required
Good Sam Emergency Road Service
PO Box 10866
Des Moines, IA 50381-0866
1-800-510-3330 Ext. 805

AAA Auto Club RV Emergency Road Service
Applications
3586 Riverside Drive
Macon, Georgia 31210 912-471-0800

Mexican Government of Tourism
1-800-446-3942

Mexico Campground
Sayulita Trailer Park
Thies and Cristina Rohlfs
Apartado 5-585 CP 06500
Mexico D.F. Mexico

Mexico information
1-900-388-7070 Ext. 325 (RVs)
1-900-388-7070 Ext. 326 (Pets)

Mexico Insurance
Lewis and Lewis
8929 Wilshire Blvd., Suite 220
Beverly Hills, CA 90211
1-800-966-6830

Sanborn Insurance
2009 S. 10th St.
MacAllen, TX 78503
1-800-222-0158

Mexico Treasury Department
1-800-446-8277

Motorhome Insurance
(Progressive - endorsed by FMCA) Okay as of
5/97
Alexander and Alexander of Michigan
3011 West Grand Blvd., Suite 700
Detroit, MI 48202-3052
Premium Quotation: 1-800-782-9885
Customer Service: 1-800-521-2942

Photos
Kodak Customer Assistance Center
1-800-242-2424

Recreation Vehicle Industry Assoc. (RVIA)
1896 Preston White Drive
P. O. Box 2999
Reston, Virginia 20195-0999

Renting an RV
Woodall's Go & Rent
1-800-323-9076

Rescue aid
Rescue & Practice Aid
County Line Ltd.
4543 Taylor Lane
Warrensville, OH 44128
888-SAV-LIFE

Revenue Canada AAA 1996
Customs and Excise
Visitor Rebate Program
Ottawa, Ontario, Canada K1A 1J5
1-800-66-VISIT (In Canada)
613-991-3346 (Outside)

RV Books

Craig Chilton
How to Get Paid $30,000 a Year to Travel
Available through Workamper News

Bill Farlow
Snowbird & Winter Texan Guide
RVing from A to Z
Freedom Unlimited,
        The Fun and Facts of Full-Time RVing
        (Co-author - Sharlene Minshall)
101 Rainbow Drive #1238
Livingston, TX 77351-9330

Janet and Gordon Groene
Living Aboard Your RV
Cooking Aboard Your RV
Box 248
DeLeon Springs, FL 32130

Gaylord Maxwell
Full-timing...an Introduction to Full-Time RVing
Available through Workamper News

Sharlene Minshall: Gypsy Press
RVing Alaska! (and Canada)
RVing Full-Time, How to Make it Happen
RVing North America, Silver, Single, and Solo
In Pursuit of a Dream
Freedom Unlimited,
        The Fun and Facts of Full-Time RVing
        (Bill Farlow - co-athor)
Suite 5024
101 Rainbow Drive
Livingston, TX 77351-9330

Bill & Jan Moeller
RV Electrical Systems
Full-Time RVing
RVing Basics
Available through Workamper News

Ray Parker
RV Having Fun Yet?
Available through Workamper News

Joe and Kay Peterson
Travel While You Work
Survival of the Snowbirds
Home is Where You Park It
Encyclopedia for RVers
Escapees, Inc.
100 Rainbow Drive
Livingston, TX 77351

Don Wright 1-800-272-5518
How to Buy and RV and Save 1,000s
Guide to Free Campgrounds

RV Campground

KOA Value Kard
P. O. Box 31734, Department D
Billings, MT 59107-1734
Internet: http://www.koakampgrounds.com/

Meri-Daes RV Park
220 W. Park St.
Marble, CO. 81623
(303) 963-1831

RV Caravans

Aztec Trails RV Tours
101 Rainbow Drive, #3182
Livingston, TX 77351

Carnival RV Caravans 1-800-556-5652

Fantasy Caravans 1-800-952-8496

Tracks to Adventure
2811 Jackson, Suite K
El Paso, TX 79930
1-800-351-6053

Point South RV Tours
11313 Edmonson Ave.
Moreno Valley, CA 92555
1-800-421-1394

Woodall's World of Travel
P. O. Box 247
Greenville, MI 48838
1-800-346-7572

RV classes

Life on Wheels Conference
University of Idaho campus
Moscow, ID 83843

RV Defensive Driving Courses

Susan Davenport
Chemeketa Community College
Salem, Oregon 97307-7070
503-399-6918

Richard Reed
1512 E Fifth Street #149
Ontario, CA 91764
909-984-7746

Good Sam Members of
National General Insurance Co.
1 National General Plaza
St. Louis, MO 63045

RV Emergency Road Service

Rapid Response Roadservice Motor Club, Inc.
P. O. Box 5100, Ste 204
Thousand Oaks, CA 91359-9925
1-800-999-7505

RV Insurance
Foremost Insurance Group 1-800-527-3905

American Modern Insurance Group
1-800-759-9008

Progressive Northwestern Insurance Company
Miller Insurance Agency, Inc.
2823 SW Glenhaven Rd.
Lake Oswego, OR 97034 1-800-622-6347

National General Insurance
One National General Plaza
P. O. Box 66937
St. Louis, MO 63166-6937
1-800-325-1190 or 1-800-847-2886

National Interstate
29328 Chaagrin Blvd.
Cleveland, OH 44122-4813

RV Maintenance
Nutz & Boltz Publications
P. O. Box 123
Butler, MD 21023-0123

RV Magazines
RV Life
Ron and Marlyn Knudson, Publishers
PO Box: 55998
Seattle, WA 98155
206-745-6556

RV Today
4005 20th Ave. W., Suite 110
Seattle, WA 98199-1291

Two-Lane Roads
Loren Eyrich, Publisher
PO Box: 23518
Fort Lauderdale, FL 33307-3518
1-888-TWO-LANE
E-mail: TwoLaneUSA@aol.com
http://www.rvusa.com/rvlife/twolaneroads

Woodall Publications Corporation
13975 West Polo Trail Drive
Lake Forest, IL 60045-5000
1-800-323-9076
For Texas RV
    Southern RV   Camp-Orama
    California RV Traveler   RV Traveler
    Northeast RV   Camping Today

RV Shopping Guide
RV Buyers Guide (1997)
PO Box: 10204
Des Moines, IA 50336-0202
1-800-309-0311
RV Consumer Group
Box 520
Quilcene, WA 98376
360-765-3846

S*M*A*R*T
Special Military Active Retired Travel Club
600 University Office Blvd.
Suite 1A
Pensacola, FL 32504
1-800-354-7681
http://www.geocities.com/TheTropics/1562/1544

Safety
Shell Answers
Shell Oil Company
P. O. Box 4681
Houston, TX 77210

Satellite Systems
Hi-Tech RV World 1-800-774-4832

Sewer System
Prest-O-Fit
P. O. Box 23929
Tempe, AZ 85285

Singles
Loners on Wheels
P. O. Box 1355SKI
Poplar Bluff, Missouri 63902

Lozark Park, Inc.
R. #2, Box 85
Ellsinore, MO 63937-9519
314-322-5298

RVing Women
PO Box: 1940
Apache Junction, AZ 85217
602-983-4678

Loners of America, Inc.
R. #2, Box 85E
Ellsinore, MO 63937-9520
314-322-5548

WIN
P. O. Box 2010, Dept. 24
Sparks, NV 89432-2010

Member Relations Department
Thousand Trails/Naco
2711 LBJ Freeway, Suite 254
Dallas, TX 75234

BOF Singles
101 Rainbow Dr.
Livingston, TX 77351-9300

Singles - FMCA
Singles International
William Preston
601 Cottage Grove Circle
Valrico, FL 33594 1-813-681-9987

Solar Electric
Noel and Barbara Kirkby
14415 N. 73rd St.
Scottsdale, AZ 85260
602-443-8520 or 1-800-999-8520

Thetford's new free copy of
"Step-by-Step Guide to Winterizing your RV
Sanitation System" 1-800-521-3032

Things to do
Death Valley '49ners, Inc.
P. O. B: 338
Death Valley, CA 92328

Elderhostel
75 Federal St.
Boston, MA 02110
617-426-8056

Thomas Shepherd Inn: (304) 876-3715
Historic Christmas Festival: (304) 876-6255

Leavenworth, Washington
509-548-5807 or http://www.leavenworth.org

Mackinac Island Chamber of Commerce
Mackinac Island, MI, 49757
906-847-6418

Rocky Mountain Cattle Moo-vers, Inc.
P. O. Box 457
Carbondale, CO 81623
(303) 963-9666.

Tire Alarms
TireMate
Land & Sea Supplies
3326 Fir Avenue
Alameda, CA 94502
1-800-521-6820

Tire care
Wintertime RV use and Maintenance (RVIA)
PO Box: 2999, Dept. WNTZ
Reston, VA 22090

Tire Safety
Tire Industry Safety Council
PO Box: 3147
Medina, OH 44258

Toll-free number to find toll-free numbers:
1-800-555-1212

Travel Club, Baja
Club Vagabundos del Mar 1-800-474-BAJA

Traveling to Mexico by Car
Mexican Government of Tourism
10100 Santa Monica Blvd., Ste #224
Century City
Los Angeles, CA 90067-4006
310-203-8191 (out of Baja book)

Trip planning - CD-ROM
Map'n'Go
1-800-452-5931
Select Street
1-800-99-CD-ROM

TripMaker
Rand McNally
1-800-671-5006

Video on winterizing
Gary Bunzer
Bunzer Consulting
P. O. Box 2074
El Cajon, CA 92021
619-441-0769

Volunteer activities
Mercy Ships
P. O. Box 2020
Garden Valley, TX 75771
903-882-0887
1-800-424-SHIP
E-mail: info@mercyships.org
Website: http://www.mercyships.org

Volunteer in Parks program
State of Alaska
Division of Parks and Outdoor Recreation
(Aug. 1996 C to C)
P. O. Box 107001
Anchorage, Alaska 99510-7001

Volunteers
Servants on Wheels Ever Ready
P. O. Box 175
Ten Mile, TN 37880

RV Habitat Gypsies
Jack and Lois Wolters
Route 1, Box 442
Columbus, NC 28722
912-924-6935, ext. 446 (O.K.)

Water Filters
General Ecology, Inc.
151 Sheree Blvd.
Exton, PA 19341
610-363-7900

Pure and Fresh Water
1-800-444-8655
Ametek
Plymouth Products Division
502 Indiana Avenue
PO Box 1047
Sheboygan, Wisconsin 53082-1047

Kinetico Water Processing Systems Inc.
3454 N San Marcos Place
Chandler, AZ 85224-1598
602-437-2474

Woodall's
RV Owner's Handbook series (3)
Woodall's Website on the Internet
www.woodalls.com

Working on the road
SkyMed International
1-800-475-9633

WORKAMPER NEWS:
Publishers, Greg and Debbie Robus
201 Hiram Road (MIN)
Heber Springs, Arkansas 72543-8747
CompuServe address: 75317,122 (RV Forum)

WORKERS ON WHEELS:
Editor/Publisher, Coleen Sykora
4012 S. Rainbow Blvd., Suite K-94 (MIN)
Las Vegas, NV 89103, 1-800-371-1440

THE CARETAKER GAZETTE:
Publisher, Gary Dunn
1845 NW Deane St. Pullman
WA 99163-9509
509-332-0806
e-mail: garydunn/@pullman.com
http://www.angelfire.com/wa/caretaker

Sharlene "Charlie" Minshall

RVing Alaska! (and Canada) (1997)

A **"How-to"** and "**Why-not**" book, that gives vehicle and mental preparation, map information, where-to-stay, when-to-go, what to take, and road conditions. Add to the practical suggestions and strong comments, the misadventures of playing with the grizzlies in Katmai National Park and canoeing the Mighty Yukon River, and you'll get information plus entertainment. 192 pages and 50 photographs.

Excerpt: Please remember, speed is directly relational to anguished springs, broken axles, chipped windshields, and creative alignment.

Excerpt: ...at the Yukon Territory and the Northwest Territories border, I drove into a totally different world. It was dark, snowy, and windy. It was more ominous looking than I wanted to admit because I didn't want to turn back. I thought hard for milliseconds, then put the Sprinter in gear, and inched toward Inuvik.

Full-Time RVing: How to Make it Happen (1997)

A **"How-to" book that lets you in on the mobile lifestyle that millions are enjoying!** What does it take to get started? What should I keep? What should I take? How do I keep relationships with family and friends intact? How do I cross borders into Canada or Mexico? What type of vehicle or health insurance is needed by a full-time RVer? What happens if I break down? How can I prevent breaking down? What is the daily life of a full-time RVer really like? 192 pages plus photographs.

Full-time RVing doesn't have to be driving the Interstates. Now you'll be able to spend extra time in the most beautiful parts of our country. Let Charlie tell you about volunteering in the Snowmass-Maroon Bells Wilderness or house-sitting in the snowdrifts of a beautiful Bavarian Village. Paraglide with this silver gypsy off a mountain in Colorado or go cattle herding on a family reunion. This book is much more than a "How-to," it's a "Why not?"

RVing North America, Silver, Single, and Solo

Follow the Silver Gypsy in her adventures into Mexico, Alaska, Canada, and all around the "lower 48." This is the daily life of a full-time RVer.

Excerpt: Tim maneuvered (ultralight) so I could look directly into a mining camp...He really didn't need to accommodate me so well. With no windshield for protection, I felt my age regress as the G's smoothed my wrinkles....Instead of landing, he flew a few feet off the ground between startled RVers...I got pictures of the plane's shadow on the ground....I felt like a hawk. Have you ever noticed they don't have wrinkles? There's a reason. 288 pgs/photos.

In Pursuit of a Dream

Find out how and why "Charlie" began her full-time RVing lifestyle. (She started almost eleven years ago, and hasn't stopped yet!)

Excerpt: I went into Baja (Mexico) with no idea I would find whales, petroglyphs, Seventeenth Century missions, and cave paintings. The bourgainvillea...sunrises, sunsets, and grande moonlit nights...were a delight....wild furry burros roamed the roads...and I saw the Pacific and the Sea of Cortez mingle at "Land's End."

Freedom Unlimited: The Fun and Facts of Fulltime RVing

(Co-author - Tech Writer Bill Farlow)   Published by Woodall's Publishing Company
Points of view from all sides of the full-time spectrum by two long-time, full-time RVing writers.

Book Description

ORDER FORM

For AUTOGRAPHED copies, complete form and send a check or money order (US Funds) to:

Sharlene Minshall
% Gypsy Press
Suite AKBK-5024
101 Rainbow Drive
Livingston, TX 77351-9330

FULL-TIME RVING How to Make it Happen...............................$12.95

RVING ALASKA! (and Canada)...$14.95

RVING NORTH AMERICA Silver, Single & Solo.........................$12.95

IN PURSUIT OF A DREAM...$ 9.00

FREEDOM UNLIMITED The Fun and Facts of Fulltime Rving
(Co-authored by Bill Farlow) ....$ 9.00

Name _____

Address _____

City, State, Zip _____

	Price	Qty	Total
FULL-TIME RVING: HOW TO MAKE IT HAPPEN	$12.95	_____	_____
RVING ALASKA! (AND CANADA)	$14.95	_____	_____
RVING NORTH AMERICA (Silver, Single & Soldo)	$12.95	_____	_____
IN PURSUIT OF A DREAM	$ 9.00	_____	_____
FREEDOM UNLIMITED	$ 9.00	_____	_____

Subtotal _____

$2 **DISCOUNT** on combo of three books   **Discount** -_____

Subtotal _____

P&H +_____

Total _____

Postage & Handling
Up to $10	$2.25
$10.01 to $20	$3.50
$20.01 to $40	$4.50
$40.01 TO $60	$6.00

Canadian orders please add $1/$20.
(Please allow six weeks for delivery)
Prices subject to change without notice.